A Reader's Guide to

ROBERT
LOWELL

A Reader's Guide to

ROBERT LOWELL

Philip Hobsbaum

THAMES AND HUDSON

For Seamus and Marie Heaney,
his friends in Ireland

The acknowledgments on pp.170–171 are an extension of the copyright page.

First published in the United States in 1988 by
Thames and Hudson Inc., 500 Fifth Avenue,
New York, New York 10110

Library of Congress Catalog Card Number 88–50133

Typeset by Q-Set, Hucclecote, Gloucester
Printed and bound in Great Britain

Contents

the sill geranium is lit
by the lamp I write by,
a wind from the Irish Sea
is shaking it —

here where we all sat
ten days ago with you
the master elegist
and welder of English.

Seamus Heaney

How is it, Robert, there in your wild land?
Within us we all bear our family graves;
How can we name the heart of sorrow's flower
As it races past us through dark cosmic waves?
Here on the stone the name that you once had rests
like discarded clothes.

Andrei Voznesensky
(translated by William Jay Smith
and Fred Starr)

You left North Haven, anchored in its rock,
afloat in mystic blue . . . And now — you've left
for good. You can't derange, or re-arrange,
your poems again. (But the Sparrows can their song.)
The words won't change again. Sad friend,
you cannot change.

Elizabeth Bishop

Preface

Every age has a poet distinguished not only for his literary power
but for his influence over younger contemporaries. Perhaps such
influence emanates not only from the individual talent but from
the spirit of the age. Yeats dominated that rising generation
whose most remarkable member was T. S. Eliot. Eliot occupied
a similar position with regard to the generation of Robert Lowell.
Lowell himself was the poet studied poem by poem and line by
line in the 1950s, the formative period of Ted Hughes, Sylvia
Plath, Anne Sexton, Anne Stevenson, Peter Redgrove and
Geoffrey Hill.

I am indebted to several of those named, as well as to Marie
Battle Singer, Arthur Terry, Seamus and Marie Heaney, and the
late John Berryman, for dialogue without which this present
book could not have been written. There is the added necessity
of acknowledging Ian Hamilton's monumental biography of the
poet. It consolidated many interviews productive of information
which, but for Mr Hamilton's industry, would have remained
inaccessible. I am also keenly aware of the work done by such
previous expositors of Lowell as Hugh B. Staples, Jerome
Mazzaro, Stephen Yenser, and Steven Gould Axelrod. A special
tribute must be paid to Dr Rex Mitchell of the Department of
Psychology at Queen's University, Belfast, for help with inquiries
into the nature of the mental illness which afflicted Lowell through
most of his life.

My study of Lowell began in 1950, when the inroads which
Hopkins and Eliot were already making into my youthful imagination were powerfully reinforced by the advent of this new
poet from the USA. That study was implemented by discussion
with my undergraduate contemporaries at Cambridge who were
equally alight with the discovery of Lowell's first publication in
Britain, *Poems 1938–49*. Its successor, *Life Studies*, was a reference

point for the London Group, and its influence can be clearly seen in the writing of George MacBeth, Edward Lucie-Smith and Peter Porter. In its turn, *Imitations* proved a constant factor with regard to that other writers' group which I formed in the early 1960s in Belfast, among whose members were the dedicatees of this book, Seamus and Marie Heaney. Their friendship was to mean a great deal to Lowell, as it must to all who are fortunate enough to know them at close quarters. I went on, later in the 1960s, to lecture about Lowell and his contemporaries at Glasgow University. An essay based on those lectures took up the fifty-eighth issue of the Scottish literary magazine, *Lines Review*, in June 1976, and laid the foundation of much that I have to say here. I ought also to acknowledge an offshoot of my lucubrations, relating to Lowell and the New Critics, that appeared in a *Festschrift, Studies in Modern English and American Poetry*, published by the University of Seoul in 1986 to honour the sixtieth birthday of Professor Chi-gyu Kim, my fellow-student with William Empson who was himself a friend of Lowell.

The present book was written under lengthening shadows on the academic scene, and could never have been completed without the help and forbearance of my colleagues at the University of Glasgow, most notably Ingrid Swanson, Patrick Reilly and Paddy Lyons. I am, as ever in my work, indebted to the resources of a generous university library and to the co-operation of its staff, especially Mary Sillitto and Jean Robertson. The final draft of my manuscript was typed, most efficiently, by Janice Mackay. Lastly, I am more grateful than I can say for the encouragement of my editorial director at Thames and Hudson, Stanley Baron, and for the support of my wife, Rosemary.

1 *Land of Unlikeness* (1944) to *Lord Weary's Castle* (1946)

The Lowell family have lived in New England since 1639 and, from 1776 onwards, based themselves largely in Boston. They proved adept at developing external structures; not only building up fortunes in trade and in the practice of law, but also making judicious marriages. For example, John Lowell (1743-1802), the 'Old Judge' as he was called inside the clan, took in succession three wives, from the Higginson, the Cabot and the Russell families respectively. He may not have married for money; but, as the chronicler of the Lowells remarks, he certainly married where money was (Greenslet, 45). The son of the Old Judge's second marriage, Francis Cabot Lowell, did more than any other member to swell the family wallets by introducing to the United States in 1812 mechanical processes in the spinning and weaving of cotton. But the branch from which the poet Robert Lowell was descended proved, in comparison, only moderately prosperous. The son of the Judge's third marriage, the Reverend Charles Lowell, had married (in 1806) a woman of Orcadian descent, and this brought into the family what was later described within its conventicles as 'the Spence negligence' (Greenslet, 117). How far this strain filtered down to the subject of the present study will be seen in subsequent pages.

The Russell-Spence line, as this branch of the family was termed, inclined towards public service, though it gave rise to literary figures as well. Robert Lowell's great-great-uncle, James Russell Lowell, succeeded Longfellow as Professor of Modern Languages at Harvard, wrote satiric poems that were famous in their time, and finished his working life as Ambassador to the Court of St James, returning to London occasionally in his retirement. The first Robert Traill Spence Lowell, James Russell's elder brother, was an Episcopal clergyman who served as the foundation headmaster of St Mark's School, Southborough, and who also wrote a novel, *The New Priest at Conception Bay*, recently resuscitated (Paddock, 81-89). His son, bearing the same name, died young, leaving little by which he could be remembered other than *his* son, born posthumously, Robert Traill Spence Lowell III. This latter, negative and subdued in personality (Clark 1979), became a naval officer and married Charlotte Winslow, daughter of Arthur Winslow, mining engineer and property-owner. The Winslows were descended from Pilgrim Fathers who had come over on the *Mayflower*, and numbered among their progeny governors and generals (Heymann, 290).

The issue of a union between a Lowell and a Winslow, Robert Traill Spence Lowell IV was marked out from the day of his birth, 1 March 1917, and was accorded the education of a Boston aristocrat. This particular Lowell, however, grew up to create his own future rather than the one his family had prefigured for him. As a matter of course he was sent to St Mark's School where his father and grandfather had gone and where his great-grandfather had been headmaster. But he did not have a distinguished career there; apart from coming low in his class at most subjects, the young Lowell was unmanageably huge in size and remarkably uncouth in manner. This brought about his lifelong nickname 'Cal', glossed by Lowell himself as a reference to the mad Roman emperor, Caligula. However, it seems at least as likely that the nickname arose from a class reading of *The Tempest* in which Lowell was cast as the savage Caliban (Clark 1979). The teacher who arranged this reading may have been the poet Richard Eberhart, the first of a series of father-figures, all literary, who took over as formative influences from the ineffectual Commander Lowell. Eberhart, then teaching at St Mark's School, had previously studied with the New Critics under I. A. Richards and alongside William Empson in England, at Cambridge. He was one of the few poets ever to be published in F. R. Leavis's periodical, *Scrutiny*. In retrospect, Eberhart described a manuscript Lowell showed him in 1935, comprising some sixty poems: 'His course was already indicated in titles such as "Madonna", "Jericho", "New England", "Death", "Easter, an Ode", "Jonah", and "Phocion". The raw power was there' (Eberhart 1947). 'Madonna' was to become Lowell's first published work, coming out in St Mark's school magazine, *The Vindex*, three months after the young poet's eighteenth birthday: 'Celestial were her robes;/Her hands were made divine;/But the Virgin's face was silvery bright,/Like the holy light/Which from God's throne/Is said to shine,/Giving the angels sight' (Hamilton, 26).

Thanks largely to Eberhart's guidance, Lowell in the autumn of 1935 entered Harvard University, with which many members of his family had been connected. However, he received little inspiration from a Faculty of English which included such respectable but chilly professors as Hyder Rollins and Bliss Perry. None of his poems appeared in the *Harvard Advocate*, nor was he allowed on the staff (Lowell 1961a). His first year seems to have been spent in the unofficial reading of modern poetry: Yeats, Eliot, Pound, William Carlos Williams, W. H. Auden. This period was further diversified by Lowell getting engaged to a woman five years his senior. The affair led to a conflict which came to a head at Christmas 1936 when, quite literally, Lowell had a fight with his father. His mother went for advice to her psychiatrist, Merrill Moore. Fortunately for Lowell, who might under other circumstances have been declared insane, Moore was himself a prolific poet. He recommended that Lowell make contact with the literary world in the shape of Ford Madox Ford, an eminent novelist and noted encourager of young talent. As it happened, Lowell had already met Ford at a Boston cocktail party and knew that he was about to go down to Tennessee to stay with a former college friend of Moore's, Allen Tate (Lowell 1961a). In the upshot, it was not so much Ford as Tate who was to prove a decisive influence. Allen Tate had been lecturing at Southwestern University in Memphis (Squires, 121) and, like Eberhart, had studied with the New Critics and was committed to a highly analytical discussion of literature. He himself had no permanent post but suggested that Lowell should leave Harvard and work under his own former teacher, the poet John Crowe Ransom, who was a professor at Vanderbilt University, Tennessee. However, shortly after Lowell's arrival in the state, Ransom accepted a Chair of Poetry newly created at Kenyon College, Ohio. This institute was an Episcopalian foundation, smaller than Vanderbilt and far less prestigious than Harvard; but Ransom calculated that the new post would afford him more opportunity for writing (Young, 269). He had already arranged that two of his best students at Vanderbilt, Peter Taylor and Randall Jarrell, should come to Kenyon with him, and he readily agreed to teach Lowell.

That summer of 1937, Lowell camped out in a tent on Allen Tate's lawn (Lowell 1959). He accompanied Tate and Ford to

writers' conferences at Olivet College, Michigan, and Boulder
College, Colorado (Axelrod 1978, 23). At the latter gathering,
Lowell met Jean Stafford who was to become one of the finest
post-war novelists, and also his first wife.

In the autumn of 1937 Lowell began his studies with John
Crowe Ransom at Kenyon College. He shared a room with Peter
Taylor, a story-writer of deceptively nonchalant distinction.
Taylor, indeed, was to chronicle Lowell's stormy relationship
with Jean Stafford in one of his most evocative fictions, '1939':
'Finally [Cal], without warning, seized [Jean] by the wrist, forcibly
led her from the room and closed the door after them . . . "Listen
to me," [Jean] began at once – belligerently, threateningly, all
but shaking her finger in his face. "I have sold my novel" '
(Taylor, 350). Apart from Taylor, Lowell's closest friend at Kenyon
was Randall Jarrell, already a graduate instructor in the college,
who went on not only to be a fine poet but America's leading
critic of contemporary verse.

However, during the Kenyon years and for some time after,
the influence of Allen Tate was strong. This can be seen in the
rhetorical patterning of the two poems Lowell published in the
first issue (Winter 1939) of a literary magazine Ransom had
started in order to put the college on the map: the *Kenyon
Review*. One of these poems, 'The Dandelion Girls', is a feverish
contemplation of mortality and, as such, bears points of resemblance to those juvenilia with which Lowell had tessellated the
pages of *The Vindex*. The form in this poem is more disciplined
though, and bears signs not only of Tate's influence but that of
the Metaphysical Poets: 'If wishes were white horses I/Under the
sirenic eyes should lie;/Or fluctuate on that charming stream/As a
windy wave-walking Christ'. This and its companion poem, 'The
Cities' Summer Death' – of which latter more hereafter – are to
be regarded as prentice-work. Ransom found Lowell's other
poems 'forbidding and clotted' (Lowell 1961a) and printed no
more until well after his pupil had graduated. The main outlet for
Lowell, therefore, had to be the undergraduate magazine, *Hika*,
which he co-edited with Robie Macauley in his senior year. Six
pieces appeared between December 1938 and February 1940,
including early versions of items that were to come out later, in a
first collection.

Ransom may not have been at this stage eager to print his
pupil's poems, but he encouraged Lowell to read the New Criticism,

on which topic he himself was writing a book. The New Critics bring out – some might say they tend to read in – an identifiable element of the classics they discuss which the most influential of them, William Empson, calls 'ambiguity'. This he defines as 'the synthesis of several units of observation into one commanding image' (Empson 1930, 2). In his turn, Tate calls this element 'tension'; an amalgam of connotation and denotation that transcends logic (Tate 1969, 65; 1976, 40-41). Lowell first encountered many of what were to become his favourite poems in the context of essays written by the critics of this school. Useful clues are provided by the poems Lowell chose to copy into his notebooks during his time at college, and immediately after (Axelrod 1978, 32; 245). He may well have read Donne's 'A Valediction Forbidding Mourning' in the setting of Tate's essay, 'Tension in Poetry' (Tate 1969, 56-71). Thus he would have met not only Donne's metaphysical image of 'gold to aiery thinnesse beate' but Tate's interpretative speculation round about it: 'Now the interesting feature here is the logical contradiction of embodying the unitary, nonspatial soul in a spatial image: the malleable gold is a plane whose surface can always be extended mathematically by one-half towards infinity; the souls are this infinity' (Tate 1969, 65). Other poems to be found in Lowell's notebooks include 'The Apparition' and 'Holy Sonnet XIII' ('What if this present were the world's last night?'). Both these poems are presented with an eye for interesting ambiguities by Empson in his *Seven Types of Ambiguity*: 'Is a man in the last stages of torture so beautiful, even if blood hides his frowns?' (Empson 1930, 184). Empson, a lifelong atheist, emphasizes the sensual aspect of the religious poems under discussion. He places Crashaw – a powerful influence in early Lowell – alongside Keats, remarking 'a saint is being adored for her chastity, and the metaphors about her are veiled references to copulation' (Empson 1930, 279). It is not surprising that Crashaw's 'Hymn to Sainte Teresa' is written out, at length, in Lowell's notebooks.

When they come to consider twentieth-century writers, the New Critics tend to privilege the modern poets who can be presented in terms similar to those that served for the Metaphysicals. Complexity, ingenuity, and paradox are the qualities that seem most in question. Essays by R. P. Blackmur (221-249) and Yvor Winters (1947, 431-459) on Wallace Stevens may have persuaded Lowell to copy out various poems by that author: 'On

the Manner of Addressing Clouds', 'Of Heaven Considered as a
Tomb', 'Le Monocle de Mon Oncle' and, especially, 'Sunday
Morning'. Something in the prose of the critics, a kind of willed
vividness, seems to have communicated itself to Lowell's verse
style in its early formation: 'The purpose of the images is to show
how they dissipate the "holy hush of ancient sacrifice", how the
natural comfort of the body is aware, but mostly unheeding, that
Sunday is the Lord's day' (Blackmur, 256); 'it places the protagonist finally and irretrievably on a small but beautiful planet,
floating like a tropical island in boundless space' (Winters 1947,
433). With regard to Hart Crane, Lowell transcribes those poems
which Winters defines as especially interesting in his essays 'The
Morality of Poetry' and 'The Experimental School' (Winters
1947, 17-29; 30-74); namely, 'Repose of Rivers', 'Voyages' II,
'For the Marriage of Faustus and Helen' II. One may infer that
Lowell's reproduction of 'Low Barometer', a poem by Robert
Bridges and hardly an anthology piece, was induced by a
remarkable essay on that author which Winters had published in
the literary magazine, *Hound and Horn*, in 1932. Lowell said, in
an interview, 'The kind of poet I am was largely determined by
the fact that I grew up in the heyday of the New Criticism'
(Lowell 1964b).

Lowell graduated from Kenyon College in June 1940, obtaining
high honours in Classics (Ransom). Three months previously, on
2 April, he had married Jean Stafford, by no means with his
parents' approval (Hamilton, 72). An editorial assistantship with
the *Kenyon Review* failed to come Lowell's way. So, on Ransom's
recommendation, Lowell went south to study at Louisiana State
University with two more of the New Critics, Cleanth Brooks
and Robert Penn Warren, while his wife worked as a secretary on
their magazine, the *Southern Review* (Cutrer, 196-197). That
way, at least, they could ensure that there was some money
coming in. Lowell also took instruction with a view to entering
the Roman Catholic church. He is said to have been reading *The
Spirit of Medieval Philosophical Experience* by Étienne Gilson
(Hamilton, 78), but there is no such book. Gilson, however,
published the Gifford Lectures, which he delivered at the University of Aberdeen, under the title of *The Spirit of Medieval
Philosophy* (1936), and this was followed by another set of lectures, delivered at Harvard, called *The Unity of Philosophical
Experience* (1938). Traces of the former may be seen in several

of Lowell's earlier poems, notably 'The Quaker Graveyard in Nantucket' and 'Cistercians in Germany'. A far more definite influence, however, stems from a further book by Gilson about the founder of the Cistercians, *The Mystical Theology of Saint Bernard* (1940). It was this book which provided Lowell with the title of his first collection, and its ascetic positives gave a Catholic gloss to what seems in Lowell to be essentially New England puritanism.

Lowell was received by Father Schexnayder into the Roman Catholic church in the spring of 1941, remarrying Jean Stafford, furthermore, according to the Catholic rites (Cutrer, 198). Stafford had already been converted and had lapsed, but Lowell acted out his religion with far more intensity than she ever did. She describes him, not without malice, persecuting another religious director: '[Lowell] mightily dismayed him, pestering him with abstruse exegeses of the sacraments as they might be applied to the modus vivendi of the New England transcendentalists, complaining of his failure to dislodge his mother from her unitarianism, demanding that I be brought to book for my failure to obey the letter of the law' (Stafford 1978). In September 1941 the young couple went to New York, where, on Father Schexnayder's recommendation (Cutrer, 201), Lowell got a job as editorial assistant to the Catholic publishing house, Sheed and Ward. Jean Stafford drafted much of her first novel, *Boston Adventure*, and carried on writing the book when, after eight months, they were invited south again to stay at Monteagle, Tennessee. Their hosts were Allen Tate (who was now freelancing) and his first wife, Caroline Gordon, herself a distinguished writer of fiction in the Southern genre. The main source of the Lowells' income at this time seems to have been derived from a family trust-fund (Hamilton, 72-82; 94). Lowell began a biography of the eighteenth-century Puritan, Jonathan Edwards, but soon turned – in the winter of 1942-43 – to the poems which were to form the core of *Land of Unlikeness*.

This title is a translation of *regio dissimilitudinis*, a phrase from St Bernard. But it is Étienne Gilson who provides the essential attitude and theme of the book:

Man lost his likeness to God in losing his virtues . . . the soul suffers, because she no longer knows how to accomplish in joy what before the first transgression she would have done without effort. Such is the condition of those who live in the Land of Unlikeness. They are not

happy there. Wandering, hopelessly revolving, in the 'circuit of the impious' those who tread this weary round suffer not only the loss of God but also the loss of themselves. They dare no longer look their own souls in the face; could they do it they would no longer recognize themselves. For when the soul has lost its likeness to God it is no longer like itself: *inde anima dissimilis Deo, inde dissimilis est et sibi.*
(Gilson 1940, 57-58)

This last sentence, the original of the preceding English one, forms the epigraph to Lowell's first collection. The whole passage is the substratum of the book: an attack on America for having fallen away from Christianity. Lowell's conversion to Catholicism gave him a weapon against his family, and this mode of ascetic philosophy afforded a fine opportunity for self-justification. In the book as a whole a degree of callowness in attitude and expression is evident, especially in the light of Lowell's later work; but critics as acute as Tate and Jarrell saw in these early efforts the stirrings of genius.

Lowell had published no verse for three years. However, in 1943 five poems were accepted by the *Sewanee Review* edited by Tate; four more were accepted by the *Partisan Review* edited by Jarrell's friend and fellow-radical, Philip Rahv; and Ransom took one for the *Kenyon Review*. These all appeared in the summer of that year; but, as early as March, Tate had recommended the collection, numbering some sixteen pieces, to the Cummington Press, Massachusetts, a small publishing house which had already brought out his own translation of the anonymous Latin poem, *Pervigilium Veneris*. The collection was accepted, with a proviso that Lowell should add a few more poems so as to bring it up to the size thought proper for a volume of verse.

Five poems were duly produced between 18 March and 2 April, and another one was hastily revised. They are called 'Concord Cemetery after the Tornado', 'The Wood of Life', 'Christ for Sale', 'The Bomber', 'Cistercians in Germany', 'A Suicidal Nightmare'. In his enthusiasm, Lowell never wrote more quickly; or more crudely. Five of the poems did not see magazine publication before the volume came out, and none of them were reprinted in any later collection. All exhibit a propensity to scold the world in language of eccentric violence, and all but one are couched in a characteristic three-stanza form. The best of the six is 'Cistercians in Germany' which describes cast-out monks filing

'Unter den Linden to the Wilhelmsplatz'. The final lines of this piece were utilized in a quite different context in *Lord Weary's Castle*.

Another batch of poems, unlike these just mentioned, achieved magazine publication: they included 'Leviathan', 'On the Eve of the Immaculate Conception 1942', 'Satan's Confession' and 'The Boston Nativity'. Over and over again, however, what seem to be attempts towards lyricism are thwarted by rancour of tone and extravagance of imagery. The manner in which 'Leviathan' had been rewritten from a draft that originally came out in *Hika* (April 1940) indicates that Lowell was attempting to follow a dictum of Allen Tate's: 'poetry . . . is the art of apprehending and concentrating our experience' (Tate 1969, 613). Therefore we read, to our astonishment, 'the ruined farmer knocked out Abel's brains'; while, in 'On the Eve of the Immaculate Conception', Lowell addresses the Virgin as 'belle and belly' and as 'celestial Hoyden'. The crude energy of these pieces becomes unacceptably grotesque when the temptation of Eve in 'Satan's Confession' is portrayed as 'Nick bends the Tree,/The Woman takes the Fall'; while, in a related poem, Moses is addressed as being 'Wet from your mummy-box'. This poem, 'Scenes from the Historic Comedy', went into *Lord Weary's Castle*, but only in truncated form. Its second and third sections were dropped, thus removing a weirdly allegorical element, and the remaining section was retitled 'The Slough of Despond': 'My way is wayward; there is no way out'.

None of the other poems so far considered was allowed, even in abridgment or revision, into *Lord Weary's Castle*. In this, Lowell showed a discrimination that was encouraged by Jarrell who went over the manuscript, selecting candidates for preferment (Axelrod 1978, 50). Three of the slighter poems that proceeded forward were 'The Crucifix', 'Salem' and 'Concord'. The theme of 'The Crucifix', the impossibility of being redeemed without the intercession of God, is represented in appropriately bleak terms – 'A stray dog's signpost' – in the last five lines which passed from one collection to the other unrevised. 'Salem', reproaching the present-day port of that name for cupidity, was the only poem allowed to pass as a whole from *Land of Unlikeness* to *Lord Weary's Castle* with no significant change. In a companion sonnet, 'Concord', critical of the town whose name it bears, there is on the other hand an extent of revision, mainly in the direction of bringing high-minded abstraction ('Gold idles here') down to earth ('Ten thousand Fords are idle here').

We move away from Boston in 'Dea Roma': the poet points out that, in spite of cupidity and barbarism, the Eternal City is still a place where the 'Fisherman' can 'bank his catch'. In revising the poem for *Lord Weary's Castle* a stanza full of melodramatic detail was dropped. However, there is an extent of ambiguity in this later version that renders unclear any reason why Rome should be more free from censure than Boston.

The tribulations of another empire are touched upon in one of the earliest of the sonnets Lowell was to cull from French history: 'Napoleon Crosses the Beresina'. The troops are unaware that 'ice/Is tuning them to tumbrils', and an epigraph to the poem, 'There will the eagles be gathered' (Matthew 24:28), refers to the defeated carcasses on the field of battle.

Two poems that deserve more attention than any so far cited are 'The Drunken Fisherman' and 'Children of Light'. The former is severely revised from 'The Dandelion Girls' (Rollins 1979a), and Lowell liked the revision well enough to send it through to *Lord Weary's Castle* with few further emendations. He also based some of his later poems on its rhythmic cadence which is itself adapted from Marvell's 'Upon Appleton House'. 'The Drunken Fisherman' stumbles over its feet more than this great original does, but the eccentricity has a dramatic function; for, in spite of the speaker's own uncertainties regarding his skill at catching fish, his hope is that he himself will be caught by the Fisher of Men. Similarly, 'Children of Light' presses Donne into service for an attack on the Puritans whom Lowell considered responsible for the commercial exploitation rife in America: 'Our Fathers wrung their bread from stocks and stones/And fenced their gardens with the Redman's bones'. In this mode, which identifies 'fence' with 'bones', we can detect not only Donne but Hopkins, Donne's nineteenth-century counterpart and a particular favourite of the New Critics. This line of wit continues through Lowell to younger contemporaries, such as Peter Porter who has a related feeling about Australian Calvinism in his 'Forefathers' View of Failure': 'Men with religion as their best technique,/Who built bush churches six days a week' (Porter, 3). Lowell's poetry is a bridge from Donne's satires and Hopkins's Dark Sonnets to the angry young men of the 1960s and beyond. Almost the only difference between the *Land of Unlikeness* version of Lowell's poem and the one that appears in *Lord Weary's Castle* is an alteration to the line 'And candles gutter in a hall of mirrors'. This last phrase is lost in favour of one that enhances a sense of place: 'And candles gutter by an empty altar'.

The best of these transition poems are three that seem ambitious in the context of *Land of Unlikeness* and are more appropriate to *Lord Weary's Castle*, for which they were eventually adapted. They are 'Christmas Eve in the Time of War', 'The Park Street Cemetery' and 'In Memory of Arthur Winslow'. The first of these was initially published in the *Partisan Review* (July-August 1943) as 'The Capitalist's Meditation by the Civil War Monument'. It appears in *Land of Unlikeness* as 'Christmas Eve in the Time of War' with, as subtitle, 'A Capitalist Meditates by a Civil War Monument'; which was the previous title. In this version the persona asks his materialist gods to buy off what looks to him like the end of his particular world. But, in their stead, another voice replies ' "I bring no peace, I bring the sword" '. This is the voice of Christ; the reference is to Matthew 11:34. A further revision appeared first in the magazine *Commonweal* (October 1946) and then in *Lord Weary's Castle*, under the title 'Christmas Eve under Hooker's Statue'. Joseph Hooker (1814-1879) was an American general who came out of retirement to lead a division on the Unionist side in the Civil War. Against this symbol of relentless belligerence is set a protagonist, no longer a fictional character but the poet speaking *in propria persona*, who inveighs against the current war; that being waged in 1942 – 'I ask for bread, my father gives me mould'. It is another reference to Matthew, this time 7:9 – 'What man is there of you, who if his son ask bread will he give him a stone?'. The poem as it appears in *Lord Weary's Castle* is cut down from five to three stanzas, the melodramatic second and fourth stanzas of the original being the ones sacrificed. A tone of complaint is subdued to one of disillusion, as though the poem were spoken by the poet himself in the guise of an older man. The speaker's bewilderment regarding the war is now answered not by Christ but by the novelist Herman Melville: ' "All wars are boyish" '. These words come from 'The March into Virginia', one of the *Battle-Pieces* that Melville had written during the Civil War. He was referring to the Battle of Manassas, but in the later poem Lowell has altered this to Chancellorsville (Staples, 91). Presumably this is because Hooker was defeated at the latter

place. One may infer from this admission of futility something
approaching a pious hope; that the world requires Christ to come
and fight the final war to abolish materialism.

In contrast with this poem, which was abridged for publication
in *Lord Weary's Castle*, Lowell expanded 'The Park Street
Cemetery' from an initial three stanzas; retitling it 'At the Indian
Killer's Grave'. There is a prosaic draft dating from 1941
(Hamilton, 76) which serves to show how deep-seated Lowell's
thoughts about his ancestors were. Some of the characteristics of
prose continue, in that 'The Park Street Cemetery' is one of the
only two poems in *Land of Unlikeness* that are unrhymed, the
other being 'Cistercians in Germany'. It is fairly loose in metre,
too, though not so much so as to approximate to free verse. 'At
the Indian Killer's Grave', on the other hand, has the heavy
rhyming and formal metric that characterized the earlier stage of
Lowell's maturity.

The *Land of Unlikeness* version, like the 1941 draft, uses a
survey of Boston tombstones to make a comment on the Founding
Fathers of New England. The stern surnames, 'Adams,/Otis,
Hancock, Mather, Revere' are framed by squalid surroundings:
'Here frayed/Cables wreathe the spreading obelisk'. This has
considerable affinity with the description of the Granary Burying
Ground as given by Jean Stafford in *Boston Adventure*. The
names in other cemeteries, says her elderly Boston aristocrat, are
second-rate: 'even Mr Emerson can't compete with Revere or
Otis'. As in Lowell's poem, however, the best names have to
compete with their environment: 'splitting gravestones', 'eroded
sarcophagi', 'the harsh garden' (Stafford 1944, 162). The affinity
between Lowell and Jean Stafford is more than that of verbal
description. Both seem to recognize the incumbents of this cemetery as destroyers, albeit destroyers in the name of national
purity. They see, further, that the past endeavours of these
Reveres and Otises are mocked by the present-day Irish who
hold 'the Golden Dome' – the Statehouse which the old lady in
Boston Adventure terms 'a perfect fright'. Amongst other matters, both authors register the fact that the formerly reigning
Puritans had been eroded by the once hated immigrants, trans-
forming Massachusetts in the process (Sullivan and O'Toole, 63).
The difference is that Stafford writes as one of these immigrants,
'lace-curtain Irish' (Stafford 1978); while Lowell, who had dropped
out of Harvard and embraced Catholicism, writes as a renegade.

The revision of 'The Park Street Cemetery' into 'At the Indian Killer's Grave' brought about an intenser degree of focus. The revised poem centres upon one particular ancestor, Josiah Winslow (1629-1680), Lowell's forbear on his mother's side. This specific Indian Killer perpetrated a war against Philip, King of the Wampanoag (Yenser, 57), which marked the end of the Indians as a national entity in New England (Axelrod 1978, 69). The increase in formality which marks Lowell's revision leads to the appearance of several literary parallels not in the earlier poem; most notably, an affinity with 'Ode to the Confederate Dead' by Allen Tate. Tate has 'The brute curiosity of an angel's stare' (1970, 17) while Lowell has 'the headstones of the dead/Whose chiselled angels peer/At you'. The Lowell poem is as deliberated as that of Tate, but it has an inner rage Tate's does not possess, perhaps as a result of Tate casting his younger contemporary in the role of a representative of the Puritans (Holder, 282). The head and hand imagery in the course of the poem – 'Philip's head/Grins on the platter' – derives from an account of the Indian king's death at Mount Hope Neck given in a letter from Richard Hutchinson (Mazzaro 1965, 49). The epigraph is from a story by Nathaniel Hawthorne who describes, in 'The Gray Champion', a figure symbolizing a veteran of King Philip's war. Lowell, however, is more condemnatory than Hawthorne, and he makes it seem as though being buried in the neglected cemetery is in itself a punishment for past misdemeanours. Even so, there are passages of rhetorical grandeur, greatly improved from the earlier version of the poem, which transcend the ostensible theme: 'A clutter of Bible and weeping willows guards/The stern Colonial magistrates'. The poem, moreover, finishes on a note of hope. It must be admitted, however, that this is glibly achieved, being only the final lines of 'Cistercians in Germany', a poem not reprinted in *Lord Weary's Castle* as a whole: 'through the trellis peers the sudden Bridegroom'. We may take this to be an image of Christ drawn from the author's theological reading (Gilson 1936, 297), though some commentators have detected an aura of the unreconstructed Indian, lingering outside the place where his persecutors are buried (Fein, 197; Williamson 1974, 34). This evidence of unresolved conflicts in Lowell's mind gives the poem, for all its melodrama, a sense of inner tragedy.

Lowell does not fully realize his theme even in the elegy for his grandfather, Arthur Winslow; though that, too, has fine passages.

Lowell's hostility to his family background forces him into a negative stand, and this causes an extent of disturbance he seems unable to control. It is as if he himself were a part of what he is condemning. Yet, whatever he felt about his ancestors, Lowell seems to have had in his childhood an affection for his grandfather; though as chronicled in the later *Life Studies*, this was tinctured with adult criticism. Even in Lowell's first attempt to write the elegy ('The Cities' Summer Death', *Kenyon Review*, Winter 1939), there is a conflict between benevolent intention towards Arthur Winslow and disquiet at the ethos from which the old man evolved. This produces some functionless distortion of language: 'Grandfather feathery as thought/Furls his flurried wrapper'. In 1942, four years after Arthur Winslow's death, Lowell produced a wholesale revision that deserves to be looked at as a new work ('Death from Cancer on Easter', *Sewanee Review*, Summer 1943): 'This Easter, Arthur Winslow, less than dead/Your people set you up in Phillips House/To settle off your wrangle with the crab'. Winslow is dying of cancer: just as cancer is the name for the astrological sign of the crab, and crabs can be caught on the Boston Basin which abuts on the hospital – Phillips House – where Winslow lies. So the longshoremen catching the crabs can be identified with Charon, the boatman who ferries the souls away from their bodies across the river Styx – here termed Acheron – except that Winslow dies to the sound of bells, imperfectly heard, proclaiming the resurrection of Christ. It is certainly clever; but the elaboration seen in this draft tends to defeat itself.

The verbal revision into the poem 'Death from Cancer', as it appeared in *Land of Unlikeness*, seems mostly to have been for the purpose of lucidity. 'Wrangle with the crab' becomes 'wrestling with the crab', and a mysterious 'Ghost/with seven wounds' is explicitly identified as Jesus. There is, however, a rise in hostility (Rollins 1979b) whereby Arthur Winslow is not so much 'borne' as 'run' 'Beyond Charles River to the Acheron/Where the wide waters and their voyager are one'. This suggests for the departed soul not resurrection but dissolution. The main difference, however, between the *Sewanee Review* version of the poem and that which appears in *Land of Unlikeness* is that three further sections are added. What is now the second section, 'Dunbarton', resembles the poem which describes the Park Street Cemetery – 'half-forgotten Starks and Winslows' – though historically the places are distinct. The third section, 'Five Years Later', deals with a return to Dunbarton where Arthur Winslow's grave is indicated in a manner which shows him to resemble his cupidinous ancestors. The final section, 'A Prayer for my Grandfather to Our Lady', seems, in spite of its title, to be spoken by Arthur Winslow himself. It is a plea for mercy, though phrased in an odd fashion: 'pour/Buckets of blessings on my burning head'. There is a reference here to Psalm 51:7, a desire to be washed whiter than snow; however, the situation also resembles that of Dives and Lazarus (Matthew 19:24; Luke 16:19-25) where the rich man is unable to enter the kingdom of heaven. Arthur Winslow is made to symbolize the commercial America that, in Lowell's view, had slipped away from God; become, in fact, the 'land of unlikeness'. It is certainly one way for Lowell to justify his own career which must, so far, have seemed to his family a history of negligence. Revision seems to be a way of finding out what he really meant, and the alterations that took 'In Memory of Arthur Winslow' from *Land of Unlikeness* to *Lord Weary's Castle* show to what extent Lowell's surrealistic tendencies were in fact a defence mechanism. 'The mirrored sun/Is booming' becomes 'the cold sun/Is melting'. Speaking of the place where Starks and Winslows rest, the line of verse 'Broken down boulders sprawl out where our fathers preached' becomes, far more lucidly, 'Their sunken landmarks echo what our fathers preached'. With *Lord Weary's Castle*, 'In Memory of Arthur Winslow' reached completion, though not fulfilment. The Winslow poems of *Life Studies* dramatize the family conflicts; and, because Arthur Winslow remains part of Lowell's background, he figures as one of 'Two Farmers' in *History*. Finally he erupts in Lowell's last collection, *Day by Day*.

Land of Unlikeness is, as we have seen, a young man's book. Many positions remain unresolved; but some of the poems could not have been revised any further without confusion setting in. For example, there is considerable doubt in Lowell's attitude towards the Puritan settlers of New England. In some poems they are pillars of virtue, especially when they trounce the English, and in others – when they kill the Redskins, for instance – they are the progenitors of all Lowell disliked in contemporary Boston. That contemporary Boston was quick enough to condemn him; but what are his positive values? The Catholicism that he puts forward contains too much gloom and disturbance to constitute an adverse critique. It is really a way of justifying some of his

personal choices. What makes the poems eccentric is their failure
to build up a motivation for their sorrow. Lowell seems to threaten
the universe saying that, if it doesn't treat him well enough, he
won't let it pass its exam (Empson 1961).

Nevertheless, from time to time the language speaks out –
plangently, specifically – in something of the way defined by the
New Critics in their analyses of Donne, Crashaw, Lord Herbert
of Cherbury, Marvell. It is not surprising that these critics and
their acolytes recognized similar qualities in this work of Lowell's.
Allen Tate wrote a preface to *Land of Unlikeness* which set the
tone of subsequent reviews: 'The style is bold and powerful, and
the symbolic language often has the effect of being *willed*; for it is
an intellectual style compounded of brilliant puns and shifts of
tone'. Discussing the book in the *Partisan Review* (Winter 1945),
Randall Jarrell called its author 'a serious, objective, and extraordinarily accomplished poet'. Conrad Aiken in his review for
the *New Republic* (23 November 1944) said '[Lowell's] angry and
violent use of Catholic symbolism is often . . . extraordinarily
effective'. Arthur Mizener (*Accent*, Winter 1945) found the
poetry 'vividly symbolic in every detail'. Even the less favourable
reviews treated the book as a serious contribution to literature,
by an author whose development would be worth watching.
R. P. Blackmur in the *Kenyon Review*, Spring 1945, said that
Lowell conceived the world as 'a place of banishment' and that
'the problem is actual to him'. Alan Swallow, Winters's publisher,
claimed (*New Mexico Quarterly Review*, Spring 1945) that *Land
of Unlikeness* used 'Tate's doctrine of tension, warped by fanat-
ical fervor'. For a slender first volume, issued in an edition of
250 copies, the quantity and quality of comment is impressive.

To some extent this degree of attention was activated by the
fact that Lowell's poems and critiques were coming out, not only
in his familiar stamping-grounds of the *Kenyon, Sewanee* and
Partisan reviews, but also in such periodicals as *The Nation*
(where Jarrell was Poetry Editor), *Poetry, Commonweal* and
Foreground. A new figure had entered the literary landscape.

Lowell needed his growing reputation. In September 1943 he
had attracted publicity of quite another kind by writing a personal
letter, as one scion of a distinguished family to another, informing
President Roosevelt that he refused to be conscripted for the
army. His ground for objection was the Allied bombing of civilian
populations which had turned a patriotic war into the putative

destruction of Germany (Heymann, 325-326). Lowell was sent to prison in Danbury, Connecticut, and served five months, emerging in March 1944 on a parole which lasted until November of that year. He and Jean Stafford then set up house in Black Rock, Connecticut, scene of several items in the next batch of poems. Jean Stafford's novel, *Boston Adventure*, came out to considerable and justified acclaim. It is a satire on Boston values; but its royalties enabled the couple in September 1945 to buy a house by Damariscotta Lake on the coast of Maine. The winter there, commemorated in a poem called 'The Holy Innocents' and an evocative prose piece, proved too harsh for them: 'icicles hanging from all the bathroom taps and great tumors and hideous fractures in the pipes' (Stafford, 1954). So they based themselves for three months in Cambridge, Massachusetts, staying with the poet Delmore Schwartz whose marriage had recently broken up (Atlas, 263-265).

Between June 1944 and September 1945, before leaving Connecticut, Lowell had written the substantive part of *Lord Weary's Castle*. He sent Jarrell the manuscript in the latter month; Jarrell sent it on to Philip Rahv, co-editor of the *Partisan Review*; and Rahv sent it to Robert Giroux, editor at the publishers Harcourt, Brace, who agreed to bring it out, naming as publication date autumn 1946 (Hamilton, 98; 108).

The Lowells settled in their home on Damariscotta Lake in March 1946. Lowell, while his wife organized carpenters and plumbers, was frequently away in New York (Heymann, 358). That summer, though, the couple played host to what Jean Stafford was to call an influx of poets. 'All those poets came to our house in Maine and stayed for weeks at a stretch, bringing wives or mistresses with whom they quarrelled, and complaining so vividly about the wives and mistresses they'd left, or had been left by, that the discards were real presences, swelling the ranks, stretching the house, *my* house (my very own, my first and very own), to its seams' (Stafford 1978). First came John Berryman, perhaps Lowell's most formidable contemporary, with his then wife, Eileen Simpson. They occupied the 'pretty guest room at the front of the house' and were not allowed to leave as originally planned: 'we felt they were pleading with us not only because they, too, were enjoying our company: It was also because they wanted not to be alone' (Simpson, 116; 132). There followed Philip and Natalie Rahv; R. P. Blackmur; Randall Jarrell and

Peter Taylor; Blair Clark and Frank Parker, schoolmates of
Lowell at St Mark's, together with their respective wives; Robert
Giroux, Lowell's editor at Harcourt, Brace (Hamilton, 114;
Heymann, 359). All these, and many others, stayed with the
Lowells in Maine. One notable guest was the estranged wife of
Delmore Schwartz, 'in her sleek, chic negligee of white linen
shorts and a long-sleeved pale-blue shirt with bogus emerald
Chanel cufflinks' (Stafford 1978). The former Mrs Schwartz went
on to New York and, in September 1946, Lowell left Damariscotta
Lake to join her. He ceased to be a Roman Catholic at this time,
and asked Jean Stafford for a divorce. His exhausted wife retired
to a clinic for alcoholics; *Lord Weary's Castle* came out in
December 1946.

Robert Lowell was awarded the Pulitzer Prize, a Guggenheim
Fellowship, an honorarium from the American Academy of
Arts and Letters; he was appointed Consultant in Poetry at the
Library of Congress; he was even photo-featured in *Life* maga-
zine. Not on his family's terms but in his own right, he was a
successful Lowell at last.

2 *Lord Weary's Castle* (1946)

Robert Lowell may have seemed to turn his back on his family traditions, but he spent most of his working life writing about them. Only a latent commitment to the path he ostensibly rejected could have impelled him into so much protestation. His adopted faith, Roman Catholicism, was worn with a difference. At Baton Rouge, Lowell had frequented such popularizers of the Thomists as Étienne Gilson, Jacques Maritain, and E. I. Watkin. He reread Gerard Manley Hopkins and wrote an enthusiastic piece about him, applauding his 'inebriating exuberance' (Lowell 1944). He reviewed T. S. Eliot's *Four Quartets*, declaring 'artistic craft is analogous to contemplative discipline, aesthetic experience is analogous to ecstasy' (Lowell 1943). Yet, whatever the technical affiliations with Catholic and Anglo-Catholic poets, *Lord Weary's Castle* remains a Puritan work. Boston values are denounced, and there is no chance for anyone to repent.

It is not anything in Hopkins or Eliot that gives the book its peculiar title, but a Scots ballad called 'Lamkin'. The eponymous hero is a mason who is refused payment by a lord, Weary, for building a castle. Thereupon Lamkin kills Weary's wife and son. In his turn, however, Lamkin is made to mourn:

> O sweetly sang the black-bird
>   that sat upon the tree;
> But sairer grat Lamkin
>   when he was condemned to die.

John Berryman commented: 'Lord Weary's castle is a house of ingratitude, failure of obligation, crime and punishment . . . The wandering blood of Cain cannot repent' (Berryman 1947). This gives us the plot of *Lord Weary's Castle* as a whole. Weary stands for Cain who, in turn, represents mankind; Lamkin is the Lamb of God who dies through man's ingratitude. Anyone but a Puritan, however, would have turned the identification the other way about.

Lord Weary's Castle, it follows, is based on a peculiar reading of the Bible: Revelation, the minor prophets, and certain books of the Apocrypha bulk large. The Founder of Christianity, on the other hand, appears largely in terms of his less promising texts: 'And whosoever shall fall upon this stone shall be broken' (Matthew 21:44); 'Depart from me, ye cursed, into everlasting fire' (Matthew 25:41). Repentance does not enter *Lord Weary's Castle*, for it is inhabited by people who, in spite of God's omnipotence, are marked out as being beyond his grace.

These poems are the progress of a kind of Lowell-ego who is best considered not as a Catholic but as an exile. Indeed, the first poem printed in the book is called 'The Exile's Return'. Its stance derives from the notion of 'a nature exiled in the imperfect' (Maritain, 32), and its imagery seems to be that of a refugee's flight in wartime. But in fact much of the poem stems (Staples, 93) from two separate passages in Thomas Mann's story 'Tonio Kröger' as translated from the German by H. T. Lowe-Porter:

(a) In the gabled streets it was wet and windy and there came in gusts a sort of soft hail, not ice, not snow . . . powerful machine-saws hissed and spat and cut up timber.
(b) He looked at everything: the narrow gables . . . the Holstenwall . . . Then he . . . went through the squat old gate, along the harbour, and up the steep, windy street to his parents' house . . . The garden lay desolate, but there stood the old walnut tree where it used to stand, groaning and creaking heavily in the wind.
(Lowe-Porter, 76-77; 108-111)

The first passage depicts a winter day in Tonio Kröger's boyhood; the second shows him returning as an adult to a town which seems to be desolate. Lowell conflates these passages to convey a sense of a figure excluded from his father's house:

> There mounts in squalls a sort of rusty mire,
> Not ice, not snow . . .
> . . . The search-guns click and spit and split up timber
> And nick the slate roofs on the Holstenwall . . .
>
> . . . guns unlimber

>   And lumber down the narrow gabled street
>   Past your gray, sorry and ancestral house
>   Where the dynamited walnut tree
>   Shadows a squat, old, wind-torn gate . . .

The Exile re-entering what seems to be the Lübeck of Mann's childhood is also Lowell returning to a desolate past. The implications of war are inserted by the poet: for example, the 'machine-saws' in the prose source are turned into 'search-guns' in the poem, and the 'walnut tree', which in Mann merely creaks with age, in Lowell has been 'dynamited'. Further, the last line of the poem reads '*Voi ch'entrate*, and your life is in your hands'. This refers to the inscription Dante records in his *Inferno* as being written on the gates of hell. H. F. Cary translates this inscription as 'All hope abandon, ye who enter here'. The 'ancestral house' of the poem, like Lord Weary's Castle in the book at large, has fallen. To re-enter is to be damned. This poem rises from deep within Lowell's autobiography, though it needs its sources to provide a structure. What Lowell rejects morally he does not discard artistically. Rather he dwells upon such material, fascinated; by his own light, therefore, courting damnation.

The second poem printed in the book is called 'The Holy Innocents'. Its topography relates to Damariscotta Lake where Lowell and Jean Stafford were living in the inhospitable winter of 'the year,/The nineteen-hundred forty-fifth of grace'. A threatening landscape – 'cindered ice below the burlap mill' – derives not only from Damariscotta Lake but from a painting by the sixteenth-century Flemish artist, Pieter Bruegel the Elder. This painter was in Lowell's eyes definitively Protestant: ' "all bawdy hoydens and horny knaves" ' (Stafford 1978). Lowell may have come across his work in the 'Carnegie set of art books' presented to his school (Lowell 1961a; Clark 1979). Bruegel's *Return of the Herd* shows cattle being driven into winter quarters. Since they are destined for slaughter, Lowell makes them the equivalent of the Innocents whose Massacre is chronicled in Matthew 2:16. The 'clinkered hill' up which they are driven is not only a local reference but also a symbol, representing time (Cosgrave, 69; Williamson 1974, 19).

A related genre-piece is 'The North Sea Undertaker's Complaint', a sonnet deriving its greens and blues from another painting by Bruegel, *Gloomy Day*. This poem is a remarkable exercise in the macabre. There is no undertaker responsible for the North Sea; but, if there were, he might well speak of 'our dumb/Club-footed orphan' and 'the martyrdom/Of one more blue-lipped priest'. Yet another sortie into Bruegel is 'The Blind Leading the Blind': based on a painting which itself is based on a Biblical text, Matthew 15:14. A further attempt by Lowell at this theme, 'The Fens', derives from a passage from William Cobbett's *Rural Rides*. In both these poems, 'The Blind Leading the Blind' and 'The Fens', it is the complacency of the peasants, representing humanity, that is under attack.

During the course of the poems printed in the earlier pages of *Lord Weary's Castle* Lowell shifts his gaze backward, biographically speaking, from Damariscotta Lake to a scene which had become familiar some eighteen months before, when he had been released from prison to fulfil the terms of his parole. Jean Stafford, as was recounted in Chapter One, had found a house at Black Rock, Connecticut, and that area furnished Lowell with the material for several of his poems. A large Hungarian population, most of them working at the Sikorski helicopter plant, worshipped at the church of this district, St Stephen's. From that church it was possible (Staples, 42) to look across to a range of black mud flats. Jean Stafford was not prepared to be romantic about this, and evoked the atmosphere dramatically in her story, 'The Home Front': 'A savage sunset ignited the windows of defense plants across the water, caused derelict heaps of rubbish to glitter blindingly, smote the khaki wings of helicopters which all day gyrated over the disheveled land'. Still, there was another aspect: 'on a clear day, the doctor could look the other way and see, far off, the live blue Sound and the silhouettes of white sailboats and gray battleships' (Stafford 1945, 105; 110).

Lowell's counterpart to this was 'Colloquy in Black Rock'. The poem begins with a caricature of industrial toil, referring parodically in lines three and five to I Corinthians 13:1 –

> Here the jack-hammer jabs into the ocean;
> My heart, you race and stagger and demand
> More blood-gangs for your nigger-brass percussions,
> Till I, the stunned machine of your devotion,
> Clanging upon this cymbal of a hand,
> Am rattled screw and footloose . . .

The 'colloquy' of the title takes place between the poet and his heart, which drives the blood about his body and is at the same time taken to be the seat of all emotions. Over and over again Lowell exclaims upon the mud: 'mud/For watermelons gutted to the crust,/Mud for the mole-tide harbour'. The theme of the poem is the power of God to elicit from degraded material something of lasting value: 'In Black Mud/Hungarian workmen give their blood'. This refers to the workers donating their blood for transfusion as part of the war effort, possibly under the auspices of the church (Staples, 42-43). It is as though they were giving their blood directly 'For the martyre Stephen, who was stoned to death'. That, in its turn, invokes the first Christian martyr (Acts of the Apostles 7:59) who is treated in the poem as though he were also the Stephen who is the patron saint of Hungary. The iterations give the poem some part of its character: 'Black Mud, a name to conjure with'; and, once the conjuration has taken effect, 'In Black Mud/Stephen the martyre was broken down to blood'. What is detritus can be redeemed: 'Our ransom is the rubble of his death'. Much of the effect lies in a mode of repetition that simulates stressed and intensive rhyming. It works upon the reader's responses in the manner of a preacher or orator, and raises what had begun as the caricature of an industrial complex to an ecstatic vision:

> Christ walks on the black water. In Black Mud
> Darts the Kingfisher. On Corpus Christi, heart,
> Over the drum-beat of St. Stephen's choir
> I hear him, *Stupor Mundi* . . .

That term, 'the wonder of the world', was originally accorded by the chronicler, Matthew Paris, to the Holy Roman Emperor, Frederick II. Here it is transferred to the composite idea of Stephen, both Protomartyr and Patron Saint and, beyond him, to the feast which the poem celebrates, Corpus Christi. The industrial complexities have dropped away – 'the mud/Flies from his hunching wings' – and what is disclosed is the personal rapture of the Exile when he sights the Holy Spirit in its act of transformation: 'my heart,/The blue kingfisher dives on you in fire'. That formulation in the second person – 'dives on *you*' – is particularly telling, in key with the overall sense of colloquy. The poem is all the more powerful for being located in a recognizable tradition. Its antecedents include 'The Windhover' by Gerard Manley Hopkins and 'Little Gidding' IV ('The dove descending') by T. S. Eliot. Behind all these is the notion of the Holy Spirit, or Paraclete. Indeed, Lowell's own poem was originally (Axelrod 1978, 54) to be called 'Pentecost': 'And suddenly there came a sound from heaven as of a rushing mighty wind' (Acts of the Apostles 2:2).

There seems to be in all this the ruling out of personal responsibility in favour of what is essentially a single sacrifice. It is unlikely that a Catholic such as Hopkins or an Anglo-Catholic such as Eliot would have felt much sympathy with this poem, whatever the affinity of style. Even so, there is a sense of illumination here that we do not find in a companion piece, 'Christmas at Black Rock'. In that poem the industrial operatives – Polish this time – seem to drag the Exile down to their caricature of 'Glory to God in the highest' (Luke 2:14): 'their juke-box booms/ *Hosannah in excelsis Domino*'. There is little that is catholic, with either a capital or lower-case initial, here. Christ is a symbol made out of evergreen, representing not continuance but death. The poem concludes 'And the green needles nail us to the wall'.

Closely related, and equally reductive, is 'New Year's Day'. '*Puer natus est*' ('Unto us a child is born', Isaiah 9:6) is first shown in terms of a kitten buried in a Christmas box, then in terms of a baby being circumcized by a representation of St Joseph in a Damariscotta burlap shack. The whole indicates the reduction in stature of the Saviour seeking to function in the fallen world, and concludes 'The Child is born in blood, O child of blood'.

Lowell's is an individual concept of the Christian Year, and marks a pattern that can be discerned throughout *Lord Weary's Castle*: in poems such as 'Christmas Eve under Hooker's Statue', already discussed in Chapter One, and in 'To Peter Taylor on the Feast of the Epiphany'. The latter poem, addressed to Lowell's Kenyon College friend, dwells upon ambiguous gifts: the Irish working folk recall the Wise Men, while the Bridgeton salespeople produce weapons of war. 'To Peter Taylor', in its turn, relates to 'The Dead in Europe', a composite monologue in which European victims of Second World War bombing make a reiterative appeal to the Virgin Mary in order that she may rescue them from the jellied fire (Fein, 165).

The pattern of the Christian Year remains discernible even
when there is a further biographical shift backwards, from
Connecticut to Boston, when the Exile returns to his boyhood
home (Staples, 95). 'The First Sunday in Lent' shows a carnival
which transmogrifies the Fall of Troy to represent the life and
folly of mankind at large. The Ferris wheel becomes a symbol for
the turning world; and all the revellers reduce to one composite
figure, a fellow-townsman who zigzags through the circus hoops,
oblivious of the fact that this is the run-up to Easter. The poem
ends, 'He is the only happy man in Lent./He laughs into my face
until I cry'.

In 'Winter in Dunbarton', a sort of epilogue to 'In Memory of
Arthur Winslow', the symbol for the world is reduced still further,
from Ferris wheel to sundial. This is a sundial, moreover, incongruously set in a world of ice and snow. Arthur Winslow himself
(here called 'father') is contracted to the dimensions of his own
cat, who went through certain predatory transactions in his time
and is now, like his late master, dead: 'curled/Tight as a boulder'.
A further epilogue, even more reductive, shows the notion of the
Boston plutocrat diminished into a second childhood, that of
Mary Winslow. In the eponymous poem, Arthur's relict is summoned, as was her husband before her, by the Chapel bells. But
in her case their call amounts to no more than an imitation of her
terrified, senile babble: 'Come, Mary Winslow, come; I bell thee
home'.

Yet other aspects of Boston culture, or the lack of it, are filled
in by 'Salem', 'Concord' and 'Children of Light'. These are *Land
of Unlikeness* poems, reprinted in *Lord Weary's Castle* with
various emendations, and were discussed in Chapter One.
'Rebellion', 'In the Cage' and 'At a Bible House' are closely
associated. The first narrates in terms of New England history
Lowell's quarrel with his father; Jarrell (1985, 147f) detected its
genesis in a *Land of Unlikeness* poem, 'Leviathan'. 'In the Cage',
a tetrametric sonnet, depicts the prison to which Lowell was sent
when he made public his objections to the war. 'At a Bible
House' shows how, even though such a resolution as the one
Lowell made may be admirable, the Chosen Person is sometimes
unprepossessing. This notion of an Elect is a clue to lead us along
the elaborately blighted landscape of *Lord Weary's Castle* to a
study of the Fall of Man, at once poetic and (almost a contradiction in terms) Calvinistic.

'As a Plane Tree by the Water' refers to a text from the Apocrypha: Ecclesiasticus 24:14 – 'I was exalted like a palm-tree in Engaddi, and as a rose-plant in Jericho, as a fair olive-tree in a pleasant field, and grew up as a plane-tree by the water'. In the poem which derives from this, the tree is defiled and the rose shattered. Further, the emphasis the poem puts upon the incidence of flies reminds us that those creatures were associated with one of the chief devils, Beelzebub (2 Kings 1:2). Most of all, the incantatory rhythm evokes a scene in order that it may be denounced:

> Darkness has called to darkness, and disgrace
> Elbows about our windows in this planned
> Babel of Boston where our money talks
> And multiplies the darkness of a land
> Of preparation where the Virgin walks
> And roses spiral her enamelled face
> Or fall to splinters on unwatered streets.
> Our Lady of Babylon, go by, go by,
> I was once the apple of your eye;
> Flies, flies are on the plane tree, on the streets.

The peculiar qualities of this poem stem from the combination of that rhythm with an elaborate sentence-structure. The continuity is further maintained by a pattern of alliteration and assonance intricate enough to form an internal system additional to the obsessive rhyming and heavy stressing: 'Darkness'/'darkness'/ 'disgrace'; 'Elbows'/'windows'; 'Babel'/'Boston'; 'money'/ 'multiplies'; 'darkness'/'land'/'preparation'/'Virgin'; etc. The overall impression is that of the city as a fair concept irredeemably corrupted: 'Flies strike the miraculous waters of the iced/Atlantic'. The city may seem to be singing for the resurrection, but 'Flies, flies are on the plane tree, on the streets'. This is an instance, not common in Lowell's earlier poems, of form being operative and not merely incidental.

A further instance is 'Where the Rainbow Ends'. Here the stanza is that which Matthew Arnold used in 'The Scholar Gipsy', a poem about an artist who decided to leave the flurry of the town and live with the travelling people. It is a stanza conducive to sonority: its rhymes are dispersed through a ten-line structure which is basically pentametric, but diversified by a short sixth line which acts as a pivot for the whole. Lowell had already used this stanza for the final revision of 'In Memory of Arthur Winslow', and his poems in this metre date in their inception from the period when he and Jean Stafford were staying with Allen Tate and Caroline Gordon at Monteagle, Tennessee, in 1942 (Axelrod 1978, 36). 'Where the Rainbow Ends', the final poem printed in *Lord Weary's Castle*, is a vision of Boston at the end of its tether as seen by, quite explicitly, the protagonist of 'The Exile's Return'. Like 'The Exile's Return', 'Where the Rainbow Ends' begins with a vision of threatening weather:

> I saw the sky descending, black and white,
> Not blue, on Boston where the winters wore
> The skulls to jack-o'-lanterns on the slates,
> And Hunger's skin-and-bone retrievers tore
> The chickadee and shrike . . .

Behind these hard gutturals and dental sibilants is the recognition that the city as a whole has been judged and found wanting. The bitter weather is a symbol of death – 'serpents whistle at the cold' – and here, as elsewhere, the serpent represents not only death but time. The Exile has no option other than to become his own sacrifice – 'The victim climbs the altar steps' – concluding, however, that through no action of his own can he be saved:

> . . . What can the dove of Jesus give
> You now but wisdom, exile? Stand and live,
> The dove has brought an olive branch to eat.

This is a note of hope, that some may be saved; and also of acceptance, that many are to be damned. The Covenant, invoked by the Rainbow of the title, does not extend to all.

A version of this concept is acted out in fictional terms by 'The Death of the Sheriff'. This, Lowell's most obscure poem, relates to Virgil's story of Laomedon who hired Poseidon, the god of the sea, to build the walls of his city, Troy (Fein, 35). When the work was done, Laomedon, like Lord Weary, refused to pay the builder. The epigraph of the poem concerns his sole surviving son, and can be translated 'Perhaps you may of Priam's fate enquire'. The line in question comes from a passage in the *Aeneid*: II 506-634. Because of Laomedon's guilt, Troy is left

vulnerable, and Priam lives on to see the city in flames. The story
as it appears in Virgil is narrated by Aeneas who escaped the
destruction and is in exile, after the event, at the court of Dido,
Queen of Carthage. He tells her that he had it in mind to kill
Helen, whom he regarded as the cause of Troy's disaster, but he
was restrained by his mother, Venus, goddess of love. She had
informed him that the Fall of Troy came not from any recent
agency but from the original failure to pay the god his due. The
drama, in other words, once set in motion, cannot be controlled
by individual will. This to some extent replicates the Fall of Man.

In the sonorous stanza-form of 'Where the Rainbow Ends',
which dealt with the Fall of Boston, Lowell attempts to rewrite
the Virgilian story. His narrator is the nephew of the Sheriff of
the title; we recall Aeneas was related to King Priam. To this
Sheriff has occurred something insupportable, fully equivalent to
the Fall of Troy. The fact of the calamity, however, does not
directly figure in the narrative; and that is why the poem seems
obscure. It may be that there is a sacrifice which pays off the debt
that is owed to the gods. It may further be that the partner of the
Aeneas-figure is Helen, although her mode of presentation
resembles far more that which in the *Aeneid* is reserved for
Aeneas's mother, Venus: 'pura per noctem in luce'; or, as the
translation by C. Day Lewis puts it, 'all glowing with light she
came through the gloom'. Possibly the connection between the
Aeneas-figure and the Helen-figure is incestuous, and it is the
recognition of this that has driven the Sheriff mad. An intention
incompletely realized by the author might cast Lowell's father in
the role of the Sheriff, Lowell's mother as Helen, and Lowell
himself as Aeneas. However that may be, 'The Death of the
Sheriff' ends with the protagonist's burial, described in terms that
imply the world has learned nothing from all its deaths:

> . . . Digging has begun,
> The hill road sparkles, and the mourners' cars
> Wheel with the whited sepulchres of stars
> To light the worldly dead-march of the sun.

A similar theme, destruction beyond volition, gives rise to a
related poem, 'Between the Porch and the Altar'. This is in four
sections. The first, a third-person narrative, describes the domin-
ation of a mother over her son; himself, the central persona of

this work. The imagery of this first section is recessive, presented as a series of cyclic serpent figures: 'the swallowed serpent, wound/Into its bowels'; 'A little golden snake that mouths a hook'. Time appears to go backward, into infancy, and this is a means of dramatizing the mother as an intimidating force. The second section, in contrast, is spoken by the son, and tells of an adulterous affair. This is framed by an image that appears first and last: that of the statue of a farmer, symbolizing an uncaring bourgeoisie, the 'cold-eyed seedy fathers'. In the third section, the Mistress, Katherine, relates her pain in her own voice: 'clear, open, and speech-like' (Jarrell 1955, 192). She dreams that she is walking through the snow to church but, finding herself without anyone to sponsor her, is unable to get in. Once again the cyclic figure predominates: 'I run about in circles till I drop/Against a padlocked bulkhead in a yard/Where faces redden and the snow is hard'. The fourth and final section is, like the second, narrated by the man: 'I sit at a gold table with my girl'. The progression is from a nightclub ironically called 'The Altar', through a race in the night against traffic lights set at red and symbolizing the Deadly Sins, to the inevitable crash. This takes the guilty couple right through the façade of a church and into a pile-up against a genuine altar at last. The holy water sprinkled at mass falls on to the car as it burns, turning the ritual into a funeral service. The wreckage is at once bier and (a reference back to the recessive imagery of the first section) baby-carriage.

The title of this poem derives from Joel, one of the minor prophets with a special propensity for denouncing mankind. One point of interest about his book is that it gave rise to the medieval hymn, 'Dies Irae', which became a climactic point for such romantic masterpieces as Berlioz's *Grande Messe des Mortes* and Verdi's *Requiem*: 'Let the priests, the ministers of the Lord, weep between the porch and the altar' (Joel 2:17). Jean Stafford has a story with this same title and, like Lowell's poem, it deals with the temptations that beset even the would-be penitent: 'The girl prayed that nothing would mar the spirit of penance which she carried like a fragile light within her' (Stafford 1945, 152). The pain of the girl in Jean Stafford's story has a good deal to do with that of Katherine in the poem by Lowell. In both, the implication seems to be that, without an almost superhuman compliance with the will of Christ, men and women – whatever their excuses – are lost.

This is surely to recognize predestination: 'the wandering blood of Cain cannot repent'. The quotation from John Berryman, already cited, might almost be a line from 'The Quaker Graveyard in Nantucket'. The poem is basically an elegy for Lowell's cousin Warren Winslow. There are various parallels between 'The Quaker Graveyard in Nantucket' and Milton's 'Lycidas' (Staples, 45ff; Dubrow; Hobsbaum 1985). Both are about young men lost at sea; both are of approximately similar length; both are couched in a stanza which, like that of 'The Scholar Gipsy', uses dispersed rhymes in the interests of sonority. Further, both poems were composed when their respective authors were just under the age of thirty.

'The Quaker Graveyard in Nantucket' is in a central tradition of elegy. It relates not only to 'Lycidas' and 'The Scholar Gipsy' but to Shelley's 'Adonais' and to 'The Wreck of the Deutschland' by Gerard Manley Hopkins. It escapes too narrow an English imprimatur by learning from poems of its author's own country near to his own time. One factor which contributes to the development of Lowell's techniques after *Land of Unlikeness* is the absorption into his verse of a good deal evident in Eliot's *Four Quartets*, especially the fusion of elegy and sea imagery of 'The Dry Salvages'. One might also point to a possible influence from Wallace Stevens, especially 'Sea Surface Full of Clouds' and the third section of 'The Comedian as the Letter C' with its vision of winter melting into a northern spring, 'in clinking pannicles/Of half-dissolving frost' (Stevens, 34). Lowell's poem gains further energy from a flexible use of prose sources, in particular Herman Melville's novel of the sea, *Moby-Dick*; indeed, it began as a pair of philosophical disquisitions in verse, 'To Herman Melville' and 'Words with Ahab' (Axelrod 1978, 55). As well as his own critical intelligence, Lowell had the advantage of that which Randall Jarrell brought to bear on the various drafts. This resulted, among other matters, in the excision from the final version of 'The Quaker Graveyard' of the attractive but otiose Napoleonic fantasy, 'Buttercups' (Jarrell 1985, 137-138).

The difference between Lowell's poem and the work of any predecessors in this mode is the paradox at the heart of 'The Quaker Graveyard'. Lowell says, traditionally enough, that death by water is a terrible thing. But Warren Winslow is a man at war, as the Quaker fishermen before him were at war against the whale. Moreover, the greed of those fishermen led them to risk their lives unwarrantably at sea. In this way, the tragedy of death by water (*The Waste Land* is another element in the poem) is a product of cupidity. Warren Winslow, unlike Lowell, was an ideal Bostonian (Fender); but the respected citizen of that pluto-cratic town stemmed from pioneers who had expropriated the indigenous Indians. In this way, too, Winslow resembles the predatory Quakers. The epigraph of the poem comes from Genesis: 'Let [man] have dominion over the fish of the sea' (1:26). The fishermen chose to take that concession to an extreme, and a sub-epigraph might well have been Chapter 16 of *Moby-Dick*: 'These same Quakers are the most sanguinary of all sailors and whale-hunters. They are fighting Quakers; they are Quakers with a vengeance'.

The poem may therefore seem a literary production, and there certainly are other antecedents to be pointed out. Nothing, how-ever, can be called inertly derivative. One notices in the accumu-lation of images and particulars the quality that Randall Jarrell terms (after Duns Scotus) 'haeccitas'(1955, 194). We can see how Lowell fertilized his raw material if we compare the first section of 'The Quaker Graveyard' with its source (Staples, 101), the description of a shipwreck victim in *Cape Cod* by Henry David Thoreau:

I saw many marbled feet and matted heads as the clothes were raised . . . the coiled-up wreck of a human hulk, gashed by the rocks or fishes, so that the bone and muscle were exposed, but quite bloodless, – merely red and white, – with wide-open and staring eyes, yet lustreless, dead-lights; or like the cabin windows of a stranded vessel, filled with sand.

This is evocative prose: Thoreau was a minor master in the associative mode of Emerson, Whitman and, later, Hart Crane. Lowell has a keener sense of form, and access to a wider tradition, but he needs Thoreau to help him with the descriptions. Warren Winslow's body was destroyed in an accidental explosion off New York Harbor and no remains were recovered (Fender; Williamson 1974, 35). It is remarkable to observe how Lowell fans Thoreau's images into poetry:

> . . . Light
> Flashed from his matted head and marble feet,
> He grappled at the net
> With the coiled, hurdling muscles of his thighs:

> The corpse was bloodless, a botch of reds and whites,
> Its open, staring eyes
> Were lustreless dead-lights
> Or cabin-windows on a stranded hulk
> Heavy with sand . . .

There is far more concentration upon the corpse than was the case with Thoreau. The exigencies of the metre lead the poet to deploy his words with an economy superior to that found in prose. Lowell's corpse is intensely physical: the 'coiled-up wreck' is personalized; and we have a sense of its previous powers in Lowell's phrase 'coiled, hurdling muscles of his thighs'. 'Hurdling' is picked up from Hopkins's 'Harry Ploughman', a powerful description of a man who is living. The corpse in Lowell's poem is not 'merely red and white' but a thing ruined. The ruin is acted out; it is 'a botch of reds and whites' (Hill). The vocabulary is sharpened: 'vessel' is anthropomorphized into 'hulk' and so assimilated to ship and corpse alike. The hulk is not passively 'filled' with sand but massively 'heavy'. In brief, though Lowell's description derives from Thoreau, it has realized its original in terms of actuality: visual, aural, tactile. The evocation of the corpse is reinforced by a tissue of references: to Elpenor in the *Odyssey* as imitated by Ezra Pound in his Canto 1: 'But thou, O King, I bid remember me, unwept, unburied' (Pound 1930). Another allusion is to Orpheus killed by the Bacchae as narrated by Ovid in his *Metamorphoses* XI. Yet a further allusion relates to the Hanged Man, Dionysus – seen by Eliot as Phlebas the Phoenician – who had to be sacrificed that the tribe might survive.

The second section of the poem broadens out from the first. That particular corpse with which we were initially confronted becomes part of a timeless seascape. The invocation, 'Sailor, can you hear?' might just as well refer to Captain Ahab and the ship Pequod – foundered while seeking the whale – as to Warren Winslow and the US destroyer *Turner*. There are lines of direct invocation: 'The winds' wings beat upon the stones,/Cousin, and scream for you'. This seems to refer ironically back to 'Lycidas': 'he . . . question'd every gust of rugged wings/That blows from off each beaked promontory' (Dubrow).

The third section broadens the area of reference still further: 'All you recovered from Poseidon died/With you, my cousin'. Man, who came out of the slime, is reassumed to it, and each man is Lowell's cousin. The implication is that the slime element represents that lust for acquisition which degrades the whole concept of humanity: this is Lowell's version of original sin. The pursuit of the whale becomes the harassment of Christ, 'IS the whited monster': 'It is because God is beautiful that things are beautiful . . . because He IS that they are' (Gilson 1936, 133). It seems that the materialism of the fishermen has perverted their religion. Even so, at the end of this third section, we hear their hymn, a version of Psalm 124:

> 'If God himself had not been on our side,
> If God himself had not been on our side,
> When the Atlantic rose against us, why,
> Then it had swallowed us up quick.'

The irony is that, as they sing this confident testimony to their knowledge of the will of God, they drown. We may be reminded of the words spoken by Jonathan Edwards, the eighteenth-century Puritan whose work Lowell had been reading: 'the waters are continually rising, and waxing more and more mighty; and there is nothing but the mere pleasure of God, that holds the waters back'. There is no complacency there, and this may make us aware of a complexity in Lowell's view of the Quakers.

The fourth section begins and ends with the Graveyard itself: 'Who will dance/The mast-lashed master of Leviathans/Up from this field of Quakers in their unstoned graves?'. The rich play of ambiguity – the poem, Jarrell noted, 'beats Empson at his own game' (Axelrod 1978, 65) – is characteristic. All sailors are the Sailor: the captain who risks his crew so that he may hear the siren voices (another reference to the *Odyssey*) is no better than Ahab who was lashed to the mast in his pursuit of the white whale, Moby-Dick. Such figures are archetypes for these Quaker fishermen who perished through greed. Their field is barren, ripe only with 'unstoned graves'; 'unstoned' because these fishermen were not martyrs; 'unstoned' also because they are, as individuals, forgotten.

The fifth section surrealizes the graveyard so that time spreads, and the carving up and rendering down of the whale (*Moby-Dick*, Chapters 61, 67) conflates with the Day of Judgment: 'In the great ash-pit of Jehoshaphat/The bones cry for the blood of the white whale'. This refers to Joel 3 which prophesies the

nations gathering in the valley of a king of Judah famed for his
savage victories, nominally on behalf of the Israelite God (2
Chronicles 20). The dead sailors, perpetrators of robbery and
destruction, hope to rise under the blood that has forgiven their
sins: the section concludes, 'Hide/Our steel, Jonas Messias, in
Thy side'. In killing the whale, the sailor has killed his prophet;
however, the prophet in his mercy may conceal the crime and so
take the sin upon himself. In being stabbed, like the whale, Jesus
hides the steel in his own flesh. We should remember, however,
that this is being spoken on behalf of the sailors, and will turn out
to be no more than a pious hope.

The sixth section moves far away from the wind-blown rocks
of Nantucket. We are in rural England at a Catholic shrine, that
of Our Lady of Walsingham, where once a vision of the Virgin
was seen. The detail of the passage, as Lowell himself indicated
in a note to *Lord Weary's Castle*, is derived from a book the
author read during his period of conversion. *Catholic Art and
Culture* by E. I. Watkin is a rhapsodic history of Church aesthe-
tics, chiefly with reference to architecture and the plastic arts. It
is done in terms of the four seasons, with the modern world
uncompromisingly represented as winter. Nevertheless, Watkin
reposes hope in a contemporary revival:

For centuries the shrine of Our Lady of Walsingham has been an
historical memory. Now once again pilgrims visit her image erected in a
medieval chapel, where, it is said, pilgrims once took off their shoes to
walk barefoot the remaining mile to the shrine and to which, there is
some reason to think, a hermitage was attached . . . The road to the
shrine is a quiet country lane shaded with trees, and lined on one side by
a hedgerow. On the other a stream flows down beneath the trees, the
water symbol of the Holy Spirit, 'the waters of Shiloah that go softly',
the 'flow of the river making glad the city of God'.
(Watkin, 170)

This is circumstantial and informative, but Lowell's verse develops the sense of place into sharp individuality by taking the facts
further and relating them to the central concept of his poem:

> There once the penitents took off their shoes
> And then walked barefoot the remaining mile;
> And the small trees, a stream and hedgerows file
> Slowly along the munching English lane,

Like cows to the old shrine, until you lose
Track of your dragging pain.
The stream flows down under the druid tree,
Shiloah's whirlpools gurgle and make glad
The castle of God. Sailor, you were glad
And whistled Sion by that stream . . .

The scene is sharpened by the use of such devices as the verb 'munching'; a word which at once conveys the leisureliness of an English lane – the pace of a grazing animal – and prepares for the rural image of the humble cattle which in Lowell represent innocence. Only by taking on such simplicity is it possible to gain the Virgin's favour. Lowell adapts the water symbols of his original to contrast with the stormy seas of Nantucket. In Walsingham, Shiloah's gurgling waters form a background for the drowned sailor, who now is seen as a penitent. It is as though he had been sacrificed in order to bring about that which is posited in Watkin, a revival of Catholicism. The inference could be that the Quaker fishermen – archetypes for Warren Winslow – were drowned not only as a punishment for their savagery but as an example to the rest of mankind.

However, the description of the effigy at the shrine does not quite come off. Watkin has 'there is no comeliness or charm in that expressionless face with heavy eyelids' (170). Lowell follows this closely: 'There's no comeliness/At all or charm in that expressionless/Face with its heavy eyelids'. But whatever the vision does in Watkin's prose, it is too inexpressive to contrast effectively with the *Sturm und Drang* which forms so large a part of Lowell's poem. Whereas Watkin goes on to posit 'an inner beauty', Lowell can only suggest that the Virgin's impassivity expresses God. In effect, he states the Virgin shares God's omniscience and the world can avail itself of this wisdom by coming to Walsingham. All this is statement, however, devoid of substantiation; and flatly written at that. The Drowned Sailor appears, then, among the penitents only as an intention. The passage seems flat compared with the rest of the poem.

'The Quaker Graveyard' ends with the aftermath of a storm. The ship has disintegrated: 'a gaff/Bobs on the untimely stroke/ Of the greased wash exploding'. As Lowell presaged in the earlier sections of the poem, man is tainted by the primeval slime. Allusions to *King Lear, Paradise Lost*, 'Lycidas' and

Étienne Gilson (1936, 216) are called in to reinforce the convic-
tion: 'sea-monsters, upward angel, downward fish'. The tone
suggests an elegaic recognition of sacrifice. Man may be dross:
but, through sacrifice, it is possible that his sin may be purged
and he himself saved. Certainly there was between God and
man, as evidenced by the patriarchs (Genesis 9:9; 17:7), a
covenant. The poem concludes:

> You could cut the brackish winds with a knife
> Here in Nantucket, and cast up the time
> When the Lord God formed man from the sea's slime
> And breathed into his face the breath of life,
> And blue-lung'd combers lumbered to the kill.
> The Lord survives the rainbow of His will.

That there is a rainbow after the storm, a promise after the
unrest, a covenant between creature and creator, we can believe.
But it is a temporary fabric compared with the everlasting
character of the creator. God goes on long after his promise to
man has been pledged: 'He wills Himself as end, and the others
only by reference to their end, i.e. in the measure in which it is
proper for other beings to participate in the Divine Goodness'
(Gilson 1924, 100). A rainbow, after all, is impermanent.

With this poem, Lowell joins his masters. One has to go to the
greatest works to find a parallel. The mode went on, too; though
in a derivative fashion. Some young poets were so overwhelmed
by Lowell's achievement that they could find no way other than
his in which to compose. Geoffrey Hill, one of the finest poets of
the generation after Lowell's, wrote directly out of 'The Quaker
Graveyard' a poem called 'An Ark on the Flood'. This was so
like its original that it has been suppressed by its author: 'Blind
sleeping trunk, he neither stirs nor turns/ For the gross vines have
knuckled to his bones'. Various items in Peter Redgrove's
sequence, 'Lazarus and the Sea', were likewise suppressed:
'There he lies, flowing with appetite along the palatable shore/
Strung like a harp with the weed and with the sound like a shell'.
For years after, when talented poets wrote either in a formal
rhetoric or about the sea, they drifted rather too near Lowell's
great elegy.

'The Quaker Graveyard in Nantucket', however, appears to
be less personal than most of the poems that offer themselves for

comparison. There is not even the reflection upon the author's
life or talent that one finds in 'Lycidas'. There is no meditation
on poetry itself, no first-person statement, nothing to identify the
author with his cousin dead at sea. Any such matters in the poem
were cut out in draft (*Partisan Review*, Spring 1945 and Winter
1946). This is characteristic of Lowell's procedure in his earlier
phase. Even when he seems most nakedly exposed, the passage
in question usually can be found to relate to another poet, a
paragraph in a travel book or historical essay, a section of the
Bible or of one of the secular classics. It is this power of
assimilation that gives Lowell a technical range and versatility of
subject matter unparalleled in the twentieth century. He is a
chameleon, a character actor of many parts and faces.

In these early poems, the concern that brings together so many
aspects of experience is essentially puritanical, to do with man's
salvation or damnation. We have seen in other poems that, in
spite of his conversion to Catholicism, Lowell had predilections
that took him along another course. His affinities with Hopkins
and Eliot do not, as has been already instanced, prevent his
bonding with Calvinists and with interpreters of Calvinism. Indeed,
another poem of this period, 'Mr. Edwards and the Spider',
began as a research into the life and writings of the eighteenth-
century minister alluded to in the title. The main sources are two
sermons by Jonathan Edwards, 'The Future Punishment of the
Wicked' and 'Sinners in the Hands of an Angry God', together
with a chapter from Edwards's juvenile study of insects written at
the request of his father and directed to a correspondent in
London. The connecting link is the relationship between the
young Edwards's observation of spiders and the allusions to
those animals in the sermons. Lowell's poem begins with the
young Edwards describing a species of spider that is carried along
by winds acting upon its spread-out skeins of gossamer. The
prose source is enthusiastic:

Of all Insects no one is more wonderfull than the Spider . . . every One
knows the truth of their marching in the air from tree to tree and these
sometimes at five or six rods Distanss sometimes . . . I know I have
severall times seen . . . multitudes of little shining webbs . . . and there
Very Often appears at the end of these Webs a Spider floating and
sailing in the air with them . . . and Once saw a very large spider to my

surprise swimming in the air in this manner, and Others have assured me
that they Often have seen spiders fly . . . the Other Difficulty is how
when they Are Once Carried Up into the air how they Get Down again
or whether they are necessitated to Continue till they are beat Down by
some shower of Rain without any sustenance . . . I have Observed that
they never fly except when the wind is westerly and I Never saw them fly
but when they were hastening Directly towards the sea . . . their Chief
time here in newengland is in the time as was said before towds the
Latter End of Aug, And the beginning of Sept, and the[y] keep flying all
that while towards the sea must needs almost all of them Get there
before they have Done . . . for at that time of Year the Ground trees
and houses the Places of their Residence in summer being Pretty Chill
they leave em whenever the sun shines Pretty Warm and mount up into
the air and Expand their Wings to the sun and so flying for Nothing but
their Ease and Comfort they Suffer themselves to Go that way that they
find they Can Go Withe Greatest Easte.

One control Lowell exerts over the breathless exuberance of the
original is to select astringently the images and details necessary
to his poem. They occur as accidents of observation in Edwards's
juvenile piece, but Lowell chooses from that piece those words
which suggest in the spiders a blithe uncaring, a frenetic activity:
'marching', 'swimming', 'beating'. These words are played off
against the slow rhythm of a stanza adopted from Donne's
'Nocturnal upon St Lucy's Day' that does much to dramatize the
manner in which the enthusiasm of the young naturalist is
checked by the stern creed of the Calvinist preacher. That is the
essential conflict within 'Mr. Edwards and the Spider'. The
young man's joy in the living creatures for their own sake is set
against the spider as example in the sermon. The Calvinist has
survived his enthusiasm:

You have often seen a spider, or some other noisome insect, when
thrown into the midst of a fierce fire, and have observed how immediately it yields to the force of the flames. There is no long struggle, no
fighting against the fire, no strength exerted to oppose the heat, or to fly
from it; but it immediately stretches forth itself and yields; and the fire
takes possession of it, and at once it becomes full of fire, and is burned
into a bright coal.
('The Future Punishment of the Wicked Unavoidable and Intolerable')

The spider, called of all insects the most wonderful by the young Edwards, is seen by the adult as noisome. Even so, Lowell notices that the naturalist is not completely lost in the preacher. The spider is compared with a damned soul pitched into hell; but, as well as being condemned, it is observed:

> On Windsor Marsh, I saw the spider die
> When thrown into the bowels of fierce fire:
>   There's no long struggle, no desire
>   To get up on its feet and fly –
>   It stretches out its feet
> And dies. This is the sinner's last retreat;
> Yes, and no strength exerted on the heat
> Then sinews the abolished will, when sick
> And full of burning, it will whistle on a brick.

This last line is an allusion to another section of the sermon. That section is adapted in this poem to make it appear that Edwards is directing his vision of judgment at his cousin, Major Hawley, an agent in the minister's dismissal from his pastorate at Northampton, Massachusetts:

> But who can plumb the sinking of that soul?
> Josiah Hawley, picture yourself cast
>   Into a brick-kiln where the blast
>   Fans your quick vitals to a coal –

The ultimate agony, voiced by Edwards and taken up by Lowell, is the failure of the senses to die. A spider cast into a fire is extinguished. A man consigned to hell suffers for all eternity:

If it were to be measured by a glass, how long would the glass seem to be running! . . . after millions of ages, your torment would be no nearer to an end, than ever it was . . . This is to die sensibly, to die and know it; to be sensible of the gloom of death.

Lowell picks out the essentials and, by a brilliant fusion of ideas, he rallies the whole poem round to a final cadence on the original theme of the spider:

If measured by a glass,
How long would it seem burning! Let there pass
A minute, ten, ten trillion; but the blaze
Is infinite, eternal: this is death,
To die and know it. This is the Black Widow, death.

The Black Widow is a particularly virulent form of spider, and so the monologue finishes on its key image. It never left the image for long. The poem as a whole is an astonishing encapsulation of the essential tenet in Calvinism: the belief that God can consign so many of his creatures to everlasting torment. This is not a matter of individuals performing evil deeds but of predestined damnation arising out of original sin; the sin inherited as a result of Adam's disobedience in the face of God. Here we have an evocative re-creation of one Puritan's life; a life expended with no ordinary degree of intensity over a startlingly narrow compass: Connecticut, Massachusetts. So far from being the victim of Lowell's satire, Edwards comes across as a species of *alter ego*. Certainly there is a congruence between the writing of this grim preacher and his presentation as effected by Lowell. It comes out even more clearly when the poem is placed in the context of *Lord Weary's Castle* as a whole. Such figures as Grandfather Winslow; 'Katherine' and her lover; Warren Winslow; the mad Sheriff; those buried in the Park Street Cemetery: all are damned.

There is, in this same context, a further Jonathan Edwards poem. 'After the Surprising Conversions' is based upon an account Edwards gave of a religious revival in Northampton, Massachusetts. It was published in London and made him internationally known. The form is that of a letter addressed to a fellow-clergyman in Boston. But where this original is dated 19 March 1737, Lowell very definitely gives the date as 22 September. This is (Mazzaro 1965, 70) the beginning of Fall. Several cases are given discursive treatment in Edwards's original narrative from which Lowell took his poem. One is that of a cripple sunk into religious melancholia; another is a child of four who repeatedly exhorted her father to perform charitable acts; yet another is a wretch who thought himself divinely instructed to help his fellow-sufferers. The most striking case, however, is that of Joseph Hawley, father of the troublemaker addressed in Lowell's other Edwards poem. This elder Hawley is termed in Edwards's narrative 'a useful and honourable person'; but he became victim to a morbid spell 'as if somebody had spoke to [him], *Cut your own throat, now is a good opportunity*. Now! now!'. In the poem Lowell lumps all these cases into one dire example which creates the impression of an ostensibly good man who fails to reach a state of grace and who is consequently damned.

The poem wears its acquaintance with Edwards rather heavily. Edwards says 'The Spirit of God not long after this time, appeared very sensibly withdrawing from all parts of the country'. Lowell adapts this to 'The breath of God had carried out a planned/And sensible withdrawal from this land'. There is a functionless change of meaning here, turning on the word 'sensible', and the movement of the verse does not seem in this adaptation to have informed the original prose with the characteristic Lowell *energia*. The final lines of the poem give up the attempt and are straight out of Damariscotta Lake (Stafford 1954): 'at dawn/The small-mouth bass breaks water, gorged with spawn'. Several interpretations are possible: that the riches of the natural world are invoked as a contrast to Calvinism (Pearce); that there are still souls to be saved and generations in need of redemption (Akey); that no one is harvesting the apples and the fish are eating their own eggs (Chambers). The obscurity is in part a result of Lowell's mode of writing. It tends towards satire, and the poem as a result seems less secure in its construction than the more self-identifying 'Mr. Edwards and the Spider'.

One has to concede that Lowell can vary considerably in efficacy when it comes to managing his sources. Even when he succeeds, success may be equivocal. 'The Ghost' derives from an elegy by Propertius, not one of those included by Ezra Pound in his book of imitations styled a *Homage* to that poet. In the poem Lowell chose to adapt, an inappropriate charge of energy is put into the verse: 'nec crepuit fissa me propter harundine custos,/ laesit et obiectum tegula curta caput' is re-created thus: 'No tears drenched a black toga for your whore/When broken tilestones bruised her face before/The Capitol'. These are harsh words to use of Cynthia and have the effect of savage denunciation, where the original suggests that a broken tile was used for no purpose more sinister than propping up the corpse's head. A touch of pathos in Propertius is turned by Lowell into a side-swipe at a dead lover!

At this early stage of producing imitations, Lowell writes better when violence is his explicit theme. 'The Soldier', one of three war sonnets originally published in the South African magazine *Common Sense* in 1945, picks up a line from an episode in Dante's *Purgatorio* V 85-129 (Prampolini) as a means of reconstructing the story of Buonconte of Montefeltro who appears in the *Inferno*, condemned for betraying the Colonna family to Pope Boniface VIII in return for a false absolution. Dante has it that his soul is taken away by an angel while his body falls victim to the Prince of Darkness. But Lowell only gives us the conflict: a lively sense of the body, never recovered from the battlefield, 'drowned face downward in his blood'.

Another adaptation, from a sonnet called 'Le Mal' by Rimbaud, was revised for *Imitations* and revised still further for *Notebook* and *History*. Discussion of this text is therefore postponed to Chapter Seven, which is concerned with the later collections. A related poem, 'The Shako', based on a translation of Rilke's 'Letzter Abend' (McIntyre, 78), infuses into a soldier's farewell a number of references – Scylla, Abel – together with a degree of melodramatic comment not found in the original.

'France' is adapted from Villon's 'L'Épitaphe'. 'Frères humains qui après nous vivez/N'ayez les cuers contre nous endurcis' is rendered, characteristically and graphically, as 'My human brothers who live after me,/See how I hang'. The adaptation is condensed from the thirty-five lines of the original into a sonnet. Even so, Lowell adds to Villon the idea that it is Abel who is hung on the gibbet; rather, that is to say, than an anonymous thief.

Another imitation, 'Charles the Fifth and the Peasant', owes as much to an equestrian portrait of the Holy Roman Emperor by Titian as to its ostensible source, the poem 'César' by Paul Valéry. Lowell shows, again graphically, the community between the Emperor and his subject; both 'middle-aged and common'.

Related to these imitations, but far superior, is '1790'. This packs an extraordinary amount of action into its twenty lines. The poem is an adaptation from *The Memoirs of Baron Thiébault* as translated by a Victorian student of languages, Arthur J. Butler (Staples 104-105). Louis XVI of France, about to be executed, is shown to be as guilty in his way as his executioners. This is the paradox adumbrated in 'Lamkin' and in 'The Quaker Graveyard in Nantucket'. The prose states the situation; the poem re-creates and dramatizes it. First, Thiébault:

Just then a lady came through the gate. She had a pretty little spaniel with her, which, before she noticed it, ran close up to the King. Making a low courtesy, she called the dog back in haste, but as the animal turned to run to its mistress, the King, who had a large cane in his hand, broke its back with a blow of his cudgel. Then, amid the screams and tears of the lady, and as the poor little beast was breathing its last, the King, delighted with his exploit, continued his walk, slouching rather more than usual, and laughing like any lout of a peasant.

Now, Lowell:

> 'What a dog's life it is to be a king,'
> I grumbled and unslung my gun; the chaff
> And cinders whipped me and began to sting.
> I heard our Monarch's Breughel-peasant laugh
> Exploding, as a spaniel mucked with tar
> Cut by his Highness' ankles on the double-quick
> To fetch its stamping mistress. Louis smashed
> Its backbone with a backstroke of his stick:
> Slouching a little more than usual, he splashed
> As boyish as a stallion to the Champs de Mars.

The distinction, as ever, is in Lowell's use of language. Particulars are shaped or altered in the interests of drama. The statement in the prose – 'the King . . . broke its back with a blow of his cudgel' – is acted out in the repeated vowel sounds and explosive alliteration: 'Louis smashed/Its backbone with a backstroke of his stick'. These graphic words – 'smashed', 'backbone', 'backstroke', 'stick' – insist upon the action, thrust it home, render it tactile. Details inessential to the pattern thus set up, such as the screams and tears of the lady, are excluded.

This poem occupied prime place in a radio discussion called 'Violence in Poetry', arranged by George MacBeth and broadcast on the BBC Third Programme, 11 December 1964. The following is from an unpublished transcript:

Edward Lucie-Smith: I would like to take up the point of the poet's reason for picking on this situation. The reason surely is that the revolution, whichever way you look at it, represents a turning-point in history, because it is the beginning of modernity. And therefore one can see why Lowell has chosen to talk about an incident in the year 1790, and one can

well see that he might expect us to moralize this incident – as indeed I think *he* does. What I don't think he does provide is sufficient signposting.
Philip Hobsbaum: What it all comes to is something very simple. Unless the poet has given us some fair amount of historical context or fictional context, the actual incidents in a poem are bound to seem arbitrary. One must know how they fit in.
Christopher Ricks: I disagree. I think that the poem isn't very good, but, on the other hand, I don't think it's *un*signposted . . . I think the 'boyish' at the end makes the point that Edward Lucie-Smith had about the kind of growing up that comes with the French Revolution. I mean that what is pre-French Revolution is boyish.
Martin Dodsworth: Well, I don't think this is the point here. What I see it really as being is a poem with very much point and very much moral – but surely the point is that you can feel pity for someone who then goes and does something which you would think was *not* pitiable, i.e. something as callous and unnecessary and superfluous as breaking the backbone of a passing dog. In the awful obviousness of the line 'What a dog's life it is to be a king', you are meant to think not twice but three times about this, aren't you . . . ?
Donald Davie: May I ask whether Martin Dodsworth is talking about the poem that he envisages Lowell is meaning to have written, or the poem that he wrote . . . ?
Edward Lucie-Smith: There's a conflict between context and immediacy. I think what Lowell is obviously trying for is immediacy.

Lucie-Smith's remark, like the poem itself, looks forward to the achievement of *Life Studies* and *Imitations*. '1790', as much as its less distinguished counterparts, 'War' and 'Charles the Fifth and the Peasant', shows a colourful alternative to the puritanism that overcasts the bulk of *Lord Weary's Castle*. But, at this juncture, it was the puritanism that told. Even readers who failed to understand Lowell's theology were carried along by the dramatic language of the poems themselves. Mostly it was the poets who showed appreciation: 'dramatic, moral, elegaic' (John Berryman, *Partisan Review*, January-February 1947); a religious poet who 'writes like a revolutionary' (Howard Moss, *Kenyon Review*, Spring 1947). The encomium of Randall Jarrell is well known: 'no poet is more notable for . . . the contrary, persisting, and singular thinginess of every being in the world; but this detailed factuality is particularly effective because it sets off, or is set off by, the elevation and rhetorical sweep of much earlier English poetry' (*The Nation*, 18 January 1947). However, some of the New Critics proper seemed bewildered. There was no review from Allen Tate, and another of Lowell's mentors, Richard Eberhart, found that the poetry of *Lord Weary's Castle* burst its formal structures (*Sewanee Review*, Spring 1947). One of a second wave of New Critics, Leavis's pupil Marius Bewley, described the whole as 'a bleak, and frequently ugly poetry' (*Scrutiny*, Spring 1950).

For Lowell himself poetry was at once a means of understanding his predicament and of justifying himself to his family. Lowell's chosen art was not only an unassailable value but a way of creating a persona strong enough to stand against the generations of Lowells and Winslows who would otherwise have absorbed him. It is important to remember that the exemplary Warren Winslow took his degree at Harvard, went to war, and was killed; while the negligent Robert Lowell became a Roman Catholic, went to prison, and survived. The contrast in itself is dramatic, and *Lord Weary's Castle* uses dramatic contrast to create its poetry. 'The poems understand the world as a sort of conflict of opposites' (Jarrell 1947). Out of this pattern of conflict emerged the dramatic monologues, still insufficiently understood, that constitute Lowell's third book, *The Mills of the Kavanaughs*.

3 *The Mills of the Kavanaughs* (1951)

The years that followed *Lord Weary's Castle* were strangely
fragmented. Before Lowell took up his appointment as Poetry
Consultant to the Library of Congress, he retreated in June 1947
to Yaddo, a writers' colony founded by philanthropists and
situated near Saratoga Springs in upstate New York. It was on a
brief visit there in 1943 that Jean Stafford had written part of
Boston Adventure. Now at Yaddo himself, Lowell worked on
what he termed a 'symbolic monologue by an insane woman'
(Hamilton, 126) which he had started as 'The Kavanaughs of the
Mills' ten years previously, during his first visit to Allen Tate
(Axelrod 1978, 81). He was unable to finish this poem even now,
but he completed drafts of others which, together with work
already done, basically added up to the volume eventually called
The Mills of the Kavanaughs. 'David and Bathsheba in the Public
Garden' was published as two separate poems in December 1946
and May 1947, and 'Her Dead Brother' in February 1947, in *The
Nation*. 'Falling Asleep Over the Aeneid' and 'Mother Marie
Therese' appeared respectively in the Winter and the Summer
issues of the *Kenyon Review* in 1948. The collection as a whole,
however, was delayed while Lowell continued to work on the
title poem. A version of this, later to be much altered, eventually
appeared in the *Kenyon Review* for Winter 1951.

At first Lowell had found his duties at the Library of Congress
congenial. He advised on books for purchase and developed the
policy of getting poets to record readings of their own works. His
choices included William Carlos Williams, Elizabeth Bishop and
Randall Jarrell. The trouble with the consultancy was its public
aspect. Lowell from time to time visited Ezra Pound who was
incarcerated at St Elizabeth's Hospital, Washington, as a result
of advocating the Fascist cause during the Second World War.
Lowell's position as Poetry Consultant led him straight on to a

Library of Congress committee where, along with Allen Tate, W. H. Auden, T. S. Eliot and others (Squires, 185), he successfully recommended Pound, in respect of the *Pisan Cantos*, for the Bollingen Prize. This decision produced a good deal of controversy, especially emanating from the political Left. Almost as a reaction against these protests, Lowell spearheaded a movement to brand Yaddo as a Communist cell on the grounds that its director, Elizabeth Ames, was a friend of the Socialist writer, Agnes Smedley (O'Connor, 11). But all Lowell's efforts succeeded in doing was to inflate a non-event to ridiculous proportions; a consequence, possibly, of the manic symptoms that were beginning to trouble him. The Pound and Yaddo crises took up much of 1949, which was itself the aftermath of a painful divorce from Jean Stafford, the petering out of the affair with the former Mrs Delmore Schwartz, and the finish of another relationship with a woman in Washington which had met with ritual disapprobation from the Lowell parents (Hamilton, 126-136).

On the positive side, Lowell's friendship with Elizabeth Bishop meant a great deal to him, and at Yaddo he had become well acquainted with other writers of distinction. There was the lyric poet Theodore Roethke whom he had first met at the Olivet Conference in 1937 (Squires, 124); the short-story writer Mary Flannery O'Connor; and the already well-known novelist and critic, Elizabeth Hardwick. These friendships were, however, counterpointed by Lowell's increasingly disturbed behaviour. A brief lapse back into Catholicism, during which Lowell went into retreat with the Trappists in Rhode Island (March 1949), was followed in April by a violent quarrel in Chicago with Allen Tate who was Visiting Professor of Humanities at the University there (Hamilton, 154-155), and by a journey shortly after to see Peter Taylor, who was teaching in Bloomington, Indiana. Lowell's manic behaviour on this visit led to his arrest, and incarceration at Baldpate, 'a small private hospital near Georgetown, Massachusetts' (Hamilton, 158). Tate wrote to Elizabeth Hardwick that in his view Lowell was dangerously violent, especially towards women. What he did not know was that she happened to be one of the few visitors Lowell himself encouraged during his three months in hospital. In fact, Lowell and Elizabeth Hardwick were married on 28 July 1949 (Axelrod 1978, 242); the shadows, however, did not disperse. By September Lowell was back in care; at the Payne Whitney Clinic, New York, where Jean Stafford had undergone treatment two years previously. When he was released, in November, the influence of the ever-forgiving Tate secured Lowell a teaching post at the University of Iowa. He went on in the summer of 1950 to lecture at the newly instituted Kenyon School of Letters (Hamilton, 167) where he was able to show Delmore Schwartz and John Crowe Ransom the revised draft of 'The Mills of the Kavanaughs', presumably the version which Ransom was to publish in the *Kenyon Review*. After this summer school, Lowell and Elizabeth Hardwick meant to go to Italy. However, Lowell's father, who had been seriously ill with a heart complaint, suddenly died. The departure was, in consequence, delayed until October. Lowell spent that month and the next in Florence, rewriting the title poem of *The Mills of the Kavanaughs* on the galley proofs of the book.

The book itself came out in the early summer of 1951 to a puzzled reception. Even the faithful Jarrell wrote of the long-gestated title poem, 'it does not seem to me successful as a unified work of art, a narrative poem that makes the same sort of sense a novel or story makes' (*Partisan Review*, November-December 1951). Richard Eberhart, a less than enthusiastic supporter of *Lord Weary's Castle*, produced a sour account: 'there is something more than puzzling, challenging if one wishes to worry it out, in the somehow undigested shooting back and forth between centuries and decades and events' (*Kenyon Review*, Winter 1952). Dudley Fitts found the title poem full of what he called 'Inoperable Particularity': 'the kind of detail that looks significant, that one worries about as a possible symbol, and that is finally rejected' (*Furioso*, Fall 1951). There were some favourable reviews, however, from William Carlos Williams (*New York Times Book Review*, 22 April 1951), and Gene Baro (*New York Herald Tribune Book Review*, 22 April 1951), the latter finding a new level of excellence in Lowell's tight integration of imagery, idea and symbol. Nevertheless, 'The Mills of the Kavanaughs' tended to be neglected in subsequent book-length studies of Lowell by, for instance, Cooper, Cosgrave, Raffel, Rudman, and Smith. Even books that took the trouble to discuss the poem were liable to come to divergent conclusions about its purport. For one critic the central figure, Anne Kavanaugh, appears to be contemplating a return to the Roman Catholic church (Staples, 60), while for another she has decided upon the mortal sin of suicide (Yenser, 95). This suggests an absence of consensus that may be the reason why the work in question was excluded from the first book Lowell published in Britain, *Poems 1938-49*. So far as the British reader was concerned, 'The Mills of the Kavanaughs' led only a fugitive existence as an appendix to a pioneer study (Staples, 116-132).

Yet, even in the face of adverse comment and subsequent neglect, it is possible to demonstrate that 'The Mills of the Kavanaughs' is a work of considerable distinction. For 'Kavanaughs' an interpretation could read 'Winslows'. The poem is just as much an evocation of Lowell's Puritan and Indian-hunting ancestors as any of the earlier poems – 'In Memory of Arthur Winslow', say, or 'At the Indian Killer's Grave'. The motto of the Kavanaughs, as of the Winslows, is 'Cut down, we flourish'. If we remember it is used ironically, that motto will serve as a key. Anne Kavanaugh is adopted by the family into which, later, she marries. Her husband is cut down in the Second World War; not killed but, apparently, disgraced. He does not flourish; neither, after his death, does she. Her whole life becomes a trance in which action takes place only in the flux of a memory out of control. The poem itself is a waking dream. It derives technically from Wallace Stevens's 'Sunday Morning', though it is built on a larger scale. Nevertheless, Lowell's poem displays the same easy flow of verse and tendency to switch from third-person dramatized consciousness to narrative in the first person. Anne Kavanaugh's meditation takes in particularly her unhappy marriage and her relationship with the Kavanaugh family.

The poem begins with her playing a symbolic game of cards against the Catholic faith which she has abandoned in favour of a union with the wealthy and Protestant Kavanaughs. Catholicism in this context is represented by the Bible and this, in turn, is identified with Phoebus, god of the sun. The cards with which she plays are termed Kavanaughs; suggesting, perhaps, the limited possibilities of the family. Her husband is repeatedly identified with Dis or Pluto. The inference must be that she loses this game, as she has always lost in the past, spending half her life away from the sun allied to a doomed family. She is identified with Persephone – a persistent line of symbolism – in the grasp of the King of the Underworld. She has become a queen, but only through marrying into the house of death. All this is expressed in verse of considerable suavity and flow:

The Douay Bible on the garden chair
Facing the lady playing solitaire
In blue-jeans and a sealskin toque from Bath
Is *Sol*, her dummy. There's a sort of path
Or rut of weeds that serpents down a hill
And graveyard to a ruined burlap mill;
There, a maternal nineteenth century
Italian statue of Persephone
Still beckons to a mob of Bacchanals.

Readers familiar with Lowell's Damariscotta poems will recognize the landscape of 'The Holy Innocents' and 'New Year's Day'; and indeed, across the meadow from the house where Lowell lived in 1946, was an imposing mansion in Federal style built by a family called Kavanagh (Simpson, 116-118).

The lady of the poem plays cards facing not only the Bible but her husband's grave on which is set his naval flag. Around her is the estate seized by the pioneering Kavanaughs from the Indians. She is twice removed from ownership; first because she is a Kavanaugh only by adoption and marriage, second because the family had no right to this usurped land. This comes across as a reinforcement of the Persephone motif, and the imagery is very near to that of Ovid's *Metamorphoses* V. One translation from Ovid has:

Not far from Henna's walls, there is a deep lake called Pergus . . . A ring of trees encircles the pool, clothing the lakeside all around, and the leaves of the trees shelter the spot from Phoebus' rays, like a screen. Their boughs afford cool shade, and the lush meadow is bright with flowers. There it is always spring. In this glade Proserpine was playing, picking violets or shining lilies. With childlike eagerness she gathered the flowers into baskets and into the folds of her gown.
(Innes, 126)

The influence upon Lowell's poem is clear:

> ' . . . Once I trespassed – picking flowers
> For keepsakes of my journey, once I bent
> Above your well, where lawn and battlement
> Were trembling, yet without a flaw to mar
> Their sweet surrender. Ripples seemed to star

> My face, the rocks, the bottom of the well;
> My heart, pursued by all its plunder, fell,
> And I was tossing petals from my lair
> Of copper leaves above your mother's chair.'

The lady addresses her dead husband. This is even more a matter of pathos when one realizes that he died insane. The mode of soliloquy instanced here predominates over the greater part of the poem, from stanza 2 to stanza 33. Only the beginning and the end show the present time in full consciousness. Mostly the poem is reverie. The marriage of Anne Kavanaugh is present mainly in ellipsis: ' "My husband was a fool/To run out from the Navy when disgrace/Still wanted zeal to look him in the face" '. We are never told what Harry – Hotspur as well as Pluto – did. But the action was bad enough to change his character and wreck all chances of peace between the couple. One may wonder why Anne Kavanaugh is harking back in this manner. There may be a clue in stanza 5: ' "*Sol*,/If you will help me, I will win the world" '. She asks the Bible for faith in order to help her struggle out of this living death. The earlier version of the poem which appeared in the *Kenyon Review* was much more heavily Catholic in its imagery. Stanza 4 in that draft has 'She dreams he is Saint Patrick come to squire/Her home from school; for there is nothing new/In their green vestments borrowed from the choir'. The identification of Harry with St Patrick involves the subsequent narrative in clumsy ramifications, including a number of ensuing references to 'life-green cassocks', 'Lincoln green', and the like. The lines about St Patrick and his vestments are replaced by 'She thinks of Daphne – Daphne who could outrun/The birds, and saw her swiftness tire the sun,/And yet, perhaps, saw nothing to admire/Beneath Apollo'. It has the effect of reinforcing the Persephone motif. Indeed, in the poem as revised, the Daphne/Apollo parallel made in respect to the protagonists continues in stanza 4 and is followed by the stanza beginning '*The leaves, sun's yellow, listen*', practically all of which appears to have been added in proof.

A similarly drastic revision takes place in what is now, as stanza 16, the fusion of two stanzas in draft. An autobiographical description (Stafford 1978) of the couple covering their kitchen walls with Mariolatrous inscriptions – 'Sancta Maria, Virgo Mater', and the like – is cut out in this conflation. A further

stanza, the present number 27, is added to reinforce the Pluto
imagery: it ends, ' "Death, carousing like a king/On nothing but
his lands, will take your ring /To bind me, and possess me to the
dust" '. Yet another crucial addition is the woman's plea, already
quoted, ' "*Sol*,/If you will help me I will win the world" '. In this
later version, that plea precipitates Anne Kavanaugh back into
the present, and into passive reflection. The Kavanaugh estate
includes spawning-ponds, but that is a further irony. Anne,
adopted as she is, is the last of the Kavanaughs. There are
children in the poem, but they are memories of herself and her
husband. In childhood she was brought up as his sister. The
implication is that the union is incestuous, as it is certainly
barren. Yet children are evoked, playing on the Kavanaugh
estate. The images previous to this eighth stanza foreshadowed
the abduction of a putative goddess of light by a king of darkness:

> The children splash and paddle. Then, hand in hand,
> They duck for turtles. Where she cannot stand,
> The whirlpool sucks her. She has set her teeth
> Into his thumb. She wrestles underneath
> The sea-green smother; stunned, unstrung and torn
> Into a thousand globules by that horn
> Or whorl of river, she has burst apart
> Like churning water on her husband's heart –
> A horny thumbnail! Then they lie beside
> The marble goddess. 'Look, the stony-eyed
> Persephone has mouldered like a leaf!'
> The children whisper . . .

There is an irony in their ducking for turtles – symbols of fertility
and emblems of love. But the only children Anne Kavanaugh has
are memories, and all they amount to – evocative though they are
– is a rehearsal of her role as Persephone, the withered statue
that she is now.

This recollection of the past has a seasonal quality, a form
adopted for large-scale narrative poems from Wordsworth in
'The Ruined Cottage' to Patrick Kavanagh in 'The Great Hunger'.
Stanzas 3-8, which introduced Anne Kavanaugh's marriage,
represented springtime. The general recollections of stanzas 10
to 14 are late spring or early summer. Summer itself occurs in
stanza 15 and goes on to 19; this section is the core of the poem.

For one thing, Anne's wedding itself takes place in June. For another, the heritage of the Kavanaughs is here explicitly identified with spoils wrested from the Indians. Anne Kavanaugh's wedding hymn, however, is the *Miserere*; she has inherited the Kavanaugh curse. The true horror of her marriage is speedily revealed. Her husband treats her churlishly, then leaves her for the war. Things have already reached a point where she is glad at his absence. But he returns mentally disturbed, a sick Pluto claiming his rights to his bride at the end of harvest. His raving about Pearl Harbor reproduces the uncertain communication of a far-off news programme on the radio, even to the interference of static. The inference is that Harry has sustained some kind of shock. But Anne Kavanaugh's kindness, such as it is, fails to restore him. By Christmas the marriage is hopelessly fractured. Stanzas 21 and 22 tell of a dream in which Anne Kavanaugh regresses to her childhood, ' "stalking in my moccasins/Below the mill-fall" '. She goes on to dream of another lover – Harry himself, but a Harry that is young and mentally unscarred. Speaking out of the dream, she treats the present Harry as a stranger. This drives him to a frenzy in which he seeks to kill her: ' " 'You mustn't choke me!' Then I thought the beams/Were falling on us. Things began to whirl./'Harry, we're not accountable for dreams' " '. But, the poem shows, we are. Anne Kavanaugh's dazzled impressions of childhood, that childhood which trapped her into being Persephone, are at one with her vision of a Harry very different from this unshaven, shaken veteran. Stanzas 20-26 form the winter of the poem, symbolic of Persephone's sojourn in the underworld. Harry's attempt to murder her, his attempt to strangle himself, an aftermath during which he is little better than an idiot – all this leaves her bound to and possessed by the dust. When the spring returns, Harry is still in a state of inanition, almost as though he had never lived. He is described, in what should have been his masculine prime, as though he were a baby – dribbling strings of orange juice, an image reminiscent of the second childhood depicted in the 'Mary Winslow' poem of the previous book.

The summer follows (stanza 31) to find Lieutenant Kavanaugh dying by his own hand, ironically enough on Independence Day. This leaves his widow to a long, dreary autumn which at length brings us to the present: 'She stands, then sits/And makes a card-house; it's as if her wits/Were overseas. The cards are Kavanaughs'.

She is their Persephone, their Queen. That summer came and
went, and she is still underground. Her last act – her only one in
the present time of the poem – is to ramble down the weedy path
to the ruined burlap mill, get into a boat, and drift down the
river, like a dying swan, or like the young Persephone taken to
the pool of Cyane, or like Cyane herself when her tears dissolved
her to water, or like Arethusa turned into a river – to instance
some of the myths and subsidiary myths suggested by this resonant
verse:

> The heron warps its neck, a broken pick,
> To study its reflection on the scales
> Or knife-bright shards of water lilies, quick
> In the dead autumn water with their snails
> And water lice . . .

The images of sexual malaise are not accidental: ' "The sticks of
Kavanaugh are buried here" ' and ' "Even in August it was
autumn" '. Like Harry Tudor, and in more senses than one, her
husband died outside the church. She herself has voluntarily
done the same, in forsaking her religion. She now belongs to the
underworld. The final lines of the poem ally her with death.
There is nothing left for her, not even an excuse: like Persephone,
she let herself go because her blood was warm – ' "And for no
other reason, Love, I gave/Whatever brought me gladness to the
grave" '. A strained marriage and a bewildered widowhood are
just deserts for – as shown in the opening lines – her play against
the Catholic faith. She has lost, and must always play the game
she follows: solitaire. Not only is she alone, without husband or
family, but she is alone in the starker, more theological sense:
she will never see God.

     This is a difficult poem, and one can see why it has been little
frequented even by admirers of Lowell. One can readily enough
fault its disruption of narrative logic, its dreams within dreams,
its bursts of violent action insufficiently motivated. It has been
suggested (Mazzaro 1969) that Harry's ship sank at Pearl Harbor
and that he was overcome with remorse because he had failed to
arrive in time. There seems to be, as with 'Between the Porch
and the Altar' and 'The Death of the Sheriff', some material
involved which the poet was unable to work into realization. It is
interesting that the Harry of the poem was a naval officer, like

Commander Lowell, and that the poem was completed – on the galley proofs – only after the Commander died. Like Harry, Commander Lowell left the navy abruptly – 'with seamanlike celerity' as *Life Studies* has it – although any 'disgrace' that may have been involved appears to exist only in the mind of his son. At this point a measure of self-blame may be involved. There seems to be a fusion of the unhappy marriage of Lowell's parents with that of Lowell himself to the Irish, Catholic and formidably motivated Jean Stafford. Certainly a good deal of Harry's presentation savours of autobiography. The poem speaks of Harry attending meetings with, of all unlikely texts, Macaulay's life of Clive 'tucked in a pocket'. There is a parallel not so much between Harry and Clive as between Lowell and Clive, in that the unmanageable boy was welcomed home as a successful man by a family 'delighted by his success, though they seem to have been hardly able to comprehend how their naughty idle Bobby had become so great a man' – 'Bobby' being the name common to both Clive and Lowell in early youth. A good deal of Lowell's poem seems to be apologia, not only with regard to his young manhood but in respect of his marriage.

A useful commentary can be found in Jean Stafford's tale, 'A Country Love Story'. Its plot resembles that of 'The Mills of the Kavanaughs' to a considerable extent. The Anne-figure is a young woman married to a professor who is mysteriously sick: 'there were times on the lake, when May was gathering water lilies as Daniel slowly rowed, that she had seen on his face a look of abstraction and she had known that he was worlds away, in his memories, perhaps, of his illness and the sanitarium' (Stafford 1945, 46). The central symbol of the story is a sleigh that has come with the place the couple have bought in Maine, west of 'a rich man's long meadow that ran down a hill to his old, magisterial house'. It is an antique, this sleigh, with snow after snow banked up against its eroded runners, going nowhere. One Christmas May recognizes that she has taken 'a weighty but unviolent dislike' (49) to her husband who has made it plain that he cannot tolerate her company. From that time she develops a fantasy about a lover who eventually crystallizes as a young man, frail and with an invalid's pallor, sitting in the sleigh.

If there are similarities between Jean Stafford's story and Lowell's narrative poem, so, it must be said, are there related opacities. The lover is as much May's notion of the professor

when young as Anne Kavanaugh's dream of a younger Harry. In
both fictions, the malady of the husband seems not only to
involve considerable disaffection but to remain a mystery to the
person concerned. Harry persists as a figure seen by the grave,
suffering woman who is at the centre of the poem. It is the
prevailing dignity and calm of the verse she speaks that is the
point. There is also the sense, felt as well in *Lord Weary's Castle*,
of a malign destiny geared to expropriate the expropriators. Like
the Winslows, the Mills of the Kavanaughs grind the Indians
small. When the Indians are exhausted, the Mills go on to grind
up the Kavanaughs. The Kavanaughs' motto is therefore seen to
be a vain boast. They are cut down; they do not flourish.

Two other works seem to have budded off from this elaborate
poem while it was in draft. 'Her Dead Brother' recounts the
incestuous love of a young woman, and does so in terms of a
search for God. It also describes her suicide by gas after her
brother's death at sea. Like Harry Kavanaugh, and indeed like
Lowell's father, the brother has seen naval action in war. Part of
the power manifest in the poem comes from the woman's
recollection of the summer idyll when her conjunction with her
brother took place. The absence of their mother which afforded
this opportunity is countered by the return of the young woman's
husband in the present time of the poem; his Packard 'crunches
up the drive'. Verbal parallels between this poem and 'The Mills
of the Kavanaughs' centre on the scene where Anne Kavanaugh,
asleep and dreaming, is nearly murdered by her husband:

> Your portrait, coiled in German-silver hawsers, mirrors
> The sunset as a dragon . . .
> ('Her Dead Brother')

>   . . . A dragon writhed around
> A knob above you, and its triple tails
> Fanned at your face . . .
> ('The Mills of the Kavanaughs', stanza 22)

> Life is a thing I own. Brother, my heart
> Races for sea-room – we are out of breath.
> ('Her Dead Brother')

> . . . Pearl Harbor's whole Pacific fleet
> Has sea-room in my mind . . .
> ('The Mills of the Kavanaughs', stanza 32)

There is a similar relationship between 'The Mills of the Kavanaughs' and 'David and Bathsheba in the Public Garden'. The latter poem is an attempt to put into a modern setting the story told in 2 Samuel, Chapters 11 and 12, where King David causes Uriah, whose wife he desires, to be sent to the forefront of battle. The first section is a dialogue in which David seems to console Bathsheba for the loss of Uriah on the grounds that her husband was the less worthy man. It is David who is the lion, David who has the power! But the second section, far more coherent, is a monologue where Bathsheba reflects that David's breaking of his vows to her in order to marry Abishag (I Kings 1) is part of the same process. His alteration derives not from strength but from that which he had previously denied, mortality. It is interesting that David's leonine energy is, as was the case with the lawless Harry in 'The Mills of the Kavanaughs', associated with childhood and, indeed, childishness:

> . . . My love, a little while,

> The lion frothed into the basin . . . all,
> Water to water – water that begets
> A child from water . . .
> ('David and Bathsheba in the Public Garden')

> . . . Here bubbles filled
> Their basin, and the children splashed. They died
> In Adam . . .
> (The Mills of the Kavanaughs', stanza 9)

A dialogue similar in some respects to Part 1 of 'David and Bathsheba in the Public Garden' is found in yet another related poem, 'Thanksgiving's Over'. The dialogue in question takes place between a man in his sleep and his wife who died some time previously in a lunatic asylum. Like 'The Mills of the Kavanaughs' and 'David and Bathsheba', this is a poem involving a considerable amount of self-reproach. The wife has been thought to represent religious ecstasy taken to an extreme, and the poem itself has been called 'a vicarious exorcism of the poet's Catholicism' (Yenser 113-114). But 'Thanksgiving's Over' is so dominated by the hysterical voice of the mad wife as to fall into imitative form (Winters 1947, 64): it is in itself what it purports to describe. The poem has certainly had its admirers: 'one of the

most horrifying that Lowell has written' (Mazzaro 1965, 84);
'technique . . . is here wholly at the service of substance' (Raffel
1981, 39). However, the main point of interest is that 'Thanksgiving's Over' picks up negative aspects of certain letters written
by Jean Stafford during the action of her divorce from Lowell
and lays them out as verse in a manner that foreshadows *The
Dolphin* poems and also the works of Sylvia Plath:

If there were tears, really, when you read my letter, if you really re-read
it, there would have been love, there would have been love and longing
and the desire to return with gifts of understanding.
(Hamilton, 125)

> . . . 'If you're worth the burying
> And burning, Michael, God will let you know
> Your merits for the love I felt the want
> Of, when your mercy shipped me to Vermont
>
> To the asylum. Michael, was there warrant
> For killing love? . . '
> ('Thanksgiving's Over')

All the poems so far discussed in this chapter equate energy
with madness and madness with childhood. In 'The Fat Man in
the Mirror', a far less significant work than the others in the
volume, the sense of childhood is grotesquely parodied. This
grotesquerie is considerably heightened from the text on which it
is based, a poem by the Austrian writer, Franz Werfel. Where
Werfel gives his protagonist a hairy chest, Lowell confronts us
with a 'Hair-belly like a beaver's house'. Where Werfel ends with
a transition from childhood to adulthood, Lowell has a kind of
manic dance-rhythm: 'Only a fat man,/Only a fat man/Bursts the
mirror. O, it is not I!'. Some of the oddity may derive from the
jerkiness of the verse translation upon which Lowell based his
poem (Snow, 5). The piece as Lowell renders it could be summed
up as the refusal of an immature spirit to accept the consequences
of growing up. There is, however, only a superficial connection
between this and the other poems in the book.

Other than this odd little sport, *The Mills of the Kavanaughs*
is, as a collection, remarkably integrated. 'Falling Asleep Over
the Aeneid' and 'Mother Marie Therese' are less ambitious than
the title poem, but they are probably the best works in the group.

Indeed, they are two of the finest monologues ever to come out of America.

'Falling Asleep Over the Aeneid', like 'The Mills of the Kavanaughs', is tinctured by Wallace Stevens: 'The sun is blue and scarlet on my page,/And *yuck-a, yuck-a, yuck-a, yuck-a*, rage/The yellow-hammers mating'. The sounds and colours project an old man in Concord into a dream based upon the Virgil text he is in the process of reading: 'Yellow fire/Blankets the captives dancing on their pyre,/And the scorched lictor screams and drops his rod'. Basically, the poem sets off an inglorious present against the heroic past. In a Stevens-like situation, the old man forgets to go to a Christian service and imagines himself as Aeneas at the pagan funeral of Pallas, an Italian prince. The poem is full of heroic reminiscence:

> The elephants of Carthage hold those snows,
> Turms of Numidian horse unsling their bows,
> The flaming turkey-feathered arrows swarm
> Beyond the Alps. 'Pallas,' I raise my arm
> And shout, 'Brother, eternal health. Farewell
> Forever' . . .

Pallas was a son of King Evander sent with some troops to assist Aeneas against the Latins and the Rutuli. He was killed by Turnus, the King of the Rutuli, but only after he had made a great slaughter of the enemy. The story occurs in Books VIII-X of the *Aeneid*; the funeral of Pallas is described in Book XI, lines 22–99. Aeneas 'chose a thousand horse, the flow'r of all/His warlike troops, to wait the funeral . . . /"Peace with the manes of great Pallas dwell!/Hail, holy relics! and a last farewell!" ' as Dryden's translation puts it. At this moment of glory, the shout and the salute, the old man wakes up: 'Church is over, and its bell/Frightens the yellowhammers, as I wake/And watch the white-caps wrinkle up the lake'.

In the transition stage between sleep and waking we see the reason for the old man's dream. He is precipitated from the funeral of the heroic Pallas, not into the immediate present, but into a childhood memory:

> Mother's great-aunt, who died when I was eight,
> Stands by our parlour sabre. 'Boy, it's late.
> Vergil must keep the Sabbath.' Eighty years!

It all comes back. My Uncle Charles appears.
Blue-capped and bird-like. Phillips Brooks and Grant
Are frowning at his coffin, and my aunt,
Hearing his coloured volunteers parade
Through Concord, laughs, and tells her English maid
To clip his yellow nostril hairs, and fold
His colours on him . . .

The Uncle Charles here is an amalgam of two of the author's
kinsmen. One is Colonel Charles Russell Lowell who 'gave
everything at Cedar Creek' and was to figure in the later volume,
History. In this poem he is accorded a single trait of his relative
by marriage, Colonel Robert Gould Shaw, who led a troop of
black soldiers to death and who is the subject of the title poem of
For the Union Dead. The funeral of this composite veteran is a
parody of that given to Pallas. Instead of 'the bird-priest chirping'
we have 'Uncle Charles' in his Federal uniform 'Blue-capped and
bird-like'. Instead of the yellow threads of the pall worked by
Queen Dido, there are the corpse's yellow nostril hairs clipped
by the English servant-girl. Nevertheless, through this diminution in stature, there remains a certain dignity. At least the
funeral is that of a hero fighting in a just cause, the abolition of
negro slavery. But the colours have now devolved upon a feeble
modern representative, an old man who misses a church service.
He must be about eighty-eight, for he remembers a funeral that
took place in 1863 (Colonel Shaw) or 1864 (Colonel Russell),
eighty years previous to the narrative time of the poem, which is
approximately the time of its being written (1947-51). So far from
wielding a heroic sword, this old man needs to cling hold of a
'parlour sabre' to keep himself from falling. For him, the
campaign to win a homeland, narrated in the *Aeneid*, and the
somewhat less heroic struggle of the American Civil War, are
alike the stuff of dreams in a degenerate present. Now he is
awake, the images of past action are so many scowling effigies,
and this is a reflection upon the myopic anti-hero, and not upon
themselves. One has, further, the feeling that Lowell's fictional
old man is as much an *alter ego* as Harry Kavanaugh who also has
inherited a faded history. It is odd that the feeling of indignation
which was directed at the acquisitors of *Lord Weary's Castle* and
the expropriators of 'The Mills of the Kavanaughs' should in this
poem be levelled at one who in his domestic life seems to be

essentially a man of peace. There is a distinct feeling at the end
that we are present at the speaker's own dissolution.

Another death is the central point of the monologue 'Mother
Marie Therese'; with the exception of 'The Quaker Graveyard',
perhaps the finest of the earlier poems. The central figure is, as
her name suggests, a worldly and secular nun, fitter to be an
empress than a mother superior. She is descended from the royal
family of Prussia, the Hohenzollerns, and has forced her aristocratic mould into the framework of an obscure convent at a place
in New Brunswick, ironically called 'Carthage'. The poem is
narrated not by this central figure but by one of her sisterhood, a
plebian and austere nun who very imperfectly understood the
superior she now talks about. Through a clever deployment of
the narrator's limitations, the character of Mother Marie Therese
comes over with considerable power:

> Our scandal'd set her frowning at the floor . . .
> . . . Christ enticed
> Her heart that fluttered, while she whipped her hounds
> Into the quicksands of her manor grounds
> A lordly child, her habit fleur-de-lys'd.
> . . . And how she'd chide her novices, and pluck
> Them by the ears for gabbling in Canuck,
> While she was reading Rabelais from her chaise.

This is one aspect of French culture satirizing another, far more
provincial. But, all the same, the Mother Superior falls victim to
her environment:

> Off Saint Denis' Head,
> Our Mother, drowned on an excursion, sleeps.
> Her billy goat, or its descendant, keeps
> Watch on a headland . . .

Her death is subject to the sort of mockery that she herself, when
she was alive, showered upon this cramped and provincial nook
of Canada with its incongruous name. Indeed, the names current
in the terrain savour of all kinds of incongruities: Saint Denis'
Head, Queen Mary's Neck. The Mother Superior irreverently
nicknamed the bell-buoy 'the Cardinal', and now it dances upon
her, while her billy goat – a symbol of sensuality – bawls. Clearly,

hers is an uneasy sleep. The tension within her character is that of
the poem at large. It derives in no small measure from the
contrast between the nostalgia with which the speaker looks back
on this worldly Superior and the Mother's own caustic disregard
in her life for religion and humanity. In the end, is Rabelais more
appropriate to a religious order than Canuck gossip? The latter
has at least the merit of being spontaneous, and certainly does
not deserve the chastisement which the Mother metes out to
offenders. We can hardly go along with the speaker's approving
remark about her Superior, 'She never spared the child and
spoiled the birch'.

The poem runs on two levels all the time. For instance, the
comments of the porpoise-bellied Father Turbot mean one thing
to the speaker and quite another to us:

> 'A sword,' said Father Turbot, 'not a saint'.
>
> 'An émigrée in this world and the next'.
>
> > 'N-n-nothing is so d-dead
> As a dead s-s-sister.' . . .

The nun who tells us this seems to imagine that she is summing
up a character of decisive force who could not be contained
within this world and whose loss is irreparable. But her description could equally well apply to a sharp-tempered worldling
unsuited to her vocation who achieved no work that would live
on after her. To provide a statement that we will understand in
spite of the speaker's misunderstandings is the most probable
role of Father Turbot in the poem; that, and bridging such lesions
in the plot as a Hohenzollern being the head of a French convent:
'an émigrée'. Certainly we see nothing but failure in the Mother's
wake; symbolized, as is usual in Lowell, by bitter weather: 'now
we freeze,/A later Advent, pruner of warped trees,/Whistles
about our nunnery slabs'. A Romantic recollection of the dead
Mother is all that survives:

> The dead, the sea's dead, has her sorrows, hours
> On end to lie tossing to the east, cold,
> Without bed-fellows, washed and bored and old,
> Bilged by her thoughts and worked on by the worms . . .
> . . . My Mother's hollow sockets fill with tears.

The speaker attributes feelings to the Mother Superior in death that she certainly never had in life. Further, the speaker shows her own impercipience by picturing the Mother tossing on the waves when, if Marie Therese had possessed a soul, presumably it would have been taken into the care of God. The lines inexorably recall Baudelaire's poem 'La Servante' which was later to be translated by Lowell as

> The dead, the poor dead, they have their bad hours . . .
> . . . These, eaten by the earth's black dream, lie dead,
> without a wife or friend to warm their bed,
> old skeletons sunk like shrubs in burlap bags . . .
> . . . My nurse's hollow sockets fill with tears.

In some ways, the adaptation in 'Mother Marie Therese' is nearer the original. The earlier version at least has the courage to call a worm by its proper name. But these two adaptations, published more than a decade apart, serve to show how much this poem of Baudelaire influenced Lowell's mind. The distinction, of course, is in the use made of the mourning properties. In 'La Servante' Baudelaire evokes and Lowell adapts the memory of a nurse who was much loved and sincerely mourned. Given the secular aspects of Mother Marie Therese, the reminiscence comes over ironically. Lowell's poem has been admired more than it has been understood.

Up to and including the collection in which this poem appeared Lowell was a master rhetorician. These highly wrought and allusive elegies were not the only barriers between Lowell's naked emotions and his readers. He created apparently fictional characters that in all sorts of ways acted out his own central impulses. These characters seem the more colourful as his personality destabilizes. Often, even without any biographical knowledge, one can sense the feeling to be highly personal. But it is rendered dramatic by the motivations accorded to the dramatis personae: Harry and Anne Kavanaugh, the sister speaking in 'Her Dead Brother', David and Bathsheba in the poem of that name, Michael and his mad German wife in 'Thanksgiving's Over', and these last two, the ineffectual old dreamer in Concord and the redoubtable Mother Marie Therese. However fragmented Lowell's life was during this period, his fictions remain astonishingly shaped. But upon this phase of activity followed a marked gap.

4 *Life Studies* (1959)

The period that led up to the publication of *Life Studies* consists of two barren areas, interspersed (in February 1953) by a brief time of writing and rewriting, and succeeded in the summer and autumn of 1957 by a major creative phase. The first of these barren areas can be dated from December 1950 when Lowell had finished *The Mills of the Kavanaughs*, quite literally on the proofs. This was the time of a European domicile lasting more than three years, the first five months of which were spent in Florence (Hamilton, 168-171). Those months proved to be a period of comparative calm, when Elizabeth Hardwick wrote most of *The Simple Truth*, a novel looking back on her residence with Lowell in Iowa, coinciding with the Benalek murder trial. Then the couple travelled to Greece and Turkey, afterwards sojourning unhappily in Paris with Lowell's widowed mother (Hamilton, 171-176). At Lowell's behest, Hardwick went on to Amsterdam, where she found an apartment for them to stay in, between October 1951 and May 1952: 'A busy, bourgeois street bordering on sloppy waters and the towers of the Rijksmuseum in view toward the west . . . How cold the house is. How we fight after too much gin' (Hardwick 1980, 97; 103). There were sundry excursions after this, but a visit to the Seminar in American Studies at Salzburg ended with Lowell having a breakdown that rendered necessary a period of hospitalization, first in Munich, then in Switzerland (Hamilton, 188-194). From October 1952, the base was Rome. However, the re-opening of the post Lowell had held in the University of Iowa drew him back to the USA in January 1953 (Hamilton, 196). Colleagues there included Paul Engle and John Berryman. A devoted acolyte among the students was the poet W. D. Snodgrass: 'The world moves like a diseased heart/packed with ice and snow' (Snodgrass, 63). It was at Iowa that Lowell broke a virtual poetic silence, revising two poems about writers which had been drafted when in Rome the previous November, and composing three poems that were to form most of Part One of *Life Studies* (Hamilton, 198). The summer of 1953 was spent teaching at the Kenyon School of Letters, held that year at Bloomington, Indiana. This was followed by a visit to John Crowe Ransom on the campus of Kenyon College at Gambier (Hamilton, 199).

One component instrumental in the composition of *Life Studies* may have been a series of conversations about the family which Lowell had with his mother when he stayed for a fortnight in Boston, buying a house at Duxbury, in January 1954: 'We were alone . . . and talked over almost everything' (Hamilton, 200). In February, however, Mrs Lowell set off by herself to Italy. At Rapallo, she suffered a stroke. Lowell, by that time teaching in Cincinnati, arrived in Italy too late to see his mother alive; she had died on 14 February (Hamilton, 202). Back in Cincinnati, Lowell underwent what seems to have been a further breakdown. He announced his separation from Elizabeth Hardwick and his imminent marriage to a music student he had met during his previous manic spell at Salzburg. He embarrassed the Faculty at Cincinnati by delivering a series of lectures on Pound and Hitler (Hamilton, 203-212). After this, ironically enough, he was committed to the Jewish Hospital at Cincinnati. This was followed by some time at Payne Whitney, New York, where he had undergone treatment five years previously. His hospitalization there and in Cincinnati extended over five months.

After his recovery, in the autumn of 1955, Lowell bought another house, 239 Marlborough Street, Boston (cf.*Life Studies*, Part Four). Ransom had recommended him to a post at Boston University, and Lowell taught there for five years. Anne Sexton and George Starbuck were among his more talented pupils (Axelrod 1978, 243); another wrote, 'a mild, soft-spoken, and myopic man, his voice lost in the hard-surfaced room, offered disconnected sentences that were more musings than messages' (Vendler). Sylvia Plath used to 'drop in on' his poetry seminar (Lowell 1966). This was his happiest period of teaching, and he had taken up writing again. The work was at first therapeutic in character: prose accounts of his mental illness alternated with prose reminiscence of family and childhood. Much of the latter was eventually distilled into the memoir which forms Part Two of *Life Studies*.

The year 1957 was marked by a series of creatively significant events. His daughter Harriet was born on 4 January. He performed in a series of recitals on the West Coast in March, appearing in different venues often six days a week, and sometimes twice in a single day (Lowell 1964a). He found he was able to adapt his poems in the very act of reading to an audience; to make them clearer (Lowell 1961a). Sometimes he shared a platform with Allen Ginsberg, a forceful recitalist, from whose performances Lowell sought to learn. The summer was spent talking with a very different kind of poet, Elizabeth Bishop, of all his contemporaries the one Lowell most admired. Thereafter *Life Studies* exploded. Between mid-August and October 1957 Lowell composed the most powerful poems in the book, using verse freer than anything he had attempted before. This was the phase which produced 'Skunk Hour', 'Man and Wife', 'Memories of West Street and Lepke', ' "To Speak of the Woe that is in Marriage" ', 'My Last Afternoon with Uncle Devereux Winslow', 'Commander Lowell', and 'Terminal Days at Beverly Farms' (Axelrod 1978, 102; Hamilton, 234). Most of these were initially published in two succeeding January issues of the *Partisan Review*, those for 1958 and 1959. Along with 'The Quaker Graveyard in Nantucket', 'Mother Marie Therese', and 'Falling Asleep Over the Aeneid', they were the greatest poems Lowell had written so far.

In *Life Studies* Lowell brought a new kind of colour into the language. There had been, to be sure, prefigurations in his previous verse: 'Fear,/The yellow chirper, beaks its cage' ('In the Cage') and 'Her Irish maids could never spoon out mush/Or orange juice enough' ('Mary Winslow'). But what in those earlier poems were flashes that illuminated a context, in *Life Studies* amounted to a triumph of style. One should, perhaps, register a qualification with regard to Part One of the book. There are poems here which could have fitted into the earlier volumes. However, it may equally be said that they serve to introduce the present one.

'Beyond the Alps' represents Lowell's valediction to Roman Catholicism. It is expressed in terms of a railway journey away from Rome, the city of God, over the Alps and on to Paris, the city of art. Two thirds of the way through the poem the railway train halts on the summit. But the city left behind, where Mussolini's skull and St Peter's sandal were in turn venerated, arouses only disgust. The current idol there is the Virgin Mary who, the Vatican has decided, was physically assumed into heaven. The outburst of applause that greets this latest dogma causes the Pope – a striking caricature – to drop his shaving mirror. His attempt to deal even-handedly with science and religion is parodied: 'His electric razor purred,/his pet canary chirped on his left hand'. Though the dawn breaks on the Alpine summit, the Exile is afforded no revelation. A Romanized paganism is no better than Rome itself: the sun-god is earth-bound, the Cyclops blinded. Minerva herself, said to have emanated from the head of Jove, is a *mis*carriage. A carriage, however, is on hand; and it takes the Exile on his way to an art which, like a Grecian urn in an unromanized mythology, gains most of its power from chronicling disintegration. A stanza, suppressed in draft, was added to later editions, but this did little more than clutter the plot with irrelevant detail. Some matter relating to the death of George Santayana was excised in draft and turned into a separate poem (Mazzaro 1965, 92-93).

In 'The Banker's Daughter', which follows in *Life Studies*, power is reduced to mere greed and calculation. The poem hiccoughs rhythmically over the details of the marriage between Marie de Medici (the 'Banker's Daughter' of the title) and Henry IV of France. These preliminaries, however, were much revised from a cluttered version published in the *Partisan Review*, May–June 1954. The finished verse gets into the familiar rumble of Lowell's couplets halfway through, after the King's death: 'Your great nerve gone, Sire, sleep without a care./No Hapsburg galleon coasts off Finisterre/with bars of bullion'. It is a debased world now. The fact that the Queen has taken a lover is justified by reference to the King's own adulteries, but meanwhile the son is adding inches to his stature. Too much of the plot, though, remains outside the poem. It is necessary for us to find out that the son, Louis XIII, later commands the assassination of the Queen's lover, Concini (Mazzaro 1965, 94). According to a note attached to this piece by Lowell himself, the Queen was exiled to a house lent her by the painter Rubens. As has happened with several Lowell poems which have a highly personal undertow, a good deal of essential narrative has been suppressed. One may point to the fact that Lowell's mother had been widowed (Yenser, 127), that her son had profited by his father's death and was further to profit by her own (Hamilton, 169; 205-206). It has been remarked (Mazzaro 1965, 93) that the final lines bear a family resemblance to those spoken by Anne Kavanaugh at the conclusion of the poem of which she is the protagonist: 'If you ever took/unfair advantages by right of birth,/pardon the easy virtues of the earth'.

The sense of political chaos suffered as personal anguish is maintained in the 'terse sonnet' (Yenser, 128), 'Inauguration Day: January 1953'. Caught in a frozen world, reminiscent of the demythologized summit in 'Beyond the Alps', are three figures: General Stuyvesant, who surrendered New Amsterdam in 1664; General Grant, who was beset by political scandal; and General Eisenhower, currently summoned to office by the Republic, 'The mausoleum in her heart'. Lowell, demonstrating that militarism in the presidency spells death, has made his own contribution to the poetry of the Cold War.

This frozen pattern of order emerges as soulless mechanism in 'A Mad Negro Soldier Confined at Munich': clocks, roll-calls, air-conditioning. In contrast to all this, the Negro is represented as an animal, floored but fighting. Lowell shows the authorities assessing their victim as being below par in terms which fore-shadow Sylvia Plath: ' "Each subnormal boot-/black heart is pulsing to its ant-egg dole" '. This character may be based on one of Lowell's fellow-inmates in the Munich military hospital where the poet was confined in August 1952; certainly it is a sympathetic portrayal. In fact, a sense of the Negro soldier as 'an embattled and alienated spirit' (Rosenthal) links the first part of *Life Studies* to Part Three, which features portraits of four writers with whom Lowell identifies.

These writers, in common with the mad Negro soldier (and indeed with Lowell himself), are essentially fighting-men. The novelist Ford Madox Ford, author of *The Good Soldier*, claimed to have been blackballed for promotion yet gassed in battle. The shabby circumstances of the writer's life are contrasted with the vaunting adventures of his fictions. In the next poem of the series, in part derived from the draft 'Beyond the Alps', George Santayana, poet and philosopher, is called an 'old trooper'. His 'cell' could be equally that of a gaol, a madhouse, or the Convent of the Little Company of Mary where, although an unbeliever, he spent the last years of his life (Santayana, 337; 348-349). The final image of the poem shows the old philosopher still in gladia-torial mood, seeing his last set of galleys under his magnifying glass as an arena 'refined by bile as yellow as a lump of gold'; in other words, satire is used for purge and purification. This makes Santayana seem oddly like Lowell. Indeed, the poem following, 'To Delmore Schwartz', is a prefiguration of what the younger poet might have become. The poem centres upon a convivial evening: Joyce and Freud, whose names pun on the English and the German words for happiness, are invoked. But in reality, the proceedings are overseen by the portrait of the drugged poet, Coleridge. In spite of its sporadic attempts towards exuberance, the poem is darkened by intimations of mortality: 'mustard gas', 'inert gaze'; the final word is 'killed'.

The last of these poems about writers, 'Words for Hart Crane', re-creates that poet as an anti-hero, 'wolfing the stray lambs'. Such a figure would be an unlikely candidate for 'Uncle Sam's phoney gold-plated laurels', such as the Pulitzer Prize. The real poets are exiles, and they cannot be apprehended passively: 'Who asks for me, the Shelley of my age,/must lay his heart out for my bed and board'. As the puns imply, to understand the poet's meaning is to take on a measure of his experience. There is a sharpness and crispness of utterance in these poems that should not go unheeded. Crane is compared not only with Shelley but with Walt Whitman and Catullus, a judgment not so strange now as it might have seemed to the readers of the *Partisan Review* for January–February 1953, where a version of this poem was published. Indeed, the four poems about writers have their own virtues as a succinct form of literary criticism.

The group has a marked degree of cohesiveness. Crane's profit is 'a pocket with a hole', while Ford's writing turns his 'pockets inside out'. Active through the four pieces is the idea that art must be pursued as a mode of perception and not as a substitute for religion. Such a pursuit brings its own penalties: 'Santayana exiled himself, Ford died in want, Crane committed suicide, and Schwartz suffered mental breakdowns similar to Lowell's' (Phillips, 22). The selection of these four figures is not arbitrary, and though critics disagree about the respective merits of the poems, each has found its advocate. For example, Staples (75) thinks 'Ford Madox Ford' 'the best of these four poems', while Standerwick favours 'For George Santayana' (*Renascence* XIII, 1960). Raffel (1981, 48) calls the Delmore Schwartz poem 'the best of the four' while Fein (69) avers that 'the best of the poems in Part Three is the last, "Words for Hart Crane" '.

Evaluations like these, emanating from such proponents of Lowell, argue a high level of distinction for the group as a whole.

The protagonists of these poems, both severally and in aggregate, issue a challenge which the rest of *Life Studies* takes up. The pageant that follows in Part Four of the book depicts the Fall of the House of Lowell (Axelrod 1978, 120). Those whom fortune seems to have chosen may not be singled out to their advantage. This appears especially in the longest poem of the book, 'My Last Afternoon with Uncle Devereux Winslow'. The character thus named does not appear until the fourth and last section of the piece. The whole poem, however, is an evocation of his doomed culture; and this context is at least as important as the man himself. The scene is presented as observed by the five-year-old Robert Lowell in the significant year, 1922. The technique of involving an innocent spectator relates to the Henry James of *What Maisie Knew* and of the autobiographical volume, *A Small Boy and Others*. So impressionistic an approach to narrative further relates to Ford's *It Was the Nightingale* (Mazzaro 1965, 105).

The child may not see that Grandfather's influence is pervasive and lethal, but that is no excuse for the reader. The images that obtrude upon the boy may, to us, seem over-statedly masculine. A thirsty alley of poplar trees parades in front of the femininity of Grandmother's rose garden and a 'scarey' stand of virgin pine: it seems to express something of the old man's relationship with his family. The décor of his house is described as being manly, comfortable, overbearing. It is shaded with screens, fitter for espionage than privacy. Its activities are monitored by an Alpine cuckoo clock 'slung with strangled, wooden game'. Everywhere are mementos of Grandfather's Victorian ego, fantastically hybrid in character (McFadden): *stogie*-brown beams, *fools*'-gold nuggets, a *Rocky Mountain* chaise longue – 'its legs, shellacked saplings'. Everything, in fact, is shellacked by Grandfather. On a hot day the maids bear cooling liquids out to the garden, but the pitcher forced upon the attention is that containing the yeasty blend of shandygaff made with Grandfather's own hands. In the face of so elaborate a mixture, it is no wonder that the 'watery martini pipe dreams' of the Lowell parents are rejected.

However, those who stay with Grandfather end up malformed, psychologically or otherwise. Grandmother is reduced to a thirsty eye hunting for a possible fourth at auction bridge. Great Aunt Sarah has been reduced from a putative bride and concert pianist to an incongruously asexual exponent of the Saint-Saëns *Samson and Delilah*; on a dummy piano, moreover, to spare Grandmother's nerves. Uncle Devereux makes his first appearance, well into the poem, as a reduced version of his father's masculine persona. There is a stricken quality about the images with which he is associated. A *sail*-coloured horse, ponds *small* as sapphires, his duck blind floating in a barrage of *smoke-clouds*: he is 'closing camp for the winter'. The posters he has kept from his student days seem *almost* life-size; they are certainly grotesque. Mr Punch is 'a water melon in hockey tights'; King Edward is at once 'ingenu and porcine'; young men in khaki kilts are 'bushwhacked'. A strange light is cast upon these pictures by the information, conveyed only in the final section of Part Four of the poem, 'My Uncle was dying at twenty-nine'. With this, the poem reaches its climax: the description of a dead man held on end, not by force of personality but by habit of class. 'He was as brushed as Bayard, our riding horse', 'his trousers were solid cream from the top of the bottle'. 'The cream of society' and 'the top drawer', Victorian clichés in themselves, are thus fused into a telling phrase. Uncle Devereux stands behind the boy like a portent, 'animated, hierarchical . . . dying'. The boy meantime plays with detritus left by 'our' farmer on the porch: a pile of earth, foundation of life, which here is 'cool'; a pile of lime, dissolver of flesh, which here is 'warm'. The boy mixes black earth with white lime; an idea running through the poem. It suggests the first dawning of adult consciousness in the boy, ripened by this impending death. The poem ends 'Come winter,/Uncle Devereux would blend to the one colour'. It seems that at least one of the hybrid entities of Grandfather's farm is finally compounded.

The irony deepens when the poem is considered in the context of *Life Studies*. No one has died at Char-de-sa during the five years of the boy's lifetime. But *Life Studies* is arranged in order of the deaths of its protagonists (Axelrod 1978, 120): first Uncle Devereux, then Grandfather Winslow; in succession, Grandmother Winslow, Commander Lowell, Commander Lowell's widow; and then, with the boy grown to manhood, his own breakdown and the disintegration of his marriage.

The two poems immediately after 'Uncle Devereux' essentially deal with Grandfather Winslow, next in the roll-call of mortality. The eye of childhood still operates in 'Dunbarton', where Grandfather continues to be vigorous among the family plots, still assuming his rights over his grandchild. He is more in command than the Commander ever was: taking the wheel, an admiral at the helm, even (metaphorically) pumping ship. In the next poem, 'Grandparents', he becomes with a cinematic shift the focus of a retrospect. He 'still' waves his stick 'like a policeman', and poor captive Grandmother 'still' wears her 'thick lavender mourning'. But this is seen from the uncertain maturity of the poet, and all seems different, the result of an altered perception. The speaker is exiled from his childhood: he can never again cuddle in his Grandfather's bed or be cherished in those all-embracing arms. The old man's dominance, fondly remarked by the child, is perceived in a different fashion by the adult: 'dipping sugar for us both', 'shooting for us both'. The grown man, at any rate, knows such collusion can never recur. Childishly, he doodles moustaches on 'the last Russian czar', as though that were a simulacrum for Grandfather. This final image is a measure of the deprecating irony of the poem. For the reader, it may not be the poet who is deprecated.

There are prose elements behind many of these poems. It is instructive to see how the anecdotage is honed into poetry through the several drafts of 'Uncle Devereux' (Axelrod 1978, 247-249). Similarly, in the prose of '91 Revere Street' Lowell describes the decline in his father's fortunes after he resigned from the Navy:

we had so many downs, so many minutes, and so many yards to go for winning a touchdown. It was just such a winning financial and social advance that my parents promised themselves would follow Father's resignation from the Navy and his acceptance of a sensible job offered him at the Cambridge branch of Lever Brothers' Soap.

The advance was never to come. Father resigned from the service in 1927, but he never had a civilian *career*; he instead had merely twenty-two years of the civilian *life*. Almost immediately he bought a larger and more stylish house; he sold his ascetic, stove-black Hudson and bought a brown Buick; later the Buick was exchanged for a high-toned, as-good-as-new Packard with a custom-designed royal blue and mahogany body. Without drama, his earnings more or less decreased from year to year.

This is factual and workmanlike, but it lacks the precision of poetry. The verse rendering of this portrait in failure reached its final plasticity (through Marvellian tetrameters, Lowell 1961a) and infused these pathetic facts with a wry humour that took Lowell's poetry a stage further from the monologues of *The Mills of the Kavanaughs*. The tragic figure here is shot through with a touching irony, quite distinct from the destructive element in which Grandfather Winslow and Uncle Devereux seem to bathe. This quality in itself would redeem 'Commander Lowell' from too close an association with what has been called Confessional Verse:

> 'Anchors aweigh,' Daddy boomed in his bathtub,
> 'Anchors aweigh,'
> when Lever Brothers offered to pay
> him double what the Navy paid.
> I nagged for his dress sword with gold braid,
> and cringed because Mother, new
> caps on all her teeth, was born anew
> at forty. With seamanlike celerity,
> Father left the Navy,
> and deeded Mother his property.
>
> He was soon fired. Year after year,
> he still hummed 'Anchors aweigh' in the tub –
> whenever he left a job,
> he bought a smarter car.
> Father's last employer
> was Scudder, Stevens and Clark, Investment Advisers,
> himself his only client.

There is genuine wit here. One hears it in the irony of the song that the ex-Naval Officer sings in his 'tub'; one sees it in the seamanlike celerity with which he left the Navy; one can bring it out by contrasting the prose which over-details the makes of the automobiles with the sharpness which points the verse: 'whenever he left a job,/he bought a smarter car'. The poetry acts out the sad but jaunty concept of a man going down with all flags flying. Its rhythms are surprisingly flexible. They are metrically free, but syncopated after the manner of jazz, and punctuated with rhymes that occur as a means of emphasis : 'With seamanlike celerity,/Father left the Navy,/and deeded Mother his property'. It is sardonic, even sour. The sourness is not, however, directed

at Commander Lowell but at the world of ruling-class Bostonians
which is too inflexible to accommodate a dreamer. In other
words, the poem is taking another bite at Lowell's ancestors. The
Commander himself is protected from the full weight of adverse
irony by the pathos which builds up through situation after situation in which he is increasingly misunderstood by his peers.

All the incongruities of Commander Lowell – the title of the
poem itself is ironic – come into play in the last section:

> Smiling on all,
> Father was once successful enough to be lost
> in the mob of ruling-class Bostonians.
> As early as 1928,
> he owned a house converted to oil,
> and redecorated by the architect
> of St. Mark's School . . . Its main effect
> was a drawing room, 'longitudinal as Versailles',
> its ceiling, roughened with oatmeal, was blue as the sea.
> And once
> nineteen, the youngest ensign in his class,
> he was the 'old man' of a gunboat on the Yangtze.

That final touch consolidates the sea imagery that is glimpsed in
hints throughout the poem. The naval officer who showed up
badly among the weekend sea dogs, the bold singer whose
anchor weighed him down in an inappropriate occupation, the
owner of a vainglorious house whose only seamanlike attribute
was a drawing-room ceiling coloured sea-blue – all these aspects
of the protagonist are subsumed in the last three lines which show
the Commander's moment of glory when for once in his life he
was the most responsible person around. The source of compassion here is the sense of time. There is pathos as well as irony in
the juxtaposition of age and youth: the boy of *nineteen*, the
youngest ensign in his class, the *old man* of a gunboat. There is
pathos even in this customary term for a commander. We are not
told what plague or battle reduced the complement of the crew to
this pass. What we know is that the point so quietly made at the
end of the poem contrasts heroically with the blunders and
vanities narrated in the preceding verses. The conflict between
potential and achievement is none the less keen because we
arrive at the end to find a picture of a man who reached his peak

too early – like Othello who beat the Turk at Aleppo – and whose life, thereafter, slid downhill all the way.

The nakedness of the poems in *Life Studies* may seem disturbing at first, but acquaintance shows them to be achieved works of art, and this is brought out if they are compared with the efforts of the so-called Confessional Poets. Sylvia Plath in her poem 'Daddy' offers too few facts about her father. He seems to have deserted his daughter (by dying!) when she was ten. The rest is fantasy: a way of motivating her hatred for him by playing a game in which the father-figure appears as a Nazi commandant:

> I have always been scared of *you*,
> With your Luftwaffe, your gobbledygoo.
> And your neat moustache
> And your Aryan eye, bright blue.
> Panzer-man, panzer-man, O You –
> (Plath 1965, 55)

Unlike 'Commander Lowell', 'Daddy' is too simplistic to wear well. The same can be said of Sylvia Plath's novel, *The Bell Jar*: 'My German-speaking father . . . came from some manic-depressive hamlet in the black heart of Prussia' (Plath 1966, 34). The heroine goes to her father's grave and '[howls] her loss into the cold salt rain' (177). One thinks in this connection of the note from the novel *Recovery*, by John Berryman, on his father's suicide: 'God was a son of a bitch who had allowed Daddy to go mad with grief and fear' (Berryman 1973, 233). There is a verse equivalent to this, 'Dream Song 384': 'I stand above my father's grave with rage' and 'I spit upon this dreadful banker's grave' (Berryman 1969, 316). One thinks, moreover, of the incipient hysteria in Anne Sexton's 'All My Pretty Ones': 'My God, father, each Christmas Day/with your blood, will I drink down your glass of wine?' (Sexton, 5). What of Maxine Kumin: 'the coffee is black as/the day of my father's death' (Kumin, 91)? What of Diane Wakoski: 'my father/made me what I am/a lonely woman' (Wakoski 1968, 20)? Examples could be multiplied. There is no shortage of attacks upon the modern American father. But their force has no support from understanding; their content lacks that precision which is a guarantee of authenticity.

Robert Lowell stands apart from the Confessional Poets, not only because of his humour and compassion, but by reason of his

colour of language and adroitness of technique. One approach to
Life Studies, not on the whole taken by the critics when the book
first came out, is its contribution to the poetry of reminiscence.
This distinctive form in twentieth-century writing is in many ways
an attempt to fill the gap left by the dislodgement of familiar
totems. In lieu of the Trinity, the Virgin, and all the saints and
martyrs, modern poets have put forward a hierarchy of admired
figures in an illuminated cloud of nostalgia. We can see more
than a trace of this in W. B. Yeats's creation of a highly personal
mythology including such incompatible heroes as Robert Gregory,
John Millington Synge, John MacBride, and MacGregor Mathers.
Ezra Pound's evocations of the 1890s and after are sufficiently
well known, especially those in the *Pisan Cantos*:

> Lordly men are to earth o'ergiven
> > these the companions:
> > > Fordie that wrote of giants
> > > > and William who dreamed of nobility
> > > > and Jim the comedian singing:
> > > > > 'Blarrney castle me darlin'
> > > > > you're nothing now but a StOWne'
>
> (Pound 1949, 15)

It would, however, be a perceptive reader who could gather at
first acquaintance that Fordie, William and Jim are, respectively,
Ford Madox Ford, W. B. Yeats, and James Joyce. The mode was
taken to its extreme by John Berryman in 'Dream Song 153': 'I'm
cross with god who has wrecked this generation./First he seized
Ted, then Richard, Randall, now Delmore' (Berryman 1969,
82); i.e., Roethke, Blackmur, Jarrell, Schwartz. One thinks also
of the doxology of tributes to Sylvia Plath by such poets as
Berryman himself, Anne Sexton, Christopher Levenson and
Erica Jong.

It is true that Robert Lowell himself derives some impetus
from the *Pisan Cantos*. But, as we saw from his poems about
Ford, Santayana, Schwartz and Crane, he is able not only to
invoke but to re-create. Further, the vivacity of his re-creation
has more than a hint of humorous scepticism which gives life not
only to 'Commander Lowell' but to its two sequels, 'Terminal Days
at Beverly Farms' and 'Father's Bedroom'. The former picks up
from 'Commander Lowell' especially its subject's defensive good

humour: 'He smiled his oval Lowell smile', 'inattentive and beaming'. This lends great point to the final lines of the poem and takes them to a pitch beyond their manifest authenticity: 'After a morning of anxious, repetitive smiling,/his last words to Mother were: "I feel awful" '. The other sequel to 'Commander Lowell', 'Father's Bedroom', conjectures, through a survey of his personal possessions, the inner life of the man. We have already seen something of this in 'Commander Lowell' when the dress sword is replaced by the ivory Annapolis slide rule. The Commander's bedroom – not the main one of the house – proves to be in direct contrast with the Victorian mausoleum inhabited by Grandfather Winslow. We find a blue kimono, a fussily shaded bedside-lamp, and a coffee-table book, *Glimpses of Unfamiliar Japan*. Yet that book itself had travelled; to the Yangtze where, like the Commander himself, it had experienced hard usage. The effect of this is something like that which occurs at the end of 'Commander Lowell'. However unassertive the Commander seems, he has seen action in circumstances – those of the Chinese Civil War in the aftermath of the Boxer Rising – which might well have tested some of his adverse critics, including his son. A further Commander Lowell poem, 'For Sale', shows his retirement cottage at Beverly Farms put on the market after his death with rather more than seamanlike celerity. The removal van follows hard upon the wheels of the hearse. The final lines are a prefiguration: 'Mother mooned in a window,/as if she had stayed on a train/one stop past her destination'.

Mother, as previously recounted, reached her terminus at Rapallo in February 1954, and returned by water back to the family cemetery. All the Italian images of 'Sailing Home from Rapallo' are hot and exotic. The shoreline of the Golfo di Canova breaks into flower, the sea-sleds blast like jack-hammers, the wake of the liner bubbles like *spumante*, and the corpse is wrapped against the heat in tinfoil like *panetone* – more properly, the dark and hard bread known as *panforte*, from Siena (Anzilotti 1979). The apparent link between this corpse, travelling first-class in a coffin modelled on Napoleon's tomb, and that of the more modest Commander Lowell, is that he, too, is wrapped up like cake; *his* tomb, though, proves to be a pink-veined slice of marble. However, its novelty makes the only Lowell in Dunbarton Cemetery stand out from the thirty or so Winslows and their collaterals. A sense of incongruity is, so to speak, relayed to the travelling grave of Mrs Lowell. The name on the Napoleonic coffin has been misspelled 'Lovel', a reversion to what may have been the authentic name of the family, found in the Battle Abbey Roll of early Normans (Greenslet, 3).

The poem 'During Fever' links the generations. Lowell sees his small daughter's uneasy stirrings in her cot and hears her mumbling 'sorry', and these put him in his own father's place. They also project him back into the discussions of that 'dim-bulb' character Lowell had with his mother when he was 'a gem-like undergraduate', still immature in his mother's eyes. Her bedroom, in contrast to that of his father, is masterful, with a hot-water-bottle reminiscent of a hip-flask, and a bed as big as a bathroom. From her sterile relationship with his father he goes further back, to her relationship with *her* father, and indicates an Electra-type explanation, her awareness of a grumbling presence behind one of his shady screens whenever one of her young men came to court her. In this way, Lowell traces a chain of instability through four generations, a bad omen for the infant uneasy during fever. The fever, of course, can be understood on a larger scale, metaphorically.

Fact is indeed raised to metaphor, if not allegory, in a trio of poems evoking people in asylum and in gaol: 'Waking in the Blue', 'Home After Three Months Away' and 'Memories of West Street and Lepke'. The first of these was written out of a period of mania following upon the August-October phase of productivity in 1957. In December, after a reading trip to Washington and New York, a series of events led to Lowell's confinement in the Boston Psychopathic Hospital. After a brief respite in January, he was admitted to the McLean Hospital outside Boston (Hamilton, 238-243). There he wrote a kind of manic love poem concerning a psychiatric fieldworker he had met. The lines about this woman were excised from the draft and later rescued for the poems '1958' (*Near the Ocean*) and 'Mania' (*Notebook*). What remained when the apparently initiating impulse was sacrificed turned into 'Waking in the Blue', a description of life at the McLean Hospital. It is a definitely anti-Victorian poem, repudiating the customs of the past, and the title may very well refer to a piece of Victorian sentiment by Thomas Carlyle: 'So here hath been dawning/Another blue Day:/Think wilt thou let it/Slip useless away?'. The days at McLean slip past uselessly, though the night-attendant reads the Ogden and

Richards study of semantics, *The Meaning of Meaning*. But there is no meaning in the lives of these Harvard drop-outs. The one-time all-American full-back, 'Stanley', tries to keep his sixty-year-old physique in seal-like litheness. 'Bobbie', member of Harvard's exclusive Porcellion Club, doesn't bother, and his nakedness exposes him 'roly-poly as a sperm whale'. The air is redolent with unfulfilled sexuality. These meaninglessly virile aristocrats contrast with the 'slightly too little nonsensical bachelor twinkle/of the Roman Catholic attendants'. The lower classes – characteristically Boston Irish – attend, as ever, on their WASP superiors: both 'Stanley' and 'Bobbie' are referred to as kings, though decidedly reduced ones. The key line of the poem deserves to be pondered: 'These victorious figures of bravado ossified young'. The joining together in unexpected congruence words that seem to have been designed for some quite separate denotation is a highly characteristic Lowell effect. 'Stanley' and 'Bobbie', like Lowell, achieved their seed-time early, and appear to have stuck there. The poet, as he describes himself, is indecently fit. Again, there is the aura of sex unused: 'Cock of the walk,/I strut in my turtle-necked French sailor's jersey'. Yet the day slips past without achievement. The atmosphere, in the end, is one of present frustration: we hear of 'pinched, indigenous faces', of shaving mirrors of metal and razors locked. It is a predicament that familiarizes the Lowell persona with the 'shaky future'.

The shaving and mirror imagery goes on in the companion poem, 'Home After Three Months Away', the piece which Lowell began during one of his weekend releases from McLean's (Hamilton, 253). After the ramrod profile of 'Stanley' in his vaguely urinous tub, we come across the contrasting image of Lowell's small daughter holding her levee; as naked as 'Stanley', but seeming a good deal more hopeful. She makes the interval in hospital seem like child's play. Indeed, the play continues: 'my child still dabs her cheeks/to start me shaving'. The 'blue' evoked in this poem is not the monotony of the asylum but – when at last she is dressed – the child's 'sky-blue corduroy'. As befits the father of a child, the speaker is treated as an adult; allowed a real mirror now, and a genuine razor. There is, however, a reverberation in the background. The poem began with a reference to an inimical nurse who tied gobbets of pork-rind on the magnolia tree for the birds. The Lowell figure is 'cured', but this means he has lost his place in the hierarchy, and is (a reference to the ambiguous conclusion of Marvell's 'To His Coy Mistress') 'frizzled, stale and small'; a gobbet, in fact. Recovery has been an exacting business: like the tulips in the coffin's-length of garden three stories beneath, Lowell has been 'bushed by the late spring snow'.

The position is, without losing any force, generalized in the last of the trio of poems, 'Memories of West Street and Lepke'. This not only re-creates a situation but the time in which it is set, that of Eisenhower, Senator Joe McCarthy, and the Cold War years. The poem begins with a self-portrait, of a man in relaxed prosperity:

> Only teaching on Tuesdays, book-worming
> in pyjamas fresh from the washer each morning,
> I hog a whole house on Boston's
> 'hardly passionate Marlborough Street'.

The quotation here comes from a lecture by William James, who used the phrase as an example of understatement (Axelrod 1978, 122). It has a leisurely and Bostonian cadence, as though temporarily Lowell has rejoined his aristocratic forbears. 'These are the tranquillized Fifties,/and I am forty': the statement has passed into currency. Lowell identifies his self-portrait with the decade: easy, hoggish, tranquillized; possessed of a prison flabbiness, in fact. From the vantage-point of this particular confinement, he recalls his period in the West Street Jail where he was placed immediately after the sentence he received in 1947 for refusing the draft; later, he was sent to Danbury. It was something of a *cause célèbre*. *That* decade was a time of idealism, and retrospectively he identifies with it: 'I was a fire-breathing Catholic C.O.'. But in gaol there is an apparent heterogeneity. Another idealist, Abramovitz, is anything but fire-breathing. He is a gentle pacifist 'so vegetarian/he wore rope soles and preferred fallen fruit'. His attempt to convert to this creed a couple of Hollywood pimps brings disaster upon him. With alliterative violence, Bioff and Brown 'blew their tops and beat him black and blue'. The prison is able to contain such disparities because it is the dustbin of society. It holds all those who, however different from one another, deviate from social norms (Smith, 74). The true focus of the poem may be found in 'Czar' Lepke; like Grandpa, the representative of an oppressively male regime – in this case, 'Murder Incorporated'. His past was violent, but his present is tranquillized, as the 1950s are tranquillized in the present time, more than a decade later, of the poem:

> Flabby, bald, lobotomized,
> he drifted in a sheepish calm,
> where no agonizing reappraisal
> jarred his concentration on the electric chair –
> hanging like an oasis in his air
> of lost connections . . .

This is a dramatic foreshadowing of the poet's own state of mind, which he equates with that of the United States at large. 'Agonizing reappraisal' was a term used, with Olympian calm, by President Eisenhower's Secretary of State, John Foster Dulles. Lowell's suggestion is that violence lies smouldering or suppurating beneath the tranquillized flabbiness (Crick, 56). What the speaker in the poem and 'Czar' Lepke the murderer look forward to is death, the oasis, the ultimate lobotomy. This represents the USA itself as a giant prison or asylum. 'Memories of West Street and Lepke' is a development of the mode of reminiscence, mainly because it has a form which includes far more than the personality it evokes. The portrait of Lepke reverberates beyond the particular character. As often happens in mid-period Lowell, the lassitude is described with such perception that the poem becomes, not a giving in to the disease, but a diagnosis of it; one that is part way towards a cure.

This is poignantly true of the two 'marriage' poems that follow in the *Life Studies* volume; and of another, closely related, 'Skunk Hour'. The first of the marriage poems, 'Man and Wife', is a complex of literary allusions. Yenser (159) relates the opening to Donne's 'The Sun Rising'; Rudman (80), with as much confidence, places it with Milton; while Raffel (1981, 54) finds the determining influence to be Pope. The Milton of the beginning of *Paradise Lost*, Book II, does indeed infuse the beginning of Pope's *Dunciad*, Book II: 'High on a gorgeous seat, that far outshone/Henley's gilt tub, or Fleckno's Irish throne . . . /Great Cibber sate'. This would make Lowell not so much Satan as a ridiculous poetaster, Satan's own caricature. Further, it is not the sun but (reversing Donne's 'The Sun Rising') the poet who is a 'busy old fool'. In yet a further reference, to 'Paleface and Red-skin', a seminal essay by one of the 'Rahvs' who are mentioned later on in the poem, he seems to be a poet aspiring to savage rebellion; but his warpaint is only dye (Lane). 'Tamed by Miltown' would suggest that Lowell is a tamed Milton descended from the Lowells who created a mill town, Lowell, in Massachusetts (Greenslet, 192); one who was tamed still more by Miltown, 'a wellknown tranquillizer' (Chambers, 9). Thus tranquillized, he lies with his wife on Mother's bed, hardly conducive to erotic passion. It is not surprising that he seems unable to make love to his wife. She shrieks out an 'old-fashioned tirade' while protecting herself against such advances as he is able to attempt: 'you hold/your pillow to your hollows like a child'; except that, of course, she is a grown woman. This situation is related back to their first meeting, when the wife was 'still all air and nerve', while the husband was even then tranquillized, in those days by alcohol: 'too boiled to make a pass'. The piece has been called a love poem (Staples, 14). It is rather a record of marital humiliation, kept from subsiding into the confessional mode by the dramatic character of the imagery – 'blossoms on our magnolia ignite' – and the network of literary allusions.

The 'old-fashioned tirade' budded off in draft from 'Man and Wife' and became a monologue, ' "To speak of the Woe that is in Marriage" '. It is framed in quotation marks three times over: title, epigraph, text. The title comes from Chaucer's Prologue to *The Wife of Bath's Tale*, perhaps the most successful monologue in English feigned to be spoken by a woman: ' "Experience, though noon auctoritee/Were in this world, is right ynogh for me/To speke of wo that is in mariage" '. Lowell's text, like that of Chaucer, is an apparent reproach to an erring husband; like the Wife of Bath, his spokeswoman imputes to her husband remarkable qualities. As with 'Man and Wife', the literary allusions help the effect of dramatic distance. It seems all there: the torrid evening which gives rise to passions of lust and anger, the natural-seeming metaphors that imply their own wry comments on the edge of caricature. This appears to be the urgent tone of the speaking voice. Yet, as the poet himself has informed us (Lowell 1961a), the poem derives from Catullus. It is a Catullus localized, updated, projected; yet still recognizable. A Victorian scholar has given us an idea of 'Oramus, si forte non molestumst' (Catullus LV) in prose:

Not though I should be moulded in brass like the fabled warder of Crete,
not though I were to soar aloft like flying Pegasus, not if I were Ladas or
wing-footed Perseus, not if I were the swift snow-white pair of Rhesus
could I overtake you: add to these the feather-footed gods and the
winged, and with them call for swiftness of the winds; – though you
should harness all these, Camerius, and press them into my service, yet I
should be tired out to my very marrow, and worn away with frequent
faintness, my friend, while searching for you.
(Cornish, 63, 65)

This section of the poem stands as a separate entity in the
manuscript (Cornish, 63), and indeed its independence seems to
have been a factor in attracting Lowell's attention. Here is the
same piece in the verse of a modern translator. He, like Lowell,
treats the passage as a separate text:

> If I were Talus, the bronze guard of Crete,
> Or Ladas, or that hero with winged feet,
> Perseus, or could borrow the sky-flight
> Of Pegasus or the two swift-hooved, snow-white
> Horses of Rhesus; add the speed of the wind
> And all the flying, feather-footed kind,
> Then yoke the lot, Camerius, together –
> And still I'd reach the end of my poor tether,
> The broken-down, bone-weary, nerve-frayed end,
> Hunting for you all over Rome, my friend.
> (Michie, 93)

The persona in Lowell, like that in Catullus, finds her husband
difficult to keep up with:

> 'The hot night makes us keep our bedroom windows open.
> Our magnolia blossoms. Life begins to happen.
> My hopped up husband drops his home disputes,
> and hits the streets to cruise for prostitutes,
> free-lancing out along the razor's edge'.

She accuses him of riotous behaviour; ' "Oh the monotonous
meanness of his lust" '. As in Catullus, the accused character
seems larger than life-size: ' "Gored by the climacteric of his
want, he stalls above me like an elephant" '. The fact that this is

really self-accusation – it is not the injured wife who wrote the poem – is disarming. The fact that the wife still finds her husband desirable is perhaps even more so. Evidently she prefers magnitude to magnanimity. An odd clue is given by the epigraph, that third contribution in quotation marks: 'It is the future generation that presses into being by means of these exuberant feelings and supersensible soap bubbles of ours'. All this swaggering, however painful to his wife, may give rise to children after all!

This is subversive, but not more so than Catullus, or indeed Baudelaire, Heine and Hölderlin. The last is co-present with other literary heroes in 'Skunk Hour', which has the richest provenance of any poem in *Life Studies* and a power of structure that survives the closest reading. The basic situation is that of a rundown seaside community – another image of America – based on Castine, Maine, where Lowell had a residence that was made over to him in 1957 by his cousin Harriet Winslow (Hamilton, 233) and where he spent the summer of that year (Axelrod 1978, 124). The characters still hanging on there are decadent and perverted, and are in the process of being replaced by more vigorous organisms. The hermit heiress, straight out of *The Country of the Pointed Firs* by Sarah Orne Jewett (Nims), dreams back to the seclusion of Queen Victoria's reign; meanwhile her tenant, a farmer, runs the town. The millionaire, looking as if he had leaped straight out of a high-class mail-order catalogue for sporting clothes, has already left. It is true that the homosexual decorator – image of the artist's role in this state of society – brightens his shop for Fall; but that very word indicates his loneliness and suggests that he has no future. In the original draft, this was made to apply to the speaker of the poem (Axelrod 1978, 250). In the final version, the speaker 'one dark night' seeks experience at a remove by spying on lovers in their cars. But love is backed up against a graveyard, 'the hill's skull', Golgotha; and the voyeur's observations are distorted by mental disturbance. Like Mephistophilis in Marlowe's *Faustus* and Satan in *Paradise Lost*, he reflects:

> I myself am hell,
> nobody's here –
>
> only skunks, that search
> in the moonlight for a bite to eat.

> They march on their soles up Main Street:
> white stripes, moonstruck eyes' red fire
> under the chalk-dry and spar spire
> of the Trinitarian Church.

Human decadence has been replaced by a lower but more vital form; the spire by (in the next stanza) the column. This is the modern world in ebb; 'a sort of greedy parody of the Eucharist' (Berryman 1964). The striking image of the red eyes marching along through the darkness has a double source. One can find it in the German poet Hölderlin, in a piece called 'Brot und Wein' ('Bread and Wine'), translated into prose thus: 'the moon is on her way in secret too; night, the dream-laden, is coming; full of stars and, it seems, little concerned with us, the astonishing one, the stranger among humans, is gleaming forth sadly and splendidly up over the mountain tops' (Forster, 293–294). The image, remarkable in itself, is reinforced by one culled from a fine poem by Elizabeth Bishop, 'The Armadillo'. Here we have a human incursion upon the animal world: careless fire-balloons set off an inferno which burns the owls' nest, scares an armadillo:

> and then a baby rabbit jumped out,
> *short*-eared to our surprise.
> So soft! – a handful of intangible ash
> with fixed ignited eyes.
> (Bishop 1984, 104)

Again we have the star as an image of fire or of eyes. One can say in passing that it is the lyric poet, Elizabeth Bishop, at once sensitive and technically adept, who is the feminine counterpart of Lowell; not the shrill lady tenants of the professional confessional. Lowell scores over Elizabeth Bishop only in range of expression. In this case, he has considerably developed his sources, distinguished though they are. It is the *Einfühlung* of his vision; an animal invasion of the human world: 'night, the dream-laden, is coming; full of stars' (Hölderlin); 'fixed ignited eyes' (Bishop); 'moonstruck eyes' red fire' (Lowell). Lowell has transformed the star image of Hölderlin and the 'ignited eyes' image of Elizabeth Bishop into a metaphor that combines moon, stars and fire to create an effect of defiance, alienation and power. This is the ultimate takeover; voiced in a muscular vocabulary:

She jabs her wedge head in a cup
of sour cream, drops her ostrich tail,
and will not scare.

The earlier stanzas are full of a quality which can be called the
Death Wish. It conditions the entire *Life Studies* cycle which is,
in reality, the picture of a society in decay. But, in portraying
such a society, Lowell does not succumb to it. It is set off and
criticized by his endlessly inventive language and by his evocative
weaving together of images from many different sources. The
subjects of these poems squander their substance, gag for air,
have faces like putty, drift flabbily, dream of Queen Victoria.
Their observer, on the other hand, is alive, alert, vividly aware of
now. This is what makes his revelatory poems so unrevelatory; of
self, that is. The central protagonist may declare himself hell, and
assert that his mind is not right. But the poems in which he says
such things are so centrally sane and accomplished that he comes
across as a dramatic character, a projection only of one aspect of
the intricate sensibility concerned.

   A good many critics who understood the previous volumes
failed to see the significance of this new one. In a letter to the
poet, Allen Tate said that all the poems about Lowell's family
were bad, termed them 'scattered items of experience', and
categorically advised against publication (Hamilton, 237).
Another of Lowell's early mentors, Richard Eberhart, found the
value of *Life Studies* to be 'historical', the 'recapitulation' of an
earlier milieu (*New York Times Book Review*, 3 May 1959).
Joseph Bennett, in the *Hudson Review* for Autumn 1959, speaks
of 'off-hand, journalistic technique. It is carelessly written'. In
Great Britain, Charles Tomlinson complained of 'inadequacies
of tone' and diagnosed 'a kind of poetic impasse' (*Listen*, Spring
1960). Donald Davie complained of a confusion between Lowell's
public role as poet and his private life, 'a spurious vitality injec-
ted into the first from a coy exhibitionism about the second'
(*Granta*, 17 October 1959). Frank Kermode claimed that the
poet was now so sure of his powers that he ignored the danger of
lapsing into 'superior doggerel' (*Spectator*, 1 May 1959). The
pejorative nature of this last phrase brought a sharp response
from two of the younger poets working at the time, Edward
Lucie-Smith and Peter Porter, who declared that this showed
Kermode to be 'sadly blind' to an exciting new way of writing

poetry (*Spectator*, 15 May 1959). Lucie-Smith followed this up
with a penetrating review in which he concluded 'these poems
suggest new ways of relating the most informal kind of English,
the spoken English of ordinary domestic conversation, to the
most formal – the language of poetry' (*Gemini*, Autumn 1959).
Philip Larkin, a poet whom Lowell had come to respect, picked
out the lightness and humour (*Manchester Guardian Weekly*, 21
May 1959), while another modern master, Norman MacCaig,
commented, 'He uses language with precision and economy'
(*Saltire Review*, Autumn 1959). A. Alvarez wrote perhaps the
most discerning review on the British side of the Atlantic:
'Instead of contorting his conflicts into a baroque theology,
Lowell exposes their beginnings in a series of ironic, and often
tender, reminiscences about the family figures who loomed large
in his childhood' (*Observer*, 12 April 1959).

Back in the United States, M. L. Rosenthal wrote for *The
Nation* of 19 September 1959 that rare item, a book review that
still holds its ground as a considered critique. Though aware of
the violence and imbalance that were the raw material of these
poems, he also points to the articulation of the whole, comparing
it with *Mauberley* and *The Bridge*; an estimate which does not
seem excessive in these days. Perhaps the most informed response
of all came from William Carlos Williams, Lowell's respected
senior, in two letters that he wrote to the author: 'You have
opened a new field. You needed that break, rhyme could not
contain you any longer, you have too much to say for that' and
'There is no lying permitted to a man who writes that way'
(Axelrod 1978, 92). Retrospectively, this ratifies what could possibly have seemed to be a negative comment in an otherwise
enthusiastic critique of *The Mills of the Kavanaughs* written in the
New York Times Book Review, 22 April 1951, when he deplored
the 'formal fixation of the line' and suggested that Lowell would
surmount 'the disaster' if he could 'break through'. Indeed, a
number of the younger poets of the time felt that this 'break
through' was what *Life Studies* constituted. However, it is worth
pointing out that several critics have noted the affinity between
Williams and Lowell growing up in the 1950s: between Williams's
'Asphodel' and Lowell's 'Man and Wife', for instance (Axelrod
1978, 93-94) or between 'Adam' and 'Terminal Days at Beverly
Farms' (Procopiow 1976). But Williams himself could never have
given this new art such impetus, and in any case the key poems of

Life Studies stand as definitive works of literature; they have absorbed their influences.

While most of the critics greeted with confused signals a collection of poems which is a monument of sanity, the unfortunate author was readmitted to the McLean Hospital in May 1959. Though released after a month, he had a summer commuting between Castine and the hospital to keep up his psychotherapy, and the outlook seemed bleak (Hamilton, 274-277). A foundation had already been laid down, however, for the next venture. As far back as 1949, Lowell had taught, at the Writers' Workshop of the University of Iowa, a course called 'Five Poets in Translation'. The writers were Rimbaud, Baudelaire, Valéry, Rilke, and Horace (Martin, 22). In 1953, as a permanent member of staff at that university, he had taken on a course teaching French poetry: 'he would describe a phrase in terms of another phrase, another poet, a group of people, a feeling, a myth, a novel, a philosophy, a country – anything!' (Baker). During his hospitalization at McLean's, after the creative outburst of the preceding summer and autumn, he was already working on translations of Montale, Ungaretti and Rilke (Hamilton, 276), and some of these were published in the *Hudson Review* for Spring 1959 and *Encounter* for August the same year. But even this could hardly have prepared the world for *Imitations*.

5 *Imitations* (1961)

Imitations is a collection of seventy poems derived from texts by eighteen authors writing in five different languages, none of them English. The technique of adaptation is related to that employed in many of Lowell's earlier poems, and to define this we can make use of a distinction, current in the Middle Ages but also relevant now. A *traduisant* is a writer who conveys the literal sense of a work; who, like Vladimir Nabokov in modern times, has 'ruthlessly sacrificed manner to matter' (Raffel 1980). A *translateur*, on the other hand, seeks to re-create the work in his own terms, often treating the original text with considerable freedom. Eustache Deschamps (1340–c.1410) in a ballade addressed to his contemporary, Geoffrey Chaucer, called that English poet 'grant translateur', and this would have been taken as a compliment. But the distinction was still understood in recent times. T. S. Eliot wrote of Ezra Pound's *Homage to Sextus Propertius* 'it is not a translation, it is a paraphrase, or still more truly (for the instructed) a *persona*' (Pound 1928, 19).

The Pound of the Propertius poems is more immediately behind the approach of *Imitations*. Lowell himself said that he tried to write live English and to do what his authors might have done, had they been writing in 1960 and in America. He achieved some notable work in this line well before *Imitations*. One thinks of 'War' (after Rimbaud's 'Le Mal'), 'Charles the Fifth and the Peasant' (after Valéry's 'César') and 'France' (after Villon's 'L'Épitaphe'). Baudelaire, as one of Lowell's most discerning critics has pointed out (Axelrod 1971), is a distinct presence in such earlier poems as 'Where the Rainbow Ends', 'At the Indian Killer's Grave' and, most explicitly, 'Mother Marie Therese'. Indeed, from the beginning, in almost nightly exercises at Kenyon (Mazzaro 1973), Lowell had used other men's texts as a springboard for his own poems. This is true even of those pieces which

on first acquaintance seem most personal. It is difficult to miss
Villon in the last part of Lowell's elegy on Arthur Winslow, and
this affinity will be discussed a little further on. We have already
seen the way in which Ovid's *Metamorphoses* entered 'The Mills
of the Kavanaughs' and the way in which 'The Death of the
Sheriff' arose out of Virgil. In *Imitations* there is a distinctive
voice, and indeed persona, with a recognizable movement of
verse and direction of vocabulary.

The first poem in the volume, 'The Killing of Lykaon', is far
more than a formal acknowledgment of Homer as the father of
European poetry. The text derives from the twenty-first book of
the *Iliad*, with a preliminary gesture towards the beginning of the
first book. Nobody, however, is going to take this as straight
translation. On the contrary, there is a personal impetus in the
sense we get of a return to the field of battle. Lowell begins 'Sing
for me, Muse, the mania of Achilles', and we have to notice the
word 'mania'. Pope in his version had 'wrath', and two different
modern translators, Richmond Lattimore and Robert Fitzgerald,
have 'anger'. But, for the Lowellian persona, battle involves
mania. Certainly the sense is rendered with Lear-like frenzy:
'You must die,/and die and die and die, until the blood/of Hellas
and Patroklos is avenged'. This first poem is a prologue to the
events, both expressed and implied, of the collection as a whole.

The book can be broken down (Yenser, 169) into seven
sections, of which 'The Killing of Lykaon' is the first. The second
section starts with 'Three Letters to Anaktoria'. Here the poet
Sappho watches with a vulturine eye the woman she loves
enjoying the affection of a man: 'all day, he sits before you face
to face,/like a cardplayer'. Sappho cannot gain the woman, so she
takes the man away; but this proves to be a Pyrrhic victory. The
sequence ends with what, in Lowell's verse, is one of the bleakest
statements of isolation modern poetry has to show: 'The moon
slides west,/it is midnight,/the time is gone –/I lie alone!'. The
theme of war, so forcefully voiced in the imitation of Homer,
recedes to the background here. It seems that the true battlefield
is in the realm of personal relationships.

These, in their turn, arise from growing up. The poem which
follows, 'Children', is set in a mysterious wood, the first of
several in *Imitations*. Its original is a late thirteenth-century work
by the pseudonymous 'Der Wilde Alexander'. Lowell remains
close, if not to the German text, certainly to the prose version

made by Leonard Forster. This may be because the allegorical
notion of children reluctant to forsake the confines of a wood is
near to some concept of Lowell's own. He retains much of the
translator's vocabulary, and several of his phrases: 'cattle gadding
about', 'their jailer tore everything off them'. There are changes,
inevitable in Lowell, in the interests of enhanced graphic quality:
'we used to go to look for strawberries' (Forster, 37) becomes
'Here we *ran swilling* strawberries'. (The italics, here and elsewhere in this chapter, indicate what Lowell has emphasized in or
added to his original.) Indeed, Lowell alters the text crucially in
at least one of its aspects. The apparently innocent detail at the
beginning, the gadding cattle, is linked up with the final phrase
identifying the lost children: 'they stood like milk cows without
any clothes'.

   That poem escorts us into the third section of the book, which
starts with a sequence based on François Villon. Lowell had
imitated the work of this poet before and seems to have felt a
considerable measure of identification with him. 'The Great
Testament', first in the sequence, is dedicated to William Carlos
Williams, itself an indication of how seriously Lowell wished his
verse to be taken. In fact, the 'Testament' in Lowell's hands is a
selection from Villon's 'Le Testament', and the whole reaches
only line 328 out of an original amounting to 2023 lines in all.
Villon's personal attacks on his enemies are omitted, as are his
detailed bequests. From what remains, two ballades, together
with a section concerning 'La belle qui fut hëaulmiere', are
excerpted to be turned into three separate poems. To these
Lowell adds a piece from *Poésies Diverses*, 'Frères humains'.
One effect is to heighten the sense of self-accusation: 'I have
loved – *all I could!* – when I try love again,/*diseases ring like bells/
through my liver and blood*' ('The Great Testament'). It is not
the Villon in Lowell, but the Lowell in Villon, that the author of
Imitations seeks out. One by-product is access to an English
verse-movement discernible in Elizabethan times, and again in
the twentieth century. Thomas Nashe has in his famous song
from *Summer's Last Will and Testament*: 'Brightness falls from
the air;/Queens have died young and fair;/Dust hath closed
Helen's eye'; and Yeats picks that cadence up in several poems,
most notably 'Easter 1916': 'Hearts with one purpose alone/
Through summer and winter seem/Enchanted to a stone' (Yeats,
204). In Lowell this comes out as 'Helen *has paid this debt –/no*

one who dies *dies well*:/breath goes, *and your eyes too*'. The power of this verse can best be displayed through a passing comparison with two of Villon's best translators. One has 'Be't Paris's or Helen's death,/Whoever dies, he dies in smart/So great he lacketh wind and breath' (Cameron 1966, 53); the other, 'Be it Paris who dies or Helen/Whoever dies dies in such pain/The wind is knocked out of him' (Kinnell, 65). Both these translators are fine poets in their own right. But it is clear that Lowell has an epigrammatic bite and rhythmic decisiveness that render his verse, whatever one thinks of it as translation, poetry; whereas the verse of Cameron and Kinnell, in this sector at any rate, is not, whatever one thinks of them as translators.

Lowell's 'The Great Testament' stops short just after this, with a sad look at the pitiful human body. Villon's 'Le Testament' goes on with a haunting ballade whose refrain is 'Mais où sont les neiges d'antan?' – 'But where are the snows of last year?' (Kinnell, 67). Lowell renders this as a separate poem, 'Ballade for the Dead Ladies'. He inserts, for Villon's 'Archipiades ne Thaïs', 'Andromeda, or Helen', thus keeping in play the serial reference to the Trojan War that runs as an underlying theme through *Imitations*. But his lament for departed beauties does not ring as truly as another excerpt from 'Le Testament', which he renders as 'The Old Lady's Lament for her Youth'. Where other poets yield to the pathos of an old woman remembering her past beauty, Lowell achieves far more of an effect by thrusting at us the spectacle of atrophy and decay. Swinburne, for instance, has in his 1878 translation 'The shapely slender shoulders small,/Long arms, hands wrought in glorious wise,/Round little breasts'. Lowell, on the other hand, spares us nothing: ' "This is how beauty *dies*:/humped shoulders, *barrenness/of mind; I've lost my hips*" '. We are reminded that it was a literary diction akin to that of Swinburne from which first Pound and then Eliot freed an older generation of poets.

Another excerpt from the original 'Testament' is 'Villon's Prayer for his Mother to Say to the Virgin'. This is a reworking not so much of Villon as of the 'Prayer' given to Arthur Winslow in Lowell's elegy on his grandfather. In *Lord Weary's Castle*, Villon is acclimatized to Copley Square: ' "The painted Paradise of harps and lutes/Sink like Atlantis in the Devil's jaw" '. In *Imitations* the counterpart is ' "a painted paradise with lutes/and harps, a hell that boils the damned" '.

The Villon sequence closes, appropriately enough, with the 'Epitaph', also attempted in an earlier volume, in which the speaker hangs as a representative of all humanity. In *Lord Weary's Castle* this came out as 'Now here, now there, the starling and the sea/Gull splinter the groined eyeballs of my sin'. The more flexible rhythms of *Imitations* may seem preferable: ' "Magpies/and crows have chiselled out our eyes,/have jerked away our beards and hair" '. The tone is not so much that of a straight translation as that of a wry comment on suffering humanity.

It is not hard to see why Lowell chose to imitate poems which reflected his preoccupations, nor why he intensified those preoccupations while imitating the poems. His first version of Leopardi, 'The Infinite', imports a violence of diction and an extent of negativism that will not be found in the original. Where Leopardi accepts the dissolution of thought in reverie, Lowell finds this a willed act involving intellectual suicide. Paradoxically, however, he sees it as pleasure: 'It's sweet to *destroy my mind/* and go down/and wreck in this sea where I drown'.

A sense of doom, which is his own importation, is localized in another Leopardi adaptation, 'Saturday Night in the Village', through an image that recurs in *Imitations*: that of a carpenter working against time. Leopardi began his poem with a girl returning home from the countryside; but Lowell's version prefaces this with – what is not found in the original – '*The day/is ready to close*', a sense of curfew which is later picked up in '*the clatter* of small bells'. For Leopardi, the evening before the sabbath has been 'stato soave' – 'a sweet state' (Whitfield, 183). Lowell's rendering is darker: '*the untroubled instant*'. In this way, Lowell foreshadows the anguish of the Sunday that is to follow, and the grind of the working days after that. One recalls the pleasurable forest of the 'Alexander' imitation, which in the end proves to be so transitory. Lowell remakes the poems he imitates: in the present instance from Leopardi, converting a village idyll into a brief oasis that already anticipates trouble to come. There is a parallel between this span of brightness and the creative moment of a poet.

A further parallel may be found in the all-too-short life of a girl, celebrated by Leopardi and lamented by Lowell (Carne-Ross), in the poem 'Sylvia'. Leopardi ends with the image of a grave, but Lowell takes this further, to a realization of the infinite: 'the grave/was the final, shining milestone/you had always been pointing to/*with such insistence/in the undistinguish-able distance*'. That is an inimitable dying fall: the final rhyme in lines of varying length is a genuine discovery. The infinite, however, has been sensed not only at the end but throughout the Lowell version. In Leopardi, Sylvia mounts the threshold of youth; in Lowell, she *leaps beyond* the limits of girlhood.

The transitory nature of life is worked almost into epic proportions in 'Sic Transit', an apocalyptic dialogue between father and son. Lowell keeps close to the German text of Johann Peter Hebel (1760–1826) as rendered by Leonard Forster, but still it is remarkably parallel in Lowell's version to 'Purgatory', a late play by Yeats. This is a further example of the way in which the adaptation of European poetry opened up for Lowell aspects of anglophone tradition. One reason for the apparent similarity between all three texts, those of Hebel, Yeats and Lowell, is the awareness, held in common by the authors, of a universe running down. In such poems as 'The Exile's Return', itself largely derived from a German text by Mann, and 'Where the Rainbow Ends', Lowell predicted the fall of Boston as surely as Hebel did that of Basle and Yeats the coming of the Second World War. The relationship between Lowell's earlier poems and this present imitation, 'Sic Transit', asserts itself compellingly; for instance:

> I saw my city in the Scales, the pans
> Of judgment rising and descending. Piles
> Of dead leaves char the air.
> ('Where the Rainbow Ends')

> . . . when the year 2000 comes around,
> all will be gone, our village will have slumped
> into its grave. In time, the plough will go
> where the church stood . . .
> ('Sic Transit')

Apart from the incidental felicities, the function of 'Sic Transit' is to act as a link between a sense of personal sacrifice and that which apprehends the destruction of a milieu. The blotting out of the city has been anticipated by the truncated life of Sylvia: 'you . . . never saw your life flower'. Both poems look forward to 'Heine Dying in Paris': 'my summer has flowered'.

'Heine Dying in Paris' is adapted from three separate poems by Heine: 'Morphine' and 'Mein Tag war heiter' are laments over the speaker's wasted youth, and they form the first and third sections respectively of the monologue, while 'Der Scheidende', which forms the second section, incorporates a satirical look at the audience:

> The curtain falls, the play is done;
> my dear German public *is goosestepping* home, yawning.
> They are no fools, these good people:
> they are *slurping* their dinners quite happily,
> *bear-hugging beer-mugs* . . .

Stylistically the German originals are distinct from one another. 'Mein Tag war heiter' is a Petrarchan sonnet, and the other two, respectively, are fourteen lines of blank verse and of tetrametric couplets. Lowell has fused them together into a stylistic unit: dramatic free verse, rhyming at times for emphasis, but mostly giving an impression of melody through echoing internal rhymes, as in the final taking leave of sensual existence:

> The hand *clangs to a close on the dominant*;
> the *champagne* glass *of orange sherbet* breaks
> on my lips – all glass; *straws in the wind*?
> *Little Aristophanes? I give my sugared leasehold on life*
> *to the great Aristophanes and author of life –*
> *midsummer's frail and green-juice bird's*-nest.

This flourish takes us well beyond the confines of Heine's 'Mein Tag war heiter'. Indeed, it puts Lowell's monologue on a plane different from most of the other *Imitations*. This is a new poem, of considerable grandeur, ostensibly on the life of Heine. It uses the poet's thoughts to see him – as is often the case in monologue – in terms of being a fictional character. There is, for example, nothing in the original about Aristophanes, 'the only ancient Greek comic dramatist whose work survives in more than mere fragments' (Thomson and Salgādo, 132). This is, however, an important point made in the poem Lowell wrote: the Deity as author of the human comedy who well understands the joke that is the poet's life. If this is a joke, it is one on a grand scale. The final line contains one of the great life images in poetry. This has, indeed, an equivalent in the original, but one that is much more cautious: 'in diesem traulich süssen Erdenneste!'. It has been translated as 'this snug, sweet earthly nest' (Branscombe, 234). Lowell has extended the familiar image into a metaphor for life which is at once fragile and desirable, sensual and valedictory. It has the effect of raising the artist to the stature of a tragic hero.

The hero is necessarily part of an artistic whole, and he often is the subject of epic narrative. This is certainly the case with respect to 'Russia 1812', imitated from 'L'Expiation' by Victor Hugo. The original is in three sections, the third of which offers a note of hope to Napoleon, the conqueror who has at last been defeated. By concentrating on the first section and excluding the other two, Lowell takes no account of any such consolation. When the Emperor exclaims 'God of armies, is this the end?', a shadow from the wings replies 'No, *Napoleon*'; and this negative is not, as in Hugo, later mollified. Lowell's Napoleon is condemned not only by his failure but by the fact that the failure is reported. In 'Russia 1812' this 'report' takes the shape of one of the finest war poems in the language, describing the retreat from Moscow:

> The snow falls, always snow! The *driving mire*
> *submerges; men, trapped in that white empire,*
> have no more bread and march on barefoot – *gaps*!
> They were no longer living men and troops.

Not only does this remind us of the winter poems of *Lord Weary's Castle* but it also draws upon an English tradition best represented by the First World War poet, Wilfred Owen: 'Men, gaps for filling/losses' ('Insensibility') and 'Many had lost their boots/But limped on, blood-shod' ('Dulce et Decorum Est').

The white empire, which submerges the Grand Army in 'Russia 1812', persists in the poem 'At Gautier's Grave'. Like the war poem, it is imitated from Victor Hugo. The younger artist who is dead, Gautier, and the elder who is alive, Hugo himself, are seen alike as warriors: 'Moi qui, plus d'une fois, dans nos altiers coupe d'aile,/Éperdu, m'appuyais sur ton âme fidèle'. This has been translated as 'I who more than once, dismayed in our proud flights, supported myself on your faithful soul' (Hartley, 84). It becomes explicitly martial in Lowell's imitation: 'I who loved you, I *who hung*/on your supporting *shoulder*, when *I fled,*/*broken*, from *the great flights*'. This is a clear reference to the flight from Moscow in the previous poem, and shows all retreats to be a retreat into death itself: 'our age that mastered the *high* wind *and wave*/expires'. The sense of mortality is brought out in Lowell through his excising some forty-two of the original's eighty-two lines, mainly those alluding to past myths and writers. What is left focuses on intellectual battle and its consequences. Even Hugo's title is changed significantly. 'A Théophile Gautier' is rendered as 'At Gautier's Grave', and the same title is given to a poem further on in *Imitations*, adapted from Mallarmé's 'Toast Funèbre'. The hint is that the poems are paired: both meditations on the death of an artist-hero. Between these two poems there are twenty-six others based on works by Baudelaire and Rimbaud. These form a fourth section and may be seen, from their content, style and position in the body of the book, to represent the dramatic centre of *Imitations*.

The first Baudelaire poem accuses the reader of vices similar to those of the poet. It is fashioned so as to bring its utterance close to that of the final Rimbaud poem imitated later on in the book. The generalized 'vermin' of Baudelaire is particularized to 'lice' in Lowell, and the devil's hissing resembles that of the sisters in Rimbaud's 'The Lice Hunters'. Lowell's imitation of Baudelaire is a statement in its own right, very much what a 1960s counterpart of Baudelaire might be deemed to have written. The relative formality of 'any poverty-stricken lecher who kisses and nibbles an old whore's martyred breasts' (Scarfe, 53) is turned to beatnik utterance in 'To the Reader':

> Like the poor *lush* who *cannot satisfy,*
> *we try to force our sex with counterfeits,*
> *die drooling on the deliquescent tits,*
> *mouthing the rotten orange we suck dry.*

The clashing of gears in Baudelaire – 'Les monstres glapissants, hurlants, grognants, rampants' (monsters 'screaming, howling, grunting, crawling') is rendered with a post-Romantic lack of decorum, without sacrificing any of the violence: '*snatch and scratch and defecate and fuck*'. Baudelaire's 'impossible' (Carruth 1962) 'monstre délicat' is rendered as 'obscene beast'; and the equally impossible 'houka' which boredom, the ugliest monster, inhales is turned into a composite act of yawning and chain-smoking. As a whole, 'To the Reader' is aligned not only with the poems imitated from Rimbaud but with Villon's 'The Great Testament' where '*the stretched veins hiss*'. There is a sense of community with the person addressed, if only in adducing the guillotine or its equivalent as a cure for the purposelessness of life.

The fourth section of *Imitations* shows through most of its course a darkening vision. The ostensible theme of 'My Beatrice' portrays the speaker being scorned by the negative elements of his world, here personified as a mob of dwarfs. In Lowell, the stress falls on the degradation of the poet. He is shown in terms of the poor player who struts and frets on the stage: ' "this . . . *ghost* of Hamlet" ', '*like Hamlet now*, I would have turned my *back*'. This second Hamlet allusion is more direct in Lowell than in Baudelaire, and perhaps the most telling lines are those that might serve as an epigraph to *Life Studies*, indicating the kinship of that book to *Imitations* (Fein, 94): ' "Let's *stop* and watch this creature *at our leisure – all sighs and sweaty hair*" '. We see here the Hamlet of Paul Scofield rather than that of John Gielgud, and it is not accidental that the most telling single line is an original Lowell formulation, a kind of artistic credo: ' "*he has to rip the lining from his soul*" '. More positive aspects of Hamlet are utilized in Lowell's versions of Pasternak, later on; but, by that time, there is an upward move towards confidence and recovery.

In this section, however, the persona seems to be entering an abyss. The seven poems that follow 'My Beatrice' form a sequence within a sequence. They are sonnet-like in many particulars, even when they are not sonnets. There exhales from them an atmosphere rich with a sense of gathering night and ebbing power. Partly this is a matter of which poems Lowell chose to imitate. Partly it is the sombre imagery which prevails in this verse. Much of the adaptation is so daring that one is better off not making a fuss about referring to the originals. One has to judge Lowell's productions by their success as new poems in English.

That is certainly the case with the first of these sonnet-like poems, 'Spleen'. The central idea is that of depression as a disease attacking a young king who is a semblance of the poet himself. Nothing can cheer this young king, neither 'gibier' ('game', i.e. hunting) in Baudelaire nor in Lowell *games* such as '*darts and tennis*'. Other distractions fall equally flat: the 'king' is not amused by, in Baudelaire, 'Du bouffon favori la grotesque

ballade' ('The comical ballad of his favourite fool': Hartley, 161);
nor, in Lowell, *'the bawdry of the pet hermaphrodite'*. As this will
suggest, everything is at once more earthy in Lowell, and also
more perverted. At the end, the climax of a series of images that
increase in force as the central figure ebbs in energy, Baudelaire's
'cadavre hébété' ('dull corpse') becomes Lowell's *'shot* corpse';
and 'l'eau verte du Léthé' ('green water of Lethe'), which flows
in the veins of the 'king', becomes *'syrup*-green Lethean *ooze'*,
which the poet *drinks*. French poetry can bear much more by way
of abstract statement than is the case in English, and therefore,
characteristically, a concept in Baudelaire becomes an image in
Lowell.

The other poems in this sequence hang even more closely
together. If we examine Lowell's versions of Baudelaire as
though they were original texts, we find them to be a counterpart
to the final section of *Life Studies*. The mood is sombre: 'Now
colder shadows . . . *Who'll turn back the clock?/* Goodbye bright
summer's *brief too lively sport!'* ('Autumn'). Image after image
reinforces this equinoctial atmosphere. Winter enters the citadel
and freezes the heart; the wood is being chopped down to build a
scaffold; 'some one is nailing a coffin hurriedly'; it is the season's
funeral. Compare this with 'I hear . . . the rapping hammer/of
the carpenter, working all night' in the Leopardi imitation,
'Saturday Night in the Village'; still more, with 'The season's ill'
('Skunk Hour') and 'Ought I to regret my seedtime?' ('Memories
of West Street and Lepke'). The originator of this last phrase is
Wordsworth, 'fair seed-time had my soul', and it runs into decay
not only in the poem 'Autumn' but in 'The Ruined Garden'
which follows: 'From now on, my mind's autumn! *I must take/the
field* and dress my beds with spade and rake/and restore order to
my flooded grounds'. This plainly shows the paradox inherent in
these poems. The primary mood is that of intense disaffection;
yet it is expressed in ordered verse. In much the same way, 'The
Flawed Bell' compares the poet's own voice with those that are
like old soldiers going unthinkingly through a prescribed drill.
Image is piled upon image; but the poet's voice prevails: '*I hear*
the death-cough of *mortality'*. The power of personality is
faithfully portrayed in Sidney Nolan's illustration to the poem
(Lowell 1968a, 44); in spite of its 'rocklike effort' to die, the voice
speaks with authority.

Sidney Nolan provided no illustration for 'Meditation' (Lowell

1968a, 46), and one can understand why. This is a curiously dispersed and conceptual poem, though none the less atmospheric for that. It begins '*Calm down*, my Sorrow, *we must move with care.*/You called for evening; it descends; it's here'. In Lowell's terms, this is almost a love poem, addressed to 'My Dearest', the lady Sorrow. One is reminded of the Yeatsian threnody: 'There was a man whom Sorrow named his friend' (Yeats, 9). It is true that the 'great bazaar' of life unfolds itself, but it proves to be a panoply of past dreams. The dead years are dressed in old clothes; regret emerges like Venus from the sea; all love, except that of Sorrow, has been a mistake. The last words of the poem appear to welcome death: 'hear the sweet night *march*'.

The last poem in the mini-sequence, 'The Abyss', is a powerful rendering of anxiety neurosis, a marvellously concrete representation of vacuity; again, there is no illustration from Nolan. 'Pascal's abyss'; '*all holes!*'; 'my spirit, haunted by its vertigo', this last recalling 'I hear/my ill-spirit sob' in 'Skunk Hour': these are at once non-semblances and statements of great power. Lowell is drawing upon certain qualities in the English language that allowed, for example, Lord Herbert of Cherbury to write a sonnet 'To Black Itself' and Rochester to write an address in verse 'Upon Nothing': 'that hadst a Being e're the World was made . . . /Great Negative'. Like Rochester, Lowell works through unexpected juxtapositions of abstract thought and concrete image: 'I *cuddle* the *insensible blank air*'. 'The Abyss', as the title would suggest, is the slough of despond so far as *Imitations* is concerned. From now on there is a sense of slow recovery.

We see it in the exuberance Lowell injects into Baudelaire's description of a swan adrift in the city. It is one of several exiles in Lowell's version of the Baudelairian rhetoric. The Trojan Queen Andromache weeps, but not by her simulated river which was constructed in order to remind her of her native Simoïs. Rather, it is the 'greasy Seine' that swelled with her tears. Baudelaire is formal; 'those . . . who suck the breast of Sorrow like a good mother-wolf's' (Scarfe, 176); Lowell lands on the lower side of black comedy: 'wolf-*nurses giving* grief a tit to suck'. This, indeed, is humanity preying on itself! Baudelaire's image of negroes is applied by Lowell to the French poet's actual mistress, Jeanne Duval, '*blindly* stamping through *puddles*'. Baudelaire's last images, of sailors abandoned on a desert island

and, more distantly, of 'those who are captive' (Scarfe, 177), are given almost a cartoon finality in Lowell: '*drowned* sailors, *fallen girls*'. This is a vision that has learned, fruitfully, from Allen Ginsberg: as an English poet says, 'a deliberate coarsening of the original effect' (Hill). But there is a range and vision here that a Beat Poet could never have accomplished.

The effect of caricature without any of the cruder concomitants is present, too, in 'The Game'. This is Lowell's version of a poem which one translator calls 'The Gambling Den' (Scarfe, 190). The gamblers in Baudelaire are 'rummaging in an empty pocket or a heaving bosom' – 'sein palpitant' (Scarfe, 191). In Lowell they are '*still* fumbling empty pockets and *false bras*' – this last phrase is a particularly apposite substitution. It is from such a 'tableau *of . . . doom*' that the 'Voyage to Cythera' takes off. 'Cythera' was the island where Venus, the goddess of love, was fabled to have been born. But a voyage there finds only the imperilling results of depravity. A hanged man is described by Baudelaire in horrifying terms: 'ferocious birds . . . had thoroughly castrated him with their beaks' (Scarfe, 224). In Lowell, this becomes a working out of a term in Baudelaire, 'ridicule pendu', which is translated only pallidly as 'grotesque gallow-bird' (Scarfe, 224). It is the implication of the French phrase that Lowell seems to bear in mind when he writes 'those scavengers, *licking* sweetmeats *from their lips*,/had hung his pouch and penis on a branch'. He replaces Baudelaire's distancing effect with a 'sequence of grim buffoonery' (Hill), and the poet cited here goes on to add that the farcical alternative, 'his bowler-hat and umbrella', is not unthinkable. It all relates back to 'Villon's Epitaph'. Lowell's substitution heightens the sense conveyed in the speaker's plea, that he hopes to be able to see his heart and body without disgust.

The poem called 'The Voyage', unlike that directed specifically to Cythera, spreads the possibilities more widely; but they remain possibilities. Going to strange seas, the travellers saw the same territories: 'we were often bored, just as you are here' (Scarfe, 243). Spiritually, too, they observed 'several religions like our own' (Scarfe, 245). Lowell's concern is to replace Baudelaire's air of universalism with 'hectic contemporaneity' (Crick, 68). For concepts such as 'the torturer delighting in his task' and 'the poison of power exasperating the despot' (Scarfe, 245), Lowell substitutes:

> *old maids who weep, playboys who live each hour,*
> *state banquets loaded with hot sauces, blood and trash,*
> *ministers sterilized by dreams of power,*
> *workers who love their brutalizing lash.*

Time and death are identified with the Wandering Jew and the Apostles; not, as in Baudelaire, opposed to them. They are as much victims of the changing situation as humanity itself. Where Baudelaire says 'en avant!' ('fare forward' or 'go on'), Lowell implements an atmosphere of hurry with ' "On, on, let's go!" '. His point is that the journey matters, not the arrival. Lowell is not merely weary of the land: his attitude is that the land rots and therefore one has no choice in going on. 'If now the sky and sea are black as ink,/our hearts, as you must know, are filled with light.' No doubt the note of hope in Lowell's 'The Voyage' is helped by its position in the total sequence of *Imitations*: the darkness is thinning. After all, what is left behind?

In so far as there is any nostalgia, it attaches itself not to place but to time. Lowell's 'The Servant' stands as a poem in its own right beside Baudelaire's original. Lowell has tidied up the plot (Carne-Ross): the graveyard in his version leads straight into the 'cold blue *half-light* of December' through which the ghostly nurse tiptoes 'as if she'd hurried from her vault'. The last phrase sits far more naturally in English verse (Lowell 1968b) than would a literal translation of the French original 'venant du fond de son lit éternel' ('risen from her eternal bed', Scarfe, 198). This recollection of a dead servant seems interestingly straightforward beside the version written ten years previously that Lowell had incorporated into his ironic 'Mother Marie Therese'. The later poem shows the solidity of *Imitations* as literature, irrespective of biography, since there is nothing that could have given rise to 'The Servant' in Lowell's own life.

In this regard, the latter half of the central section, which is devoted to imitations of Rimbaud, differs from the poems just discussed. There are all kinds of touches that bring the work of the wild young French homosexual nearer to the early experiences of the Boston Brahmin. Indeed, one could say in the case of 'Nostalgia', a poem based on Rimbaud's 'Mémoire', that Lowell filled a Symbolist meditation with his own sense of having been deserted by his father and with his dread of being taken over by his mother. One reading of the Rimbaud original suggests that the 'elle' of the poem refers to the river, 'and that the successive images evoked by the poet-speaker are dependent upon the changing appearance of the river landscape according to the movements of the sun from morning until dusk' (Perloff 1973, 64). It may be considered, however, that the figure who in the Rimbaud poem stands erect in the neighbouring meadow (Bernard, 200) represents 'the perverse human will' (Perloff 1973, 66). Here, if anywhere, Rimbaud may be referring to his mother whose husband left her when the poet was six (Bernard, xv). In any case, Lowell conflates the 'she' which may refer to the river and the 'she' which may refer to the mother in order to create his own image of a child's unhappiness. We have, in an edited prose translation, 'the weed sinks, and having the blue Heaven for a canopy, takes for curtains the shade of the hill and of the arch' (Bernard, 199). In a verse translation this runs: 'She/dark, having the blue sky as a canopy, calls up/for curtains the shadow of the hill and the arch' (Wallace Fowlie, cited Perloff 1973, 78). In Lowell it comes out thus: '*His mother* had the blue sky for *parasol*,/yet begged the arched bridge and the hills for shade'. This idea of the mother is identified with 'She, cold and *black*, *flew*. Rushed after her lost man!'. The child feels apart, both from the mother weeping and from the muscular figure for whom she weeps. He rows along the river but cannot escape, his boat stuck fast: 'its anchor *dug* for bottom;/the *lidless* eyes, *still* water, *filled with* mud'. There are evident *Life Studies* connections (Ehrenpreis), especially with 'My Last Afternoon with Uncle Devereux Winslow', 'Commander Lowell' and 'During Fever', in the way in which the child's awareness of disaffection is conveyed.

Again, the likeness between the mother-figure of the Rimbaud poem, 'Les Poëtes de sept ans' and that of Lowell's own mother is heightened. This is partly done by substituting sharper for less sharp detail. Partly, also, it is achieved by the breaking down of narrative continuity into a structure not dependent on formal requirements (McLachlan). The point may be put succinctly by comparing the opening of a translation of the poem made by Norman Cameron with that of the imitation, 'The Poet at Seven', written by Lowell. The point to be noticed is how sprung, in comparison with Cameron, the verse of Lowell is:

And so the Mother, shutting up the duty-book,
Went, proud and satisfied. She did not see the look

In the blue eyes, or how with a secret loathing wild,
Beneath the prominent brow, a soul raged in her child.
(Cameron 1942, 27)

When the timeless, daily, tedious affair
was over, his Mother shut
her Bible; her nose was in the air;
from her summit
of righteousness, she could not see the boy:
his lumpy forehead knotted
with turmoil, his soul returned to its vomit.
(Lowell)

Lowell creates a ferocity in the child that shows, even more
powerfully than is the case with Rimbaud, that the only refuge
from the mother and her authoritarianism is in fantasy. Rimbaud's
romances are about life in the great desert: 'forests, suns, shores,
savannahs' (Bernard, 125). Lowell has 'sunrises, buffaloes, jungle,
savannahs!'. The intrusion of the buffaloes in the vegetative
context suggests a mélange rather than an exact place: 'one
becomes conscious of the exciting confusion of second-hand
but strongly felt experiences rushing in on the child's mind'
(McLachlan). Even more striking is the personal impress Lowell
gives Rimbaud's narrative towards the end, telling of the child
lurking in the dark and reading his novel. Bernard translates this
as 'vertigo, collapses, retreats in disorder, and pity!' (127), and it
is rendered by Lowell as 'dizziness, *mania, revulsions*, pity!'. We
see how the word 'mania' is picked up from 'The Killing of
Lykaon' at the beginning of *Imitations*, and realize that we are
past the stage centre of the book, on to an erratic voyage out of
the abyss.

This is seen in the next poem, 'The Drunken Boat', which has
more than an echo of preceding poems in the *Imitations* sequence
(Yenser, 184–185); most obviously, of 'The Voyage': 'Through
the unknown, we'll find the new'. There are, also, links with 'The
Game': 'those who . . . *crowd full sail into the blue* abyss', where
the imagery is Lowell rather than Baudelaire. There are links
with 'Nostalgia', 'my boat *stuck fast*', and with the preceding
poem, 'The Poet at Seven': 'he lay alone on pieces of unbleached
canvas,/violently *breaking into* sail'. 'The Drunken Boat' is
considerably abridged from the Rimbaud original. In particular,

it has been noted (Chadwick) that a crucial stage is deliberately
left out; the part which Bernard translates as 'I long for Europe
with its age-old parapets' (170). The effect in Lowell is to reduce
the Rimbaudian conflict to a quarrel between fantasy and a
recognition of fact. It is not the cry of Rimbaud: 'if there is one
water in Europe I want, it is the black cold pool where . . . a
child . . . launches a boat' (Bernard, 171). It is rather a statement
of irreducibility: '*Shrunken* and black *against* a twilight *sky,/our*
Europe has *no* water. *Only a* pond'. The paper boat launched by
the child in Lowell's poem is also the fantasy ill-equipped to
battle against the Lowell and Winslow commercial interests.

There follow imitations of some sonnets Rimbaud wrote on
the road to Belgium when he was running away from school and
hoping to find work on a newspaper. These resemble in their
relative superficiality the adaptations found in *Lord Weary's
Castle*. They are colourful, but do not have the informing rage
that characterizes the *Imitations* proper. Nevertheless, the sonnets,
generically titled 'Eighteen-Seventy', carry on the underlying
theme of war, and link the unworthy Louis Napoleon (Napoleon
III) with the comparatively exalted Napoleon I of the Hugo
imitation, 'Russia 1812'. These sonnets are, perhaps, at their best
when they pick up themes of earlier poems. For example, 'On
the Road', a Jack Kerouac title substituting for 'Ma Bohème',
takes us back to a Kerouac prototype, the central figure of
'Words for Hart Crane': 'I was your *student*, Muses. What affairs/
we had together! My only pants were a big hole'. In other words,
this is an early Beatnik, and Lowell introduces details in the spirit
of Hart Crane. While Rimbaud has 'I felt drops of dew on my
forehead like vigorous wine' (Bernard, 111), Lowell gives us a
fused image. 'The *rain's cheap* wine was *splashing* on my *face*'.

Rimbaud's satire against the emperors, on the other hand, has
an authenticity for which there is no parallel in Lowell. Even so,
Rimbaud in 'Morts des Quatre-vingt-douze' has 'Dead men . . .
who . . . trampled under your clogs the yoke' (Bernard, 101),
while Lowell has the more telling composite '*when tyrants
trampled on humanity,/you broke them* underneath your wooden
shoes'. Others among these sonnets have similar virtues. The one
which in *Imitations* is called 'Evil' had an earlier version, 'War',
in *Lord Weary's Castle*, and was revised into a later version called
'The Evil'. This appeared in *History*, and all three are discussed
in Chapter Seven, which is concerned with that book. The

chapter in question also includes a discussion of a sonnet Lowell based on 'Rages des Césars', called 'Napoleon after Sedan' in *Imitations*, revised for *Notebook* as well as *History*.

This pivotal fourth section of *Imitations* ends, as it began, with a victim being tormented by demons. In 'The Lice Hunters' there are two sisters searching a child for vermin. Rimbaud's poem is based on two 'aunts', actually the aunts of his teacher, Izambard (Bernard, xvi), who took care of the young poet after his abortive trip to Paris and before the journey to Belgium in 1870. In Lowell, this is a powerful instance of a juvenile being preyed upon by adults:

> Wine of idleness *had flushed his eyes*;
> somewhere a child's harmonica pushed its sigh
> *insanely through the wearied lungs* – the rise
> and dying of his *ceaseless* wish to cry.

We should take this not as a translation but as a conclusion. It finishes the central section of *Imitations*. The section, itself a succession of journeys into fantasy, is flanked on either side by poems concerning Gautier, as if to emphasize the fact that not only this part of the book but the book as a whole forms a meditation on a subject central to Lowell: the artist as hero. Lowell, in his version of the Mallarmé poem on Gautier, chooses to reverse the emphasis in Hugo and put the weight not on Gautier's work but on his being remembered as a person. In this, Lowell differs not only from the Hugo original but from that by Mallarmé: '*His tombstone ornaments the garden path* –/here is the only true and lasting light'. Ironically, this imposing tomb is the prototype for a series of resurrections.

In the first of the imitations drawn from Rilke, 'A Roman Sarcophagus', the matron is brought back; and, since in Lowell she is Etruscan and not Roman, she has a greater distance to come: 'Where's the intelligence/to galvanize this dead presence?'. The answer is implied in the nervous flexibility of the verse, linking carved stone with water as a symbol of endurance (MacIntyre, 136):

> That would be water
> glittering *like geysers*,
> *the tarpon's or marlin's mermaid flash*,
> water delivered
> from the imperial aqueducts.

Another adaptation, 'The Cadet Picture of my Father', is dedicated to Lowell's psychiatrist in New York, Viola Bernard; and one can see why. The Rilke original is turned to a portrait of Lowell's own father, 'that deep young midshipman': 'There's absence in the eyes. The brow's in touch/with something far'. The dead are brought back: there are clear links, not only with the Hugo and Mallarmé poems on Gautier, but also with the haunting qualities of such Baudelaire versions as 'The Abyss' and 'The Voyage' (Fein, 104): 'The hands are quiet, they reach out towards nothing . . ./as if they were/the first to grasp distance and disappear'. A similar quality invests a companion poem, 'Self-Portrait', which in its turn relates to the self-disclosures based on those of Rimbaud: 'A *scared* blue child is peering through the eyes'.

The dead are brought back for a purpose: to disappear again. In 'Orpheus, Eurydice and Hermes', the archaic, epigraphic quality of the original (Simon) is sacrificed to concrete and specific reference. The moral seems to be that creativity arises only out of imperfection. Orpheus knows that a failure to keep his bargain with the god 'would be the ruin of this work/*so near perfection*'; meaning the return of Eurydice to life. But his work as an artist is more important to him. He cannot be certain that Hermes is following him with Eurydice, so 'as *a matter of fact/he knew* he must now turn to them'. It is Lowell's drama rather than that of Rilke: the poet sacrifices his happiness in order to advance his work. The loss of Eurydice gives him a theme for his poem, as her reinstatement would not. That is an indication of the sub-text below *Imitations*, and below *Life Studies* as well. In Rilke, Hermes, 'the god of messengers' (Bridgewater, 41) is sorrowful. In Lowell, he stands as an image of reproach: '*His caduceus was like a shotgun on his shoulder*'.

The fifth section of *Imitations* concludes with a group of ten poems founded upon texts by Montale. After Baudelaire and Rimbaud, Montale is the poet who, in terms of quantity, figures the most in the book. 'Dora Markus', 'one of the most poignant love elegies of all time' (Cambon, xxiii), is a portrait of a Jewess mysteriously kept alive by some unknown chance. Lowell attaches himself with a kind of frenzy to the properties of Montale's world (Carne-Ross), thus making this study in exile his own. Lowell's evocation of Jewish restlessness is highly individual, as a comparison with a good English translation will show. David P.

Young has 'And here where an ancient life/is dappled with a soft/
oriental worry' (Cambon, 47). This, while lucid enough, is not as
searching as Lowell: 'Here where the old *world's way of surviving*/
is *subtilized* by a   *nervous/Levantine* anxiety'. To produce this
equivalent to 'ansietà d'Oriente' is, as a distinguished authority
on translation has commented, 'one of those windfalls of which
one says the translator has pinned down what the original could
not' (Belitt, 62).

Even further along this line, 'Hitlerian Spring' is ruthless in its
realism. The liberating hope of spring has failed; the festival of
the patron saint of Florence has become a blood-sacrifice; for the
Führer rides through the streets with his henchmen. Montale
finishes the poem with a hopeful gaze into the future (Simon),
but Lowell cuts from a reminiscence of winter – '*the sharpness of
driving snow*' – to a gesture bordering on despair. A translator,
Maurice English, puts this as 'O this ulcered/Spring will still be
festival, if it can freeze again/in death that death!' (Cambon,
147). The poem goes on to hope that a breath of dawn will
appear, no longer bearing wings of terror. There is, however, no
going on in Lowell's adaptation. The ulcered spring is the end,
and it is rendered harshly: '*April's reopened wound is raw*!'.

It is a wound that bleeds through Lowell's version of the
Montale poem he calls 'The Coastguard House'. From the first
he makes his original a starting-point for his own pain. The initial
phrase is his own: '*A death-cell*?'. He goes on to intensify the
particularity present, though decorously so, in Montale. The
speaker in the poem revisits the coastguard house by himself,
whereas on a previous occasion he had been there with the
woman he loved. Her remembered presence colours the present.
Montale's repeated 'tu non ricordi' ('you don't remember')
registers in Lowell's verse as 'You didn't *take it to heart*' and 'You
haven't *taken my possession to heart*'; a reproach, rather than a
reminiscence. One admirable translation has 'O the skyline in
retreat where, flaring,/the tanker's light shows rarely on the
verge!' (Cambon, 75). Lowell turns this into a self-lacerating
image of loneliness: 'Oh the *derelict* horizon,/sunless except for
the/*orange hull* of a *lonely, drudging* tanker!'. We should not
worry too much about the source of *derelict* horizon; rather, in
the end, we should read his 'adaptation' as an original poem.

The family resemblance between *Imitations* and other Lowell
poems persists. The description of lightning and storm in 'Arsenio'

reminds one critic (Whittemore) of *Lord Weary's Castle*: 'Roof-
high, winds *worrying winds/rake up* the dust, *clog the chimney
ventilators,/drum through the bald, distracted little squares*'. Certainly, it is more Lowell than Montale, and the latter poet is said
to have remarked that the images intrinsic to his original had
been brought to the surface, like knots emerging from wood
(Rizzardi). The storm seems to provide rebirth but, in the end,
offers, as its only release, death. This is, however, death of a
peculiar nature. An American critic (Rudman, 102) has proposed
the lines at the end of 'Arsenio' as Lowell's own motto: *'it's a sign
that this is* the hour *for letting go*/of the life *you were always*
disposed to throttle'.

The basic plot of Montale's 'Notizie dall' Amiata' already has
certain affinities with the Lowellian sensibility. The image of the
porcupine sipping at a stream, placed at the end of the poem,
irresistibly invokes 'Skunk Hour'. Perhaps the atmospheric opening of 'Notizie dall' Amiata' is somewhat muffled (Raffel 1981,
118): 'Soft mists/ that climb from a valley/of elves and mushrooms
to the diaphanous cone/of the crest cloud over my windows'
(Cambon, 83). Lowell, in his 'News from Mount Amiata',
'stretches the Italian' (Raffel 1981, 120) but is much more
definite about line-endings and avoids unhelpful ambiguities:

> *A sick smoke* lifts from *the elf-huts* and *fungi* of the valley –
> *like an eagle* it climbs our mountain's *bald* cone,
> and *soils* the windows.

'Sick smoke' and 'soils' are further verbal discoveries.

Imitation led Lowell into new territory. He is as fine a poet of
the city as Baudelaire himself; but his focus on the countryside
was narrow, privileging mainly the gloomier aspects. Montale
and, in the penultimate section of the book, Pasternak, seem to
have put him to the test. Perhaps Lowell responded to what
Leavis called Montale's 'effect of spontaneous naturalness' (*The
Listener*, 16 December 1971). In a poem after Montale's 'L'anguilla',
it is the unlikeness between the eel and the woman that is
exposed. Montale says 'can you consider her not your sister?'
(Simon) or 'in this/not recognize a sister?' (Cambon, 159; Barnstone, 310). But Lowell has 'can you call her Sister?', which is a
rhetorical question expecting the answer 'no'. He has linked with
the original 'L'anguilla' another poem, 'Se t'hanno assomigliato',

which brings into comparison with womanhood notions of other creatures. Both are published as a single poem in two sections, called 'The Eel'. Montale adumbrates similarity; Lowell, contrast.

The fifth section of *Imitations* is rounded off by 'Little Testament'. As the title suggests, it is an answer to a key poem of the second section, 'The Great Testament', after François Villon. The differentiation is clear enough. Lowell's adaptation from Villon is in itself despairing and is followed by prayers, epitaphs and elegies for friends cut off in their prime. In contradistinction, the 'Little Testament' is invested with ghosts, invocations, and, above all, the enlivening memories which characterize the Montale adaptations as a group. Compared with *Life Studies* and the earlier *Imitations*, 'Little Testament' is full of positive concepts; positive even when defined through negations:

> Each knows his own: his pride
> was not *an escape*, his humility
> was not *a meanness*, his *obscure*
> *earth-bound flash*
> was not *the fizzle of a wet* match.

Lowell's poem has been considered (Belitt, 65) an 'effect' arising out of Montale's 'cause'. The insistence upon man's achievement, as distinct from the defeatism of the earlier *Imitations*, has likewise been applauded (Yenser, 190). The rainbow, unlike other manifestations of that phenomenon in Lowell, is now the covenant between man and man, representing 'the creative intensity of the poetic sensibility' (Yenser, 189).

The sixth section builds upon this enhancement of life, and its mixture of positive and negative is caught in a phrase from one of the Pasternak imitations: '*my resurrection in the* spring'. Imitations or not, these are among the happiest poems Lowell ever wrote. The theme of the renewing season is brought out strongly in, of all months, 'September'. As in 'My Last Afternoon with Uncle Devereux Winslow' and the Baudelaire imitation, 'Autumn', a summer house is boarded up: '*The carpenter's gavel* pounds *for new and naked roof-ribs*'. But the mood of the poem, unlike those others, is to leave the past behind and strike out towards a new terrain.

The climax of the section comes with the mini-sequence Lowell calls 'The Seasons'. It is a composite based on five

separate poems by Pasternak. Here, the coming of spring is
explicitly identified with poetic inspiration. According to Babette
Deutsch's translation of the poem 'Spring', poetry is a recording
device: 'O poetry, be a Greek sponge supplied/With suction
pads, a thing that soaks and cleaves' (Pasternak 1958, 274).
Lowell takes the hint, but goes further in suggesting that poetry
actually re-creates the landscape in absorbing it: 'Poetry is like a
pump/with a suction-pad that *drinks and drains up/the clouds*'.
The poem on spring is followed by one on summer which in some
ways parodies this: 'The earth is swollen and *smelly*,/the pasture
is a sponge;/as if it were August the *far off* night ripens/*and rots in
the elm-dissected* field'. Here 'smelly', 'far off' and 'elm-dissected'
are all Lowellian concepts. The caricature element continues,
with an edge of violence, in the third poem, which is concerned
with autumn. 'Pasternak's storm picture has to be made more
frantic' (Gifford): 'The lilac bush is *a black scarecrow*./From hill
and sky armfuls of lightning/*crash* on the station-agent's cottage/
to *smash* it with light'. This resembles the landscape-with-crows
of 'Waking in the Blue' (Rudman, 98); but it has more positive
energy. There is a quality of vision in the way this poem ends:
'Something in my mind's/most inaccessible corners/registers the
thunder's illumination,/stands up, and steadily blinks'. It is that
'something' that illumines, also, the poem after. Though winter
follows, already it is rushing towards spring. In C. M. Bowra's
translation, this reads: 'As always, with overcoat unbuttoned,/
With muffler about his chest undone,/He pursues before him the
unsleeping/Silly birds and chases them on' (Pasternak 1958, 263).
Lowell identifies the 'he' explicitly, adding earthy details as a way
of making this onset specific: 'With *unbuckled galoshes*, with a
muffler/*flapping* from his unbuttoned coat,/*March bulls ahead,
and makes rushes* at the frivolous, *frenzied* birds'. This resurrection is carried forward into a reprise of the first poem in the main
sequence: the season has returned to spring, with its 'astonished
pines' and sense of 'the age . . . breaking'. It is all 'inexorably
beginning again' (Yenser, 194). The vision of the poet as a
gladiator at the end – which is also the end of the mini-sequence
'Seasons' – leads on to the almost clownish celebration found
in 'Sparrow Hills', brought out with a thoroughly Lowellian
exuberance.

    Pasternak's original has been much translated. C. M. Bowra
renders the last two lines of the third stanza as 'Look how in the

heights thoughts seethe into white bubbles/Of fir-cones, woodpeckers, clouds, pine-needles, heat' (Pasternak 1958, 260).
George Reavey, on the other hand, has 'See how thoughts gather
high in a white froth/Of woodpeckers, clouds and heat, pine cones
and needles' (Barnstone, 433). Lowell is close to the latter, but
he solves the rhythmic problem, which is inherent in catalogue,
more adroitly: 'Look, conception bubbles from the bleached
fallows;/fir-cones, woodpeckers, cloud, pine-needles, heat'. The
whole sixth section of *Imitations*, and this poem in particular,
seems to celebrate the continuity of life (Yenser, 195): 'the
piebald clouds spill down on us like a *country woman's* house-
dress'.

Another aspect of springtime vitality is given play in a poem
called 'Wild Vines', feigned to be written by the eponymous hero
of Pasternak's novel, *Dr Zhivago*. Max Hayward and Manya
Harari translate: 'A cape covers our shoulders/And my arms
circle you' (Pasternak 1961, 579). Lowell brings out the implications idiomatically, and with a sense of drama: 'one raincoat
covers both our shoulders –/*my fingers rustle like the wild vine
around your breasts*'. The tendency towards imagery favouring
love and rebirth is a kind of answer to the recurrent theme of
death in the first four sections of *Imitations*.

This imagery is highly explicit. Pasternak's 'In the Woods', as
translated by Bowra, begins: 'A lilac heat was heavy on the
meadow,/High in the wood cathedral's darkness swelled./What
in the world was left still for their kisses? /It was all theirs, soft
wax in fingers held' (Pasternak 1958, 262). Lowell sharpens this
considerably, partly to bring it into line as a reply to his own
version of 'Der Wilde Alexander': 'A lilac heat *sickened* the
meadow;/high in the wood, a cathedral's *sharp, nicked groins./
No skeleton obstructed the bodies –/*all was *ours, obsequious wax
in our fingers*'. This effort is not isolated. The poem that follows
is one of the Zhivago pieces called by Hayward and Harari 'The
Wedding Party' (Pasternak 1961, 580–582). Lowell's title is 'The
Landlord', and the point has been made (Yenser, 195) that its
last line specifically answers the end of the 'Der Wilde Alexander'
imitation, 'Children'. That poem ends with transmogrification:
'they stood like milk cows without any clothes'. 'The Landlord',
on the other hand, closes with a change that is really rebirth:
'the dissolution of ourselves into others,/like a wedding party
approaching the window'.

Lowell's selection of poems adapted from Pasternak finishes with what is at once the most exposed view of the artist as hero and also the most 'original' poem in *Imitations*: 'Hamlet in Russia, A Soliloquy'. It is a cento of three Pasternak pieces, but so adapted as to be independent of them. One is the title poem of Pasternak's third book of verse. George Reavey's translation begins: 'Sister my life, to this day overflowing,/You burst on all things with springtime rain,/But men with watch fobs are highly fastidious/And, like snakes in the grass, politely sting' (Barnstone, 433). In Lowell's hands, this gains a Wordsworthian echo: ' "My sister, life!/*the world has too many people for us,/the sycophant, the spineless* –/politely, like snakes in the grass, they sting" '. Lowell utilizes only two out of the six stanzas this poem affords. The idea seems to be to give an impression of an artist retreating from the crowd. As a whole, the poem has been admirably summarized: 'the narrator thinks of escaping social and artistic obligations by imagining himself on a lake, far away from the stage of social and artistic obligations. He imagines himself out there in nature just before he is to receive his cue to go in front of the audience and perform' (Fein, 109). This is an answer to earlier poems: ' "I am *content* to play the one part *I was born for*" ' may remind us of 'Heine Dying in Paris'. There is an explicit Hamlet reference in 'My Beatrice', but 'Hamlet in Russia' itself is much more positive. The latter part of the poem derives from a Zhivago piece which in the Hayward and Harari translation ends stoically: 'Yet the order of the acts is planned/ And the end of the way inescapable' (Pasternak 1961, 570). To take another translation, Reavey has: 'But the acts have been ordained,/Irreversible the journey's end' (Barnstone, 438). Lowell's Hamlet, however, is quite as volatile as that of Shakespeare. The drama in his last lines vibrates with a determination that is worth defending:

> 'The sequence of scenes was *well thought out*;
> *the last bow is in the cards, or the stars* –
> but I am alone, and *there is none* . . .
> All's drowned *in the sperm and spittle* of the Pharisee –
>
> To live a life is not to cross a field.'

The artist, be he Heine or Hamlet or Lowell, takes a voyage; yet he still finds himself in front of the audience.

The concluding poem of *Imitations* deserves to be classified as a section in itself. It is an adaptation of Rilke, 'Pigeons', and is a summation of the book, and of Lowell's writing up to this point. The pigeon who flies out and gets battered is the one who really understands: 'Still, only by suffering the rat-race in the arena/can the heart learn to beat'. For one critic this sentiment is false and childish (Hecht). Certainly it is romantic: one thinks of the tattered writers in the third part of *Life Studies*: 'that worn arena, where the whirling sand/and broken-hearted lions lick your hand' he wrote of George Santayana. Probably gladiators are childish, but for Lowell they represent a heroic stance – artistic, as well as martial. The image persists all the way through *Imitations*: 'my twin gladiator beauties' ('Heine Dying in Paris'); 'we saw . . . the fight, the tumult, the arena' ('At Gautier's Grave', after Hugo); 'this retarius throwing out his net' ('The Voyage'); 'The overpaid gladiator must die in earnest' ('The Seasons'). The imagery of birds, of woods, of the seasons themselves, would repay kindred attention. A sub-text concerned with Troy runs through the book. There is 'The Killing of Lykaon' as prelude; then 'Helen forgot her husband and dear children/to cherish Paris/ . . . the murderer of Troy' ('Three Letters to Anaktoria'); 'Helen has paid this debt' ('The Great Testament'); 'Say in what land, or where is . . . Helen' ('Ballad for the Dead Ladies'); 'the meanest little Philistine living/in Stukkert-am-Neckar is luckier/than I, the golden-haired Achilles' ('Heine Dying in Paris'); 'Andromache, fallen from your great bridegroom,/and now the concubine and baggage of Pyrrhus' ('The Swan'); 'reptilian Circe with her junk and wand' ('The Voyage'); 'once more I see the galleys bleed with dawn,/and shark with muffled rowlocks into Troy' ('Helen', after Valéry); 'the gods' Homeric laughter' ('September').

This is subsumed in the final poem which, like the first one in the book and the one at the centre, 'The Poet at Seven', features the key word, 'mania': 'the ball thrown almost out of bounds/ . . . miraculously multiplied by its mania to return' ('Pigeons'). The key word is sounded explicitly three times, but there is more to it than this: the book is full of the instances of mania: 'a hollowness in my ears/thunders and stuns me' ('Three Letters to Anaktoria'); 'you'll lose yourselves;/your pleasure will end in bawling' ('Children'); 'What lives in me is death' ('Heine Dying in Paris'); 'Winter has entered in my citadel:/hate, anger, fear' ('Autumn'); 'I'm drunk on water. I cry out too much' ('The

Drunken Boat'); 'the rise/and dying of his ceaseless wish to cry' ('The Lice Hunters'); 'Lucky grace,/how could you help knocking your brains out!' ('You Knocked Yourself Out', after Ungaretti); 'Like snowmen, they melt in your mind's white glare' ('The Chess Player', after Montale); 'He is out of his senses, he musses his mop of hair./He is buried in his mind's mush' ('The Seasons').

The theme of *Imitations*, then, is a romantic one. Ennui spells death; mania brings enlightenment; suffering is the matrix of poetry. This is self-justification: quite as much as T. S. Eliot's doctrine of impersonality, though at the opposite end of the spectrum. There is undoubtedly an extent of incoherence in the theory, and it is ethically open to assault. Its justification, however, lies in the quality of the work produced; and Lowell's 'Heine Dying in Paris', 'Spleen', 'The Servant', 'Russia 1812', 'The Seasons' and 'Pigeons' – to name only a few – are among the finest poems in the language. At his most apparently personal, Lowell is most literary. *Imitations* nevertheless has to be read as a set of original texts. One would not, after all, take Johnson's *The Vanity of Human Wishes* as a transcript of Juvenal, or Fitzgerald's *Rubáiyát* as a transcript of Omar Khayyám; and it is to this genre that the poems in Lowell's collection belong. From various European poets Lowell has extracted themes congenial to his troubled spirit, and made them his own. He has adapted a range of poets to his own characterization; for him, the mask is the face. Critics who have catechized these texts in terms of infidelity to originals have succeeded only in unearthing criteria that are irrelevant. It is by the efficacy of the verse that the poems of *Imitations* stand or fall. The point can be made by comparing the work of any competent translator with that of Lowell. The first of the quotations below, a translation of Baudelaire's 'La servante au grand coeur', merely limps in verse:

> If, in the evening, by the singing fire,
> I saw her sit down, peaceful, in her chair:
> If, some December night of cold and gloom,
> I found her in a corner of my room,
> Pensive, arriving from eternity
> To watch me, now a man, with mother's eyes,
> What could I answer that Godfearing soul,
> Seeing from hollow lids her tears fall?
> (Richardson, 175)

The second quotation, from Lowell's imitation of Baudelaire, has movement and continuity. The verse dances:

> The oak log sings and sputters in my chamber,
> and in the cold blue half-light of December,
> I see her tiptoe through my room, and halt
> humbly, as if she'd hurried from her vault
> with blankets for the child her sleepless eye
> had coaxed and mothered to maturity.
> What can I say to her to calm her fears?
> My nurse's hollow sockets fill with tears.

6 *For the Union Dead* (1964); *Phaedra* (1961); *The Old Glory* (1964); *Prometheus Bound* (1969); *The Oresteia* (1978); *Near the Ocean* (1967)

Lowell's own history provided the plot in *Life Studies*. *Imitations*, on the other hand, was shaped by the writings of others. But the poems comprising *For the Union Dead*, even when determined by external structures, fail as sustained works. Largely it is a question of movement. There are strong lines, even strong passages, but no masterpieces.

Lowell was in McLean's Hospital when *Life Studies* came out to a decidedly mixed reception in May 1959. His treatment finished in June, but the only poem completed that year was 'The Drinker' (Hamilton, 274), a highly uneven performance. Unlike the best of *Life Studies*, its diagnosis is at one with the disease: 'The man is killing time – there's nothing else./No help now from the fifth of Bourbon/chucked helter-skelter into the river'. Most of the piece behaves as though the truthful setting down of fact amounts to poetry. Nevertheless, almost miraculously, it works up to a conclusion that has something of the *Life Studies* charisma:

> Is he killing time? Out on the street,
> two cops on horseback clop through the April rain
> to check the parking meter violations –
> their oilskins yellow as forsythia.

An authority on poetic closure comments, 'The assertion with which the poem had opened . . . now becomes a question, no less ambiguous, ironic, or unstable. Having posed it . . . the speaker does not answer, but instead turns to glance outside the window – and changes the subject' (Herrnstein Smith, 252). The claim has been made that, like 'Returning', this is one of the

finest pieces in the collection (Smith, 91). The latter poem
certainly shares the disconsolate mood of its companion, looking
backwards to 'The Exile's Return' and forwards to *Day by Day*,
where it recurs in a revised version, 'Homecoming'.

Even so, the prognosis after McLean's was not good. 'When I
finished *Life Studies* I was left hanging on a question mark'
Lowell commented at the Boston Arts Festival for June 1960
where he had been asked to read a new poem (Lowell 1964b).
Recent work had included a belated Life Study, 'The Old
Aquarium'; also an ode with the title 'One Gallant Rush: The
Death of Colonel Shaw' (Axelrod 1978, 158–159). Robert Gould
Shaw had been chosen in 1863 to lead the first black regiment
organized by a Northern State. This was decimated in the Civil
War when attacking the outermost defence of the Charleston
harbour (Kavanagh; Axelrod 1978, 163). Colonel Shaw was
buried by the Confederates with his negro troops, presumably as
an insult. After hostilities ceased, his father successfully resisted
efforts to have the Colonel ceremonially reinterred, saying 'a
soldier's most appropriate burial place is on the field where he
has fallen' (Burchard, 143). Lowell sought to link the two
sketches, 'The Old Aquarium' and 'One Gallant Rush', partly in
response to some work done at the time by Elizabeth Hardwick
on the letters of William James. It was James who, in 1897, had
unveiled a bas-relief by Augustus Saint-Gaudens commemorating
Shaw and his soldiers. The oration had included phrases such as
'one can almost hear them breathing' and monuments 'reared on
every village green' (James, 40; 42); sincerely meant, no doubt,
but unmistakably clichés. Lowell gains little by incorporating
them into the resultant poem, 'For the Union Dead'. He benefits
more tangibly from the cool scepticism with which, in an essay of
the same period, his wife questioned Boston's claims to tradition:
'the cars are double-parked so thickly along the narrow streets
that a moving vehicle can scarcely maneuver . . . old Boston, a
culture that hasn't been alive for a long time' (Hardwick 1962,
159). Lowell has: 'The Aquarium is gone. Everywhere,/giant
finned cars nose forward like fish'.

In spite of this obvious connection, one may doubt whether
the two sketches, rewritten to form a whole, are effective. The
poem starts intimately: 'The old South Boston Aquarium stands/
in a Sahara of snow now/ . . . Once my nose crawled like a snail
on the glass'. This is at odds, however, with the public address of

the middle section: 'He is out of bounds now. He rejoices in man's lovely,/peculiar power to choose life and die'. It has been suggested (Kavanagh) that Robert Lowell was explicitly answering an ode, inscribed on Shaw's monument, written by his nineteenth-century collateral, James Russell Lowell: 'He leads for aye the advance,/Hope's forlorn-hopes that plant the desperate good/For nobler Earths and days of manlier mood'. Another precursor is the 'idealist, angry' (Axelrod 1978, 167) 'Ode in Time of Hesitation' by William Vaughn Moody: 'This delicate and proud New England soul/Who leads despisèd men, with just-unshackled feet'. But Lowell does not so much answer his predecessors as assimilate to their mode of rhetoric. One need not doubt that they meant what they said. But that, as was seen with William James, is no guarantee of success. There is also an explicit rivalry with Allen Tate, whose 'Ode to the Confederate Dead' sustains its oratory with a rhythmic confidence Lowell, at this juncture, could no longer match. In any case, the most damaging comparison comes from Lowell's own work. One telling image of Shaw in 'For the Union Dead' is 'He has an angry wrenlike vigilance', but this is no more than a recension of the bird imagery recalling the 'Uncle Charles' of 'Falling Asleep Over the Aeneid': 'blue-capped and bird-like'. In the earlier poem we find a confrontation of the unheroic present by a heroic past. Even to say that, however, suggests how cobbled 'For the Union Dead' seems by way of contrast. Lowell's technique is no longer able to bridge the gap between 'the garage's earthquake' (stanza 6) and 'Two months after marching through Boston/half the regiment was dead' (stanza 7). It cannot cover the distance between Colonel Shaw 'riding on his bubble' (stanza 16) and the Negro children that appear on the speaker's television set (stanza 15). In the end, there is insufficient energy to fuse together Lowell's memory of the old Aquarium and his well-researched history of Colonel Shaw.

Nevertheless, the poem was enthusiastically received at a reading in the Public Garden, under the sponsorship of the Boston Arts Festival, by an audience of 4000. It was added to a 1960 edition of *Life Studies* reprinted by Vintage Books in paperback together with *The Mills of the Kavanaughs*. 'For the Union Dead' has been canonized in academic discourse ever since: 'One of the great American poems of this century' (Moore 1973); 'one of the finest poems Lowell has written' (Ricks). For most critics, it is the pivot of the book (Rudman, 133; Fein, 125); for some, the book is the pivot of his *oeuvre*: 'the sustained moment when the whole Lowell enterprise comes into focus' (Pearson).

The next poems to be written came eighteen months later, towards the end of 1961 (Hamilton, 293). They are comparatively slight. A 'fragment left over from the *Life Studies*' (Fein, 115), 'Alfred Corning Clark', commemorates a school friend at St Mark's. It pairs off with 'Eye and Tooth', a poem Lowell described reductively as 'my farewell to contact lenses' (Hamilton, 293). More importantly, there is a tie-up between the verse of the latter poem and the impressionistic prose of an essay, 'William Carlos Williams', that appeared in the *Hudson Review*. It is Lowell's tribute, in lieu of an obituary, to his friend, whom he knew to be dying:

An image held my mind during these moments and kept returning – an old-fashioned New England cottage freshly painted white. I saw a shaggy, triangular shade on the house, trees, a hedge, or their shadows, the blotch of decay . . . Inside the house was a birdbook with an old stiff and steely engraving of a sharp-shinned hawk. The hawk's legs had a reddish-brown buffalo fuzz on them; behind was the blue sky, bare and abstracted from the world.
(Lowell 1961b)

The poem is, in comparison, functionlessly ugly in sound and jerky in movement:

> Nothing can dislodge
> the triangular blotch
> of rot on the red roof,
> a cedar hedge, or the shade of a hedge.
>
> No ease from the eye
> of the sharp-shinned hawk in the birdbook there,
> with reddish brown buffalo hair
> on its shanks, one ascetic talon
>
> clasping the abstract imperial sky.

What people are likely to take away from the poem is not this versification of a perfectly adequate prose lament, but rather the painfully physical account of conjunctivitis: 'My whole eye was sunset red,/the old cut cornea throbbed'. Sylvia Plath, whose poetry Lowell later referred to as 'controlled hallucination, the autobiography of a fever' (Lowell 1966), would seem to have learned from this poem of 1961. However, as with 'For the Union Dead' itself, essential connections remain unmade. The intention is brave enough: an attempt to motivate dispersed anxiety, and so render it an elegy on friends passing. But the main element of the elegy, that concerned with the dying William Carlos Williams, had already been woven into a prose so seamless that the tired Lowell of *For the Union Dead* could not revamp it into verse.

Similarly, Lowell sought to versify a story, 'In the Village', by Elizabeth Bishop. Once more, it is the prose that has the cadence and the verse that jerks and halts:

A scream, the echo of a scream, hangs over that Nova Scotian village. No one hears it; it hangs there for ever, a slight stain in those pure blue skies, skies that travellers compare to those of Switzerland, too dark, too blue.
(Bishop 1953)

> A scream, the echo of a scream,
> now only a thinning echo . . .
> As a child in Nova Scotia,
> I used to watch the sky,
> Swiss sky, too blue, too dark.
> ('The Scream', Lowell)

The connection between an echo of the scream and the stain in the sky is lost in Lowell's poem. It is impossible to gauge what Lowell thought he had achieved by hacking into verse a story so exquisite in its English prose.

Two other poems in this late-1961 group, 'Middle Age' and 'Fall 1961', show the sense of unease manifest in 'The Drinker' as well as in 'Eye and Tooth' and the Corning piece. 'Middle Age' has a sketch of Lowell's father, of interest as looking forward to *Day by Day*. 'Fall 1961' ends with an image of wild spiders culled from a letter to Randall Jarrell detailing some of the young Harriet Lowell's talk (Hamilton, 296). It owes at least as much, however, to the terminal section of Tate's 'Ode to the Confederate

Dead', which in hindsight seems to have been the upas tree of
this volume.

Perhaps 'Water' and 'The Old Flame' are the most interesting
poems of the 1961 group. The former is compounded from
images of coldness and is born out of Lowell's relationship with
Elizabeth Bishop. This had been reified by the month she spent
with him in November 1961. The poem speaks of a non-situation:
'Granite quarries', 'bleak/white frame houses', 'the water was
too cold for us'. On Lowell's side the relationship would seem to
have been unsatisfactory because of the lack of sexual fulfilment;
Elizabeth Bishop was a lesbian. Unrelated to biographical fact as
it is, the poem stands out as an achieved lyric, far superior to the
political attempts of the collection. Further, unlike 'The Scream',
it is touched with something of the felicity of Elizabeth Bishop's
style, and is not unworthy to be compared with such poems as
'The Imaginary Iceberg', the fourth of the 'Songs for a Colored
Singer', and, perhaps most of all, 'A Summer's Dream'. However,
to make such a comparison shows up by way of contrast the lack
of poise in other poems of this later period. 'The Old Flame', for
instance, is a recension of Jean Stafford's 'A Country Love
Story', discussed in Chapter Three: 'No one saw your ghostly/
imaginary lover/stare through the window'. But this only indicates
that, like 'For the Union Dead' itself, 'The Old Flame' had
essentially been done before. A more impressive use of the
Stafford piece was made in 'The Mills of the Kavanaughs'.

Lowell can hardly be supposed to have had his mind focused
on the poems of *For the Union Dead*. He moved from Boston to
New York in September 1960, responding to a Ford Foundation
grant for the study of opera (Hamilton, 280). He decided, in the
process, to give up teaching at Boston University where he had
been for the previous five years. In New York he came under the
influence of Viola Bernard, the psychiatrist to whom one of the
Rilke imitations was dedicated, and underwent hospitalization
for manic-depressive disorder at the Columbia-Presbyterian
Medical Center in March 1961 (Hamilton, 285). But he also
became an honoured guest at President John F. Kennedy's White
House gatherings of savants, and undertook a tour of Brazil and
Argentina in the summer of 1962. The tour proved disastrous,
and resulted in further hospitalization, this time at the Institute
for Living, in Hartford, Connecticut (Hamilton, 303). He was,
however, able to return home – which was now an apartment on

West 67th Street, New York – by November, and to start a new teaching job, at Harvard, in February 1963 (Hamilton, 303). This would mean commuting two days a week for four months each year. Between November 1962 and February 1963, before taking up this post, he had added to the poems of 1961 several new pieces (Hamilton, 304). But 'Jonathan Edwards in Western Massachusetts' did nothing not previously accomplished by 'Mr. Edwards and the Spider': 'you saw the spiders fly/basking at their ease,/swimming from tree to tree'. 'Hawthorne', written for the centenary edition of that author's work, draws as a means of description upon the unfinished romance, *Septimius Felton* (McCall). 'His head/bent down, brooding, brooding/eyes fixed on some chip,/some stone, some common plant' is verbatim from the prose, and no more distinguished. Such close proximity is the converse of the procedure in *Imitations*, and argues an inventive failure.

Two studies in time and memory, 'The Lesson' and 'Those Before Us', have something in common with another item in this group, 'Night Sweat'. The latter, comprising two sonnets, is the only poem in *For the Union Dead* comparable in quality with 'Water', the key piece of the group of 1961. Unlike that predecessor, 'Night Sweat' looks forward to the final phase. Part of the impetus (Axelrod 1978, 143) seems to have come from an essay on Yvor Winters that Lowell wrote for *Poetry* April 1961 where he paid particular tribute to that poet's 'The Marriage': 'And, in commemoration of our lust,/May our heirs seal us in a single urn,/A single spirit never to return' (Winters 1960, 62). Lowell retunes this to suggest the turmoil of creativity: 'always inside me is the child who died,/always inside me is his will to die –/one universe, one body . . . in this urn/the animal night sweats of the spirit burn'. This cry for help is echoed in 'The Flaw', where his sense of imperfection, 'some mote, some eye-flaw', is contrasted with the dead certainty of 'old wives and husbands', an enviable and impossible permanence similar to that found in the poem by Yvor Winters. Another poem relating to 'Night Sweat' is the more fragmented 'The Neo-Classical Urn', and a tenuous connection relates this latter piece to 'Caligula', where Lowell satirizes his boyhood self-identification with the mad Roman emperor.

Other such connections can be made among the items in this book. The 'severed head' of the poem bearing that name relates

to the severed head 'swung/like a lantern in the victor's hand' at
the end of 'Florence'. The lacerated vision of 'Eye and Tooth'
and 'The Flaw' relates to the anguish of 'Myopia: a Night'. Two
poems, related in their tameness, 'Buenos Aires' and 'Dropping
South: Brazil', come out of the wild trip to South America.

It would seem, from all this, that the reviewers made too much
of the political interests said to form a sub-text to the book.
Comparing Lowell's imagination with that of a great historian, as
G. S. Fraser did (*New York Times Book Review*, 4 October
1964), certainly boosted his status, but one could hardly call this
criticism. 'The entire book is an exequy for all broken alliances,
picked wedlocks, leagues betrayed' (Richard Howard, *Nation*, 26
October 1964); that too, is exaggerated.

Between March 1960 and January 1965, much of Lowell's
energy went into writing and seeing to the production of various
plays. There had already been a version of Racine's *Phèdre*, a
commission for the Classic Drama series (Bentley). It was
published as *Phaedra* in 1961, and consequently associated with
Imitations. But its contorted and melodramatic verse cannot be
felt either to interpret the original or to add a genuine play to the
language. 'What he does, every time, is to bring into the
open . . . the sexual meanings which Racine's language conceals
under the politic abstractions of *bienséance*' (Cruttwell). The
critic in question cites the scene where Phèdre tries to seize
Hippolyte's sword in order to stab herself. 'Au défaut de ton bras
prête-moi ton épée:/Donne!' has been translated 'Then lend your
sword to me. – Come! Give it now' (Henderson). But Lowell has
'Look, this monster, ravenous/for her execution, will not flinch./I
want your sword's spasmodic final inch'. That 'spasmodic' is
especially dubious. Here, as elsewhere in Lowell's *Phaedra*, an
effect which depends upon decorum is lost, without any felicity to
act as compensation.

Most critics would agree that not *Phaedra* but *The Old Glory*
is the main contribution Lowell made to the theatre. This is a
trilogy, based on stories by Hawthorne and Melville, which came
directly out of the period, 1960-61, spent studying opera. Indeed,
even before the Ford Foundation grant, Lowell had in contemplation a libretto based upon Melville's 'Benito Cereno' (Hamilton,
280). After a period of intense theatre-going in New York,
Lowell retreated in the summer of 1961 to the Castine holiday
house made over to him by his Cousin Harriet, and completed by

September, not indeed an opera libretto, but a play. This, together with two other plays, became a topic of discussion between the author and the British director, Jonathan Miller. An experimental reading of the three plays was given in the late summer of 1963. 'After a year's preparation and further fund-raising they were given a full-scale production in November 1964' (Miller, x). This was at a church converted to a theatre, the American Place. Before the first night, one of the plays, 'Endecott and the Red Cross', was dropped. It was to be expanded and presented later as a full-length piece at the American Place on 18 April 1968 (Procopiow 1984, 50). Another play, 'My Kinsman, Major Molineux', fell out when the production was transferred to Greenwich Village 'for a regular off-Broadway run' (Weales).

The trouble is that Lowell was dealing with masterpieces of prose fiction, and to adapt them into dramatic verse would have required a creative effort of the order of *Imitations* itself. 'My Kinsman, Major Molineux' is one of the greatest works of fiction ever to come out of America, but Hawthorne couched it in an essentially narrative prose, and its dialogue is very much an adjunct to that narrative. A good deal is lost when Lowell puts the narrative into the stage directions and versifies the bare bones of the dialogue to stand for the play.

He resumed his walk, and was glad to perceive that the street now became wider, and the houses more respectable in their appearance. He soon discerned a figure moving on moderately in advance, and hastened his steps to overtake it. As Robin drew nigh, he saw that the passenger was a man in years, with a full periwig of gray hair, a wide-skirted coat of dark cloth, and silk stockings rolled above his knees. He carried a long and polished cane, which he struck down perpendicularly before him at every step; and at regular intervals he uttered two successive hems, of a peculiarly solemn and sepulchral intonation. Having made these observations, Robin laid hold of the skirt of the old man's coat, just when the light from the open door and windows of a barber's shop fell upon both their figures.

'Good evening to you, honored sir,' said he, making a low bow, and still retaining his hold of the skirt. 'I pray you tell me whereabouts is the dwelling of my kinsman, Major Molineux'.
(Hawthorne)

[A MAN enters from the right. He wears a full gray periwig, a wide-skirted coat of dark cloth and silk stockings rolled up above the knees. He carries a polished cane which he digs angrily into the ground at every step. 'Hem, hem,' he says in a sepulchral voice as he walks over to the barber shop. The TWO BARBERS appear, ONE with a razor, the OTHER with a bowl of suds]

MAN IN PERIWIG   Hem! Hem!

ROBIN   Good evening, honored sir,
                     Help us. We come from out of town.

MAN IN PERIWIG   A good face and a better shoulder!
                     Hem, hem! I see you're not from Boston.
                     We need good stock in Boston. You're lucky!
                     meeting me here was providential.
                     I'm on the side of youth. Hem, hem!
                     I'll be your guiding lamp in Boston . . .

ROBIN   I have connections here, a kinsman . . .

MAN IN PERIWIG   Of course you have connections here.
                     They will latch on to you like fleas.
                     This is your town! Boy! With that leg
                     you will find kinsmen on the moon.

ROBIN   My kinsman's Major Molineux.

(Lowell)

The Lowell quotation is only a small part of a scene, padded out with dialogue which seeks atmosphere and finds instead otiosity. Probably no one could have adapted the story which, as F. R. Leavis was wont to say, is as profound an allegory as anything in English.

Herman Melville might have proved more amenable: two notable films and a distinguished opera have been adapted from his work. However, 'Benito Cereno' offers intractable problems. For one thing, it is static. There has been a mutiny, and that mutiny is explained, through various depositions, in the concluding pages of the tale. But the only action presented in narrative terms is Cereno's leap from his ship to the American captain's boat, and Lowell, in his adaptation, cuts this out. He adds, however, all kinds of irrelevance; from the jocose figure of the American mate, Perkins, to a credo from the black leader of the mutiny. This latter contribution is particularly unfortunate. Melville's Babo resolves to end his days in an Iago-like silence: 'Seeing all was over, he uttered no sound, and could not be forced to. His aspect seemed to say, since I cannot do deeds, I will not speak words'. Lowell, avoiding silence, gives his Babu a final speech, but it is naively explicit and irrelevant to the basic narrative:

[BABU steps back, and quickly picks up a crown from the litter]
    This is my crown.
[Puts crown on his head. He snatches BENITO'S rattan cane]
    This is my rod.
[Picks up silver ball]
    This is the earth.
[Holds the ball out with one hand and raises the cane]
    This is the arm of the angry God.
[Smashes the ball . . . Holding a white handkerchief and raising both his hands]
    Yankee Master understand me. The future is with us.

In reply, the American captain shoots the mutineer's body full of bullets. This is a clumsy device and trivializes the conflict. Yet there is not, and cannot be, any equivalent to the final paragraph of Melville's 'Benito Cereno':

Some months after, dragged to the gibbet at the tail of a mule, the black met his voiceless end. The body was burned to ashes; but for many days, the head, that hive of subtlety, fixed on a pole in the Plaza, met, unabashed, the gaze of the whites; and across the Plaza looked towards St. Bartholomew's church, in whose vaults slept then, as now, the recovered bones of Aranda: and across the Rimac bridge looked towards the monastery, on Mount Agonia without; where, three months after being dismissed by the court, Benito Cereno, borne on the bier, did, indeed, follow his leader.

The production of *The Old Glory* at the American Place was successful, winning five Obie awards for the 1964–65 season, including one for the best play. However, the critics confused the literary and performative aspects of the event: 'the triumph of *The Old Glory* is total, flowing centrally from Lowell's magnificently literate text' (*Newsweek*, 16 November 1964); 'it heralds the arrival . . . of one who may very well come to revolutionize the American theater' (Brustein). This latter derives from a note published in the original edition of the trilogy. Though it was later replaced by a comment from the director, the note provided a response to what was obviously a remarkable production: 'Roscoe Lee Browne, alternating between Calypso sunniness and sinister threat as Babu . . . Frank Langelli as Cereno, his eyes continually lowered in shame, his voice morose and rich' (Brustein).

A not dissimilar warmth of response may have been deserved by *Prometheus Bound*, which Peter Brook commissioned on behalf of the Royal Shakespeare Company. Lowell worked on this through the summer of 1966 (Hamilton, 347), and it opened on 9 May 1967 at the Yale Drama School, where Lowell's advocate, Robert Brustein, happened to be dean. The play was no doubt helped by Jonathan Miller's production and by the fact that the leading role was undertaken by Kenneth Haigh, who had more than ten years previously created the part of Jimmy Porter in *Look Back in Anger*. With Haigh 'an angry, ageless Prometheus' (Heymann, 435), *Prometheus Bound* ought to have been impressive, especially in its more exalted moments:

What did men know of houses built of brick, and turned to face the sun? They swarmed like ants, though with far less order, through a sunless underground of eroding holes. Leafless winter, flowering spring, and fruitful summer were all one season to them. The stars looked down on them like an aimless sprinkle of water drops running out into nothing. I taught men the rising and the setting of the stars.

Beside this, the verse translation of a fine poet, Paul Roche, seems a little wordy and rhythmically lax: '[Men] Knew no brick-built homes to front the sun,/No woodwork; but beneath the soil/They lived like tiny ants recessed in sunless holes;/No measured sign for winter, flowery spring,/Nor summer full of fruit;/Without a clue they practiced everything,/Until I showed the stars to them,/Their rising and their set –/So difficult to calculate' (Roche, 46).

Perhaps verse is an impediment in translating Aeschylus. Certainly Lowell's poetic adaptation of *The Oresteia*, commissioned by the Lincoln Centre (Lowell 1964b), is inferior to *Prometheus Bound*. The first two sections, 'Agamemnon' and 'Orestes', date from the early 1960s. At the same period, an attempt at a third play in the cycle, 'The Furies', was abandoned after only a few pages. *The Oresteia* as a whole was never discussed and revised as other Lowell manuscripts were (Bidart); nor, at the time, was it produced. The verse of the first two plays in the cycle seems, in its compressed effect of caricature, to be a kind of answer to the measured and literary version, which Lowell himself especially admired, of Richmond Lattimore. One could point the contrast as being between 'O hail, blaze of the darkness, harbinger of day's/shining' (Lattimore) and 'What am I seeing? The sky's on fire' (Lowell). The third part of the trilogy, however, is distinctly more verbose than the other two; far more like translatese. This is obvious in the priestess's opening speech: 'What happens from now on must be left to Apollo;/he heals by divination, clarifies the darkest omen –/he purifies the house of his servant'. Lowell does not seem to have consulted the sketches he wrote in the early 1960s. However, some readers will find them, fragmented though they are, more promising: 'I've done what I could. I am terrified./Oh Apollo, my healer, you know everything./You can do everything. Save your servant!'.

By the later 1960s, however, the failure of an individual play, or even the adverse response to a book, made little difference to the upward swell of Lowell's reputation. With the death of Robert Frost, Lowell became America's unofficial Poet Laureate. That meant anything he did was news, especially if it savoured of opposition to the government. Lowell first accepted, then publicly repudiated, an invitation from President Lyndon B. Johnson to take part in a White House Arts Festival (*New York Times*, 3 June 1965). *Time Magazine* made a fuss about this, quoting Lowell as saying, 'I . . . can only follow our present foreign policy with the greatest dismay and distrust' (11 June 1965). This referred to the current war in Vietnam and the possibility of nuclear conflict. It was followed by a statement sympathizing with Lowell's stand signed by Hannah Arendt, Lillian Hellman, Alfred Kazin, Dwight Macdonald and fourteen others who, unlike Lowell, had not been invited to President Johnson's Festival but who wanted, nonetheless, to show solidarity (*New York Times*, 4 June 1965). Lowell's stand might have held public significance if he had made any study of the matter. But the resultant 'commotion' (as *Time* put it) derived from nothing more substantial than the aura that had by now gathered around the great poet. This was fostered by his New York domicile and proximity to socio-cultural sounding-boards.

A further non-event was the failure of Lowell to become Professor of Poetry at Oxford. This post is virtually honorary, secured by the votes of Oxford graduates holding the degree of

138   ROBERT LOWELL

Master of Arts. The election in which Lowell was involved took
place in February 1966, and the successful candidate was a poet
almost twenty years Lowell's senior. Edmund Blunden had made
his reputation just after the First World War. Lowell had termed
the earlier work of this poet 'regional . . . wonderfully concrete'
but went on to describe a later volume, *Shells from a Stream*, as
'careless, academic, and sentimental' (Lowell 1946). Edward
Lucie-Smith fanned the flames on Lowell's behalf, suggesting
that 'Lowell made "modernism" accessible again, and saved
English poetry from death by stagnation' (*Spectator*, 28 January
1966). This remark, as Lucie-Smith undoubtedly foresaw, drew
out various backwoodsmen: '[Lowell] wrote in a streamlined
contemporary idiom; and that is what the journalists, clerks
and advertising men who manipulate poetry in England like';
'Blunden . . . does have the advantage of being intelligible and
grammatical, which is more than can be said of . . . Robert
Lowell' (James Reeves, Derek Hudson: *Spectator*, 4 February
1966). All this only went to strengthen Lowell's hold on the
British cognoscenti, no matter what the electors at Oxford might
have decided.

After his main burst of playwriting finished in early 1965 and
these various public disturbances petered out, Lowell seems to
have been weary and vulnerable. No one can doubt the sincerity
of his concern with the Harlem race riot of July 1964, which gave
rise to his poem, 'The Opposite House' (Axelrod 1978, 182–83);
no one, either, can doubt his horror as the White House drew the
country deeper into war with Vietnam. Lowell retreated to
Castine for the summer of 1965 and wrote a set of poems which
was to form the basis of *Near the Ocean*: 'Waking Early Sunday
Morning', 'Fourth of July in Maine', 'Near the Ocean' and
'Central Park'. The first three, and to some extent the last, are
linked thematically and metrically, and really constitute one
poem: a rambling, diary-like affair. This is plainly to be seen, as
regards subject-matter and rhythm, in the draft stanzas that did
not find their way into the published version of 'Waking Early
Sunday Morning':

> Time to dig up and junk the year's
> dotage and output of tame verse:
> cast-iron whimsy, limp indignation,
> liftings, listless self-imitation,

> whole days when I could hardly speak,
> came barging home unshaven, weak
> and willing to show anyone
> things done before and better done.
> (Hamilton, 328)

Of course, this is a rejected stanza, and the finished 'Waking Early Sunday Morning' has received respectful attention. 'The free-associative monologue of a poet on his Creator's day of rest . . . At the same time it is a philosophical meditation on energy and reality-transcending experience – "breaking loose" – in man, a *summa* of its modalities and origins' (Williamson 1974, 116). That is a great deal of weight to put upon lines such as 'Pity the planet, all joy gone/from this sweet volcanic cone'. The earth cannot be termed a 'cone'; it is not by any means entirely 'volcanic'; and the word 'sweet' requires backing if it is to take its place, like the bird's-nest image in 'Heine Dying in Paris', as a concept of life. In comparison with the difficult but rewarding poems of *Lord Weary's Castle*, this recent work seems drained.

'Waking Early Sunday Morning' and its companions, 'Near the Ocean' and 'Fourth of July in Maine', stem from a poem of Lowell's, admired by R. P. Blackmur, 'The Drunken Fisherman'. This is not alone among the early works in seeming to have a derivation from Marvell's 'Upon Appleton House'. That seventeenth-century work affords many instances revealing insight and invention, but suffers from being a plasm from which four or five individual poems could have been distilled. As it stands, 'Appleton House' is a notebook. But it is still superior in texture to 'The Drunken Fisherman'; and immeasurably so to, say, 'Fourth of July in Maine'. A juxtaposition may help to make the point:

> For now the Waves are fal'n and dry'd,
> And now the Meadows fresher dy'd;
> Whose Grass, with moister colour dasht,
> Seems as green Silks but newly washt.
> No *Serpent* new nor *Crocodile*
> Remains behind our little *Nile*;
> Unless it self you will mistake,
> Among these Meades the only Snake.
> ('Appleton House')

Now the hot river, ebbing, hauls
Its bloody waters into holes;
A grain of sand inside my shoe
Mimics the moon that might undo
Man and Creation too; remorse,
Stinking, has puddled up its source;
Here tantrums thrash to a whale's rage.
This is the pot-hole of old age.
('The Drunken Fisherman')

And now the frosted summer night-dew
brightens, the north wind rushes through
your ailing cedars, finds the gaps;
thumbtacks rattle from the white maps,
food's lost sight of, dinner waits,
in the cold oven, icy plates –
repeating and repeating, one
Joan Baez on the gramophone.
('Fourth of July in Maine')

In the end, 'Fourth of July in Maine' is no more than a chatty letter to Cousin Harriet, and 'Near the Ocean' the (frequently obscure) Marvellizing of Lowell's own 'Man and Wife'. Lowell records that he had started one of the *Life Studies* in Marvell's four-foot couplets and Elizabeth Hardwick had responded with 'Why not say what really happened?' (Lowell 1963). Lowell remarked at the time that the metre prevented any honesty on the subject. The fact that he reverted to this same metre in *Near the Ocean* indicates not dishonesty but tiredness. The form, as we have seen, does nothing for the subject.

Lowell's tendency in this phase is to rely upon literary antecedents as a crutch. In so far as 'Central Park' differs from the other poems in the sequence, it is because Marvell has been forsaken in favour of Williams (Eulert):

to the right
from this vantage, the observation tower
in the middle distance stands up prominently
from its pubic grove
(Williams 1963, 69)

> each precious, public, pubic tangle
> an equilateral triangle,
> lost in the park, half covered by
> the shade of some low stone or tree.
> ('Central Park')

Lowell's dependence here is an indication of power in ebb. He wrote no new poems between the summer of 1965 and that of 1966, when he was preparing *Near the Ocean* for the press. The volume was bulked out by the inclusion of a number of imitations of Dante, Juvenal, Horace, Quevedo and Góngora, dating from the summer of 1962. These had not been thought worthy of inclusion in *For the Union Dead* (Hamilton, 348). The versions of Quevedo and Góngora are cruder and more forced than anything to be found in *Imitations*. There are reminiscences of *Lord Weary's Castle*, but the controlled rhetoric of that volume has given place to a cacophonous play on words. A representative comparison can be made between this, from the earlier book:

> Augustus mended you. He hung the tongue
> Of Tullius upon your rostrum . . .
> ('Dea Roma')

and this, from *Near the Ocean*:

> You search in Rome for Rome? O Traveller!
> in Rome itself, there is no room for Rome . . .
> ('The Ruins of Time')

The longest poem in the book is Lowell's version of the Tenth Satire of Juvenal. It suffers, as none of the *Imitations* proper do, from competing with a version that has established itself in the English language as a major classic. By giving his version the same name as that by Samuel Johnson, 'The Vanity of Human Wishes', Lowell calls in unfortunate comparisons:

> Unnumber'd suppliants crowd Preferment's gate,
> Athirst for wealth, and burning to be great;
> Delusive Fortune hears th'incessant call,
> They mount, they shine, evaporate, and fall.
> (Johnson)

> How many men are killed by Power, by Power
> and Power's companion, Envy! Your long list
> of honors breaks your neck . . .
> (Lowell)

The next longest poem is a version of Dante's *Inferno*, Canto XV: 'Brunetto Latini'. But here, once more, Lowell is up against a mighty rival: the free adaptation that forms the dialogue in 'Little Gidding', the last of T. S. Eliot's *Four Quartets*:

> Since our concern was speech, and speech impelled us
>   To purify the dialect of the tribe
>   And urge the mind to aftersight and foresight.
> (Eliot)

> In one word, we were scholars in our time,
> great men of letters, famous in the world
> we soiled and lost for our one common crime.
> (Lowell)

The trouble is that the adaptations in this book are not imitated from foreign sources so much as translated. This means that Lowell was unable to take over the poets he was adapting and turn them into personalized masks. The results consequently lack personality: they are neither fair translations nor imaginative imitations. As one student of both Dante and Lowell put it, 'He took a direction that was not congenial to his talents and abilities' (Prampolini).

Near the Ocean came out in the spring of 1967. According to Lowell himself, there is a theme that holds the volume together; the relationship of ancient Rome with modern America. But in fact the poems fall into two categories, those adapted from the classics and those which are loose meditations upon chiefly religious topics. The collection amounts to seven poems and six translations: of which Hayden Carruth said 'one can scarcely find a complete sentence from stanza to stanza, but only phrases, expletives, stabs of meaning' (*Hudson Review*, Autumn 1967).

Nevertheless, *Near the Ocean*, like *For the Union Dead*, has continued as a classic, especially among university critics. This either indicates the critics' disaffection from poetry; or that a Lowell tamed from the intensities of *Life Studies* and *Imitations*

fits appropriately into the academic pantheon. ' "Waking Early
Sunday Morning" is a masterpiece of prosody, tone, and disastrous
likelihood . . . What we are given . . . is the great poem of the
sixties' (Richard Howard, *Poetry*, September 1967); 'Here is the
confluence of Lowell's Rome and his America . . . The title
poem is a beautifully unpredictable, yet integrated and controlled, handling of the loyalties of love' (Daniel Hoffman, *The
Hollins Critic*, February 1967).

Howard and Hoffman represented the applause of a rising
generation, and Lowell needed it. His friends and mentors had
departed in a regular embassy of death. Williams and Roethke
had died in 1963; Eliot, Blackmur and, most tragically of all,
Jarrell, in 1965; Delmore Schwartz in 1966. Lowell himself had
been hospitalized for mental breakdowns in December 1963,
January 1965, December 1965 and December 1966 (Hamilton,
306; 318; 343; 356). Berryman, to whom Lowell turned in what he
felt to be his isolation, was himself depressed, clinically alcoholic,
and writing his latest *Dream Songs* during a sabbatical year,
1966–67, in Dublin. This was a mourning-journal in verse, whose
power Lowell at once admired and was shaken by (Hamilton,
351): 'Let Randall rest, whom your self-torturing/cannot restore
one instant's good to, rest' (Berryman 1969, 15). Lowell was to
echo this in one of the strangest poems of his own next phase:
'black-gloved, black-coated, you plod out stubbornly,/as if asleep,
Child Randall, as if in chainstep'. Battered and stripped of his
friends, yet acclaimed as hardly any American poet had been
before him, Lowell staggered into a new period of composition.
In spite of his problems, he was to discover fluency.

7 *Notebook 1967–68* (1969); *Notebook* (1970); *History* (1973); *For Lizzie and Harriet* (1973); *The Dolphin* (1973); *Day by Day* (1977)

Robert Lowell was afflicted with a manic-depressive illness, in his time known as cyclothymia. At least from the age of thirty-two, the period of his first hospitalization, he was subject to a yearly cycle of moods that reached its crisis each December, or sometimes January. The symptoms included hyperactivity, extreme verbosity, pressure of speech, grandiosity, manipulativeness, irritability, euphoria, hypersexuality, threatening behaviour, and religiosity. The first six of these are listed as common to all in a sample of manic patients assessed by Gabrielle A. Carlson and Frederick K. Goodwin. The other symptoms were apparent in from fifty to ninety per cent of the sample. All biographical information available suggests that Lowell's behaviour patterns in his annual state of disturbance occurred well within the parameters defined by Carlson and Goodwin and their successors in the study of what is now termed bipolar disorder; bipolar, because the unfortunate patient is trapped in a cycle between elation and depression.

In the late 1960s, bipolar disorder was established as endogenous (Bratfos and Haug), which meant that the victim had little choice as to his behaviour. The illness, however, proved to be preventable by treatment with lithium carbonate (Prien, Klett, Caffey). Lowell began this treatment after being discharged from McLean's Hospital in the spring of 1967 (Hamilton, 359). It was not so successful as it might have been had he followed his doctor's instructions. But he found it impossible, especially when in company, to leave off alcohol (Tillinghast; Williamson 1979). Even so, Lowell functioned more or less effectively through a busy 1967 and 1968.

At the end of *Notebook 1967–68*, Lowell has a note in prose that chronicles what were for him the main events of those years. They include the Vietnam War, the Six Days' War between the Arabs and the Israelis, the French Students' and Workers' Uprisings, and the Russian occupation of Czechoslovakia. Lowell himself was involved in the Pentagon March of 21 October 1967; in Eugene McCarthy's campaign for the Democratic Presidential nomination; and the Demonstrations and the Democratic Convention in Chicago, 25–29 August 1968. Those public events served to counterpoint Lowell's deteriorating domestic life. A further outlet from the latter was provided by Proustian or Chekhovian forays into the past: Lowell always had a lively memory. Concerns such as these directed the shape of his 1969 volume of verse.

Notebook 1967–68 has been more talked about than read. It has had no circulation in Britain and, apart from its early months of publication, little in the USA. Yet it is an important book; at least as much as *For the Union Dead*, and more than its own immediate successors. There are few poems in this collection one would term major, but it has a raw charm as the verse chronicle of a year. The technique was in part based on the *Paterson* of William Carlos Williams, where heterogenous materials were cobbled together to form an intermittently poetic *bricolage*. Partly *Notebook 1967–68* derives from the *Dream Songs* (see Chapter Six), buckled variants of the sonnet form that John Berryman had begun writing in California in the early 1960s.

Possibly the lithium treatment encouraged in Lowell what was an unprecedented fluency. Certainly a degree of self-criticism was removed, and this may also be connected with the loss of Randall Jarrell, who had died in 1965.

Notebook 1967–68 was termed, when it came out, 'a sonnet sequence which Lowell wishes us to take as a single continuous poem' (Leibowitz). That is not quite true: the *Notebook* is neither 277 separate poems nor one sequence. Rather, it is a series of fifty-eight sequences, ranging in scale from one to seventeen items apiece. It is as though the individual sonnet could no longer accommodate Lowell's new-found loquaciousness.

It all begins with a group of four sonnets about Lowell's daughter, Harriet, who had attained the age of ten in the same year as her father was to reach the age of fifty. The group of poems is strongest when it focuses on the middle-aged parent, 'offering a child our leathery love'. The sonnets here are uncharacteristic of the book as a whole, being relatively formal and richly rhymed. They are followed by a sequence of fourteen items called 'Long Summer'. This is based on Lowell's holiday home at Castine, and indicates the tensions beneath the surface of the ageing Lowell-Hardwick ménage. The best of these sonnets is the first, beginning 'At dawn, the crisp goodbye of friends', but there are some winning moments elsewhere in this mini-cycle. For instance, the second sonnet has the excited 'this night, this night, I elfin, I stonefoot,/walking the wildfire wildrose of those lawns'. Number 14 has 'each day now the cork more sweetly leaves the bottle,/except a sudden falseness in the breath,/passive participation, dogged sloth,/angrily skirting greener ice'. It seems that the 'long summer' atmosphere is tainted. One thinks of Seamus Heaney's similarly domestic sequence, 'Summer Home', which indeed may have learned from Lowell's example.

After a tribute to Hardwick's friend, Mary McCarthy, comes a sequence of four retrospective sonnets, 'Searchings'. These invoke Lowell's childhood, 'the boy, held over in the hollow classroom,/sanding down *RTSL*, his four initials, slashed/like a dirty word across the bare, blond desk' ('1'). 'Dream of the Fair Women', a sonnet on its own, prefaces a sequence of five sonnets about dreams, still reminiscent of the past: ' "After my marriage, I found myself in constant/companionship with this almost stranger I found/neither agreeable, interesting, nor admirable" ' ('4. The Next Dream'). This 'stranger' is Commander Lowell, ironized by Mrs Lowell's patter, which Lowell himself drew from a notebook kept by his mother in 1937 (Hamilton, 385). The lithium treatment may have brought out symbolism inaccessible to Viola Bernard and the Freudians: Lowell identifies with a birth trauma his obsessional need to write. The typing paper he uses, a variety named Onion Skin, 'seemed to scream,/as if Fortuna bled in the white wood,/first felt the bloody gash that brought my life' ('7').

This, quite understandably, leads on to sex. 'Through the Night', the next sequence, seems to be an account of an extra-marital affair, one of several into which Lowell entered during his weekly two-night-stands at Harvard (Bell, 162; Heymann, 471–472). The exiguous verse-technique is something with which we grow familiar in Lowell's later work. By now the poet has settled into loose, unrhymed fourteeners, extended into sequences of two, three or more items, as the subject overflows the form.

Such informality does not preclude random felicities, such as (in number 3 of the sequence) 'the window/holds out its thin, black terminal disk of joy'.

There follows a pairing of two retrospective items, 'The Muse'. The first is based on an extra-Harvard reading party at Nantucket in 1935. The second – the first poem on the arts in the book – stems from the work of the German satirical painter, George Grosz. It seems to bear in mind especially such water-colours as *Beauty – thee I praise* (1919) or *Suburb* (1920): 'the receding hairlines of those nettled cunts/severed like scalplocks by the stroke of a brush'. It was this kind of poem that served as a contrast to the *tendresses* of *Notebook 1967–68*, not greatly to the advantage of that volume. Touching upon artistic or political matters is well enough when the concerns engage the author's feelings. The two-item elegy on Jarrell echoes Lowell's own essay about that writer. 'He has the harsh luminosity of a Shelley' (Lowell 1967) creatively links up with the vision of Jarrell's shade offering Charon, boatman across the River Acheron, an obol. Its counterpart, the poem '2. Randall Jarrell: 1914–1965', has 'with harsh/luminosity grasping at the black coin of the tunnel'; an allusion to Jarrell's mysterious death in a pedestrian road accident.

But Lowell is not so felicitous when it comes to public affairs. 'Munich, 1938' trivializes the Hitler-Chamberlain encounter. His poem on the subject prefaces a six-piece sequence called 'October and November'. This is based upon the March to the Pentagon, an anti-Vietnam demonstration that took place in Washington on 21 October 1967. It has what may be termed the ring of authenticity:

> . . . An MP sergeant kept
> repeating, 'March slowly through them. Don't even brush
> anyone sitting down.' They tiptoed through us
> in single file, and then their second wave
> trampled us flat and back . . .
> ('The March')

A good deal of the 'political' writing in *Notebook 1967–68* is like that, depending for effect on plain statement of more or less interesting fact in unrhymed sonnet form. There is a poetic irony in the two 'March' poems – this is the second – being followed by one in memory of Lowell's collateral ancestor, 'Beau Sabreur'

('5. Charles Russell Lowell: 1835–1864'). That *nom de guerre* was applied to Charles Russell Lowell, nephew of Lowell's great-grandfather and also of James Russell Lowell. Charles Russell, like his own relative by marriage, Robert Gould Shaw, lost his life fighting the Confederacy: 'he had, *gave* . . . everything/at Cedar Creek'. An echo of his fame had been previously heard in 'Falling Asleep Over the Aeneid'.

Four political sonnets, collectively titled 'Autumn in the Abstract', follow; and, in their turn, are succeeded by 'Symbols'. This six-item sequence consists of episodes which, like Lowell's sojourn in Danbury Jail for refusing the draft, are biographical, or which, like Mao Tse-Tung's cure for lepers, are horrific. But the best of the 'Symbols' links up with the Pentagon March, and it is probably also the finest poem in *Notebook 1967–68*. It is called '1. The Well':

> The stones of the well were sullenly unhewn,
> none could deny their leechlike will to stay –
> no dwelling near and four square miles of flatness,
> pale grass diversified by wounds of sand,
> the grass as hard as rock and squeezed by winter,
> each well-stone rounded as an ostrich egg,
> strange for unfinished stone. It seemed a kind
> of dead chimney . . .

This has a power which comes from intent observation relayed in minute description. One feels that here is a localizable well. Beyond that, there is an aura of significance. But if the well is significant, what is it significant of?

The poem cannot be altogether comprehended from the text before us. A clue, however, is afforded by Norman Mailer's book, *The Armies of the Night*. This is an account of the Pentagon March in which Mailer, like Lowell, took part. Against a great deal of comment in ratio to not very much tangible description, Mailer says:

Lowell's poetry gave one the sense of living in a well, the echoes were deep, and sound was finally lost in moss on stone; down there the light had the light of velvet, and the ripples were imperceptible. But one lay on one's back in this well, looking up at the sky, and stars were determinedly there at night, fixed points of reference; nothing in the

poems ever permitted you to turn on your face and try and look down into the depths of the well, it was enough you were in the well – now, look up! The world dazzled with its detail.
(Mailer, 137)

With this fairly undistinguished piece of prose as a compulsory footnote, the poem swims into focus. It is a reinforcement of ego: the poet takes over and uses elliptically what an admiring acolyte says of his poetry. Some of the imagery, that to do with crowds for example, is clearly picked up from the surrounding context:

> . . . The halting trespasser
> was free to pitch the bucket, drinking cup
> and funnel down the well – his neighbor's bucket
> through bottomless, thin black hoops of standing water,
> and plenty of elbowroom for scuttled gear;
> room to reach the bottom, unnoticed, uncrushed . . .
> It's not the crowds, but crowding kills the soul.
> ('1. The Well')

Lowell's good poetry was a reconnaissance into the deep . . . one went down with the idea one would come back with more . . . the intent silence of a group of near a few hundred men.
(Mailer, 137–138)

But we have only to compare this poem with 'Mr. Edwards and the Spider' to see how limited it is. The raw material is inherently uninteresting: Norman Mailer has regard neither for style or idea, he lacks a coherent body of philosophy, and his revolt against society is essentially negative. The Jonathan Edwards poem, on the other hand, stands on its own feet as a revelation of character and a comment involving a major field of doctrine. It would do so if one knew nothing about the character of Edwards nor the doctrine his life's work embodied. '1. The Well', as we have seen, is little more than a description, precise in its detail, but labouring under a sense of portent never completely to be delivered. Even so, it is one of the few good poems to be found in the *Notebooks*.

More easily comprehensible, and almost as distinguished, is 'The Heavenly Rain', a sonnet on its own which serves as a transition from 'politics' back to the poetry of reminiscence. Like 'The Well', it has a characteristic, quiet cadence: 'The rain falls down, the soil swims up to breathe,/the squatter sumac, shafted in cement,/flirts its wet leaves to heaven like the Firebird'. With one of Lowell's glances at girls, 'always young as last week', we move on to the seven sonnets of 'Charles River', which harks back to Lowell's youthful affair, when he was at Harvard; the one that culminated in his fight with his father. This sequence lives chiefly in its topography, and reminds us how Lowell, for all his travelling, belonged essentially to Boston: 'And now, the big town river, once hard and dead as its highways,/ rolls blackly into country river, root-banks, live ice,/a live muskrat muddying the moonlight' ('2'). For Lowell, the clock every now and again reverts to 1936. His striking his father is 'never to be effaced'.

Memories of the family intersperse the sequences. But such poems as 'For Aunt Sarah' and 'My Grandfather' really relate to *Life Studies*; where, however, in such poems as 'My Last Afternoon with Uncle Devereux Winslow', the essential work of portraiture has already been done. At this stage of *Notebook 1967–68*, one feels that the verse is flagging. In a series of six sonnets called 'Names', familiar Lowell heroes are not so much re-created as invoked: Cato, Alexander, Napoleon, among them. The latter is no improvement on the Hugo imitation, 'Russia 1812'. Lowell is stronger in the present, even if the present affords nothing more than a clandestine affair. That is the case (Bell, 155) in the sequence called 'Harvard', itself echoing 'Charles River': 'a silk stocking, blown thin as smog, coils in a twig-fork,/dangling a wire coathanger, rapier-bright' ('1'). A kind of postlude to this Harvard sequence is formed by a trio of sonnets called 'Alcohol'. They are really a single sonnet that has outgrown its bounds. The point can be made by excerpting a single line from each of the three sonnets in question: 'Brown hours, they stream like water off the back' ('1'); 'Pale ale, molar drain . . . I face the men's room mirror' ('2'); 'Nature might do her thing for us; so they swore' ('3').

Paratactically, but not logically, we reach a further retrospect, 'In the Forties': 'The back-look? Green logs sizzled on the fire-dogs,/painted scarlet like British Redcoats. June/steamed up in greenness' ('1'). The meaning of this escaped a reviewer in the *Times Literary Supplement* (10 August 1973) who found Lowell's striving for intensity resulted in the compression of an idea already tightened to the limit. The poem will remain incomprehensible to any reader not conversant with 'The Mills of the Kavanaughs': ' "And there was greenwood spitting on the firedogs,/That looked like Hessians. It was June, and Maine/Smouldered to greenness" ' (stanza 15). The other poems of 'In the Forties' are also taken from 'The Mills of the Kavanaughs': stanzas 34 and 36, respectively. They seem more lucid in their narrative context; more so, at least, than when extracted arbitrarily and placed in *Notebook 1967–68* to serve, perhaps, as a tribute to Jean Stafford. It is also possible that the first of the three sonnets looks forward to 'The Downlook' in *Day by Day*.

There follows 'The Literary Life, a Scrapbook', a sonnet on its own, which links a recollection of 'My wife' (probably Stafford) who 'caught in that eye blazes', with the sequence 'Sleep'. This latter is composed of three sonnets about the poet at Harvard: 'Six straight hours to teach on less than three hours' sleep' ('2'). One former student speaks of Lowell's 'soft voice, sometimes impossible to hear, the reticent approval-seeking mannerisms, the tilted head, crooked glasses' (Baumel). His powers of projection could hardly have been helped by the current inamorata whom he addresses in 'Sleep' as 'you standing up on your bed/in your Emily Dickinson nightgown, purely marveling/whether to be sensible or drown' ('3'). But in the ensuing 'Blizzard in Cambridge', another detached sonnet, he rises from 'the blindness of teaching to bright snow' and escapes to 'the train home,/rolling with stately scorn'. 'Home' is back in New York; there he spends 'Christmas and New Year'; this latter, the title of the following eight-sonnet sequence. It is full of domestic survival and underlying disturbance: 'How could we nurse one family glass of Bourbon/through two half hours of television news?' ('3. The Dialogue'). The poet asks himself, still on this rueful note, 'Can I go on loving anyone at fifty?' ('6. The Book of Wisdom').

The answer transpires in the next sequence, 'Mexico', the twelve-part chronicle of another foray out of domesticity (Bell, 184), this one identified with an exotic landscape: 'We sit on the cliff like curs, chins pressed to thumbs,/the Toltec temples changing to dust in the dusk' ('4'). We are never far from a sense of mortality. It is to be found in the 'dust/dusk' juxtaposition; also in the poet's wry self-appraisal: 'I, fifty, humbled with the years' gold garbage' ('1'); 'how can I love you more,/short of turning into a criminal?' ('12'). This latter recognition shrouds the Mexico sequence, and the *Notebooks* themselves, at large.

A couple of historical sonnets, 'Canterbury' and 'Killiecrankie', show military grandeur in death, before the heart dies again in another New York sequence, 'Midwinter'. The first of the six sonnets comprising this set is thought to be addressed to the widow of President Kennedy (Hamilton, 388): 'I, though never young/in all our years, am younger when we meet' ('1. Friend across Central Park'). Once more Lowell engages in retrospect in a two-poem set, 'School', when he yet again invokes his Kenyon College friends, Peter Taylor and the endlessly-regretted Jarrell. The latter asks from a dream, ' "tell me,/Cal, why did we live? Why do we die?" ' ('2').

A nod towards the Israel of 1916 and another to that of 1969, presumably inserted as an afterthought to commemorate Lowell's visit there in the latter year, precede a series of seven sonnets called 'Writers'. These attempt to reify Eliot, Pound, Ford, Williams, Frost and, among the living, Tate. A meditation on age, 'Those Older', consisting of three sonnets, follows. There is then a two-sonnet description, in terms of the frozen Hudson River, of a relationship iced over. This is followed by a two-part reverie, based on one visit to a conference in Venezuela and another to Ivan Illich's cultural centre in Mexico, called 'My Death'.

'February and March', the next sequence, is by comparison obscure. The reference appears to be European, featuring the poet Mallarmé ('4. Le Cygne') and the painters Cuyp and Rembrandt. The sonnet about this last is partly taken from *The Nude* by Kenneth Clark, commenting on the spirituality that can be shown to exist in an ample, heavy body (Clark 1956, 340–342; Branscomb). Yet in those months of 1968, the months of the title, Lowell was very much on the campaign-trail. He was supporting Eugene McCarthy, whose campaign manager was Lowell's school-friend, Blair Clark (Larner, 35), in a bid for the Democratic presidential nomination. What had Rembrandt to do with that?

But there is no obvious logic in *Notebook 1967–68*. A two-item set, 'Pastime', flashes back once more to boyhood; the three-hander that follows, 'April 8, 1968', refers in its title to the date of the assassination of the black Civil Rights leader, Martin Luther King. Yet the first of the sonnets concerned deals with a breaking domesticity and the second is a soliloquy drawn from words uttered by the young Harriet Lowell, while the third pictures the poet climbing down a rope in order to save his life. This last is an image used by Dickens to betoken the paranoid nightmares of Jonas Chuzzlewit. The three poems together are best read as an indictment of cautious bourgeoisie.

The other side of the bourgeois is brought out in 'Mania', a two-piece set. The first item consists of lines that did not get into 'Waking in the Blue' and that had already occurred as a sonnet called '1958', published in *Near the Ocean*. Its appearance there elicited a letter from the addressee of the original draft. This letter, in its turn, was adapted as a further sonnet, '1968': 'What I write to tell you is what a shining/remembrance of someone, of you, to hold of . . . me' ('2. 1968'). The habit of using personal correspondence grew upon Lowell in years to come. The twelve-part sequence, 'April', that follows has a tendency in this direction. There are allusions to private conversations and to biographical incidents. This goes along with a curiously breathless form of notation: 'The headache, the night of no performance, dusk of daybreak:/limping home by the fountain's Dionysiac gushes' ('2. Europa'). The reference is to yet another affair, any reason for whose disclosure remains beyond the text. '6. The Misanthrope and the Painter' would remain equally obscure if Sidney Nolan had not glossed the line 'When I am in a room, Wyeth is invisible'. Apparently it refers to a Boston girlfriend of Lowell's claiming 'When I'm in the room Rothko disappears' (Hamilton, 387). Even with the gloss, though, the poem is inconsequential. Still less consequential are poems whose backing reference remains withheld, perhaps for ever: '5. The Dialogue'; '7. Even Such'; '8. The White Goddess'. All these seem to derive from passing conversations; and '9. Sappho' might also seem to, if one did not know the poem is based on an adaptation of Sappho that was the second item in *Imitations*.

There may be some form of submerged plan in *Notebook 1967–68* indicated by the way in which the poems that are public and historical interrupt those that are more individually emotive. Each of these alternative modes is in its turn interrupted by retrospections into a highly personal past. But the public poems are the least interesting of the collection. A thirteen-part sequence called 'Power' features Attila, Count Roland, Tamerlane, and Richard III, among others. The narrative, however, is anecdotal. As ever with Lowell, no special insight is shown into the power politics that never ceased to fascinate him. The sequence ends in

desperation, with Lowell admitting ('13. New Year's Eve 1968')
that the year was 'written/in bad, straightforward, unscanning
sentences'. He declares himself to be left with a typescript 'like a
Rosetta Stone'. The reference here is to an ancient stone, found
in the Nile Delta in 1799, and seeming to be a mass of chaotic
inscriptions; yet it formed the key by which the Egyptian
hieroglyphics were deciphered. This may be a clue as to how
Lowell wanted his *Notebooks* read. But it is noticeable that here,
as elsewhere, there is an escape from intellectual inquiry into
topographical description: 'The slush-ice on the east water of the
Hudson/rose-heather this New Year sunset'.

'April's End', a five-part sequence, also seems to be a kind of
release from thought: '1. King David Senex' personalizes an
historic figure in a way that relates him to the author; 'Night
Sweat' and 'Caligula' recall poems from an earlier book, *For the
Union Dead*. 'Eloges to the Spirits', a four-piece set, and a
detached tribute to Norman Mailer, are followed by 'May', a
sequence of seventeen sonnets loosely based on the student
demonstration at Columbia in 1968. '1. The Pacification of
Columbia' sounds the note of impending trouble, while '2.
Violence' deplores the necessity to take a stand. The anonymous
'3. Leader of the Left' is pitted against the university President,
himself personified as 'the old King': '4. The Restoration'. The
sequence then broadens out to an uneasy equation of external
power with emotional life. A tribute ('5') to General de Gaulle,
the French wartime leader, rubs flanks with an attack ('7') on
'The New York Intellectual', said to be the critic, Irving Howe
(Hamilton, 388). Conversations are drawn upon ('10. Another
Doctor' – 'Heidegger' in revision); a further affair is hinted at ('13.
Civilization'); a placatory poem, '15. The Picture (For Elizabeth)',
is followed by a random-seeming reflection, '17. Memorial Day',
that ends the sequence with 'fathomless profundities of inanim-
ation'. This apparent inconsequence is interrupted by a trio of
sonnets on Robert Kennedy, brother of the late President,
himself assassinated during his own bid for supreme office. The
ensuing sequence of eleven poems, 'To Summer', includes invocations of Jonathan Edwards, Casanova, Genghis Khan, Attila
the Hun (again!), and Louis the Sun-King, together with tributes
to Louis MacNeice, Theodore Roethke (rewritten from *Near the
Ocean*), Eugene McCarthy ('I love you so . . . Gone?'), Harpo
Marx, Milton, and Stalin. The link would seem to be a correlation

between performance in politics and performance in the arts. The Stalin poem – 'What shot him clawing up the tree of power?' – has been admired (Fein, 171–172), though one cannot help feeling, as with so much of Lowell's political writing, that his text would have benefited from the acquisition of further knowledge on the topic. His questions are rhetorical, even frenetic; not genuinely exploratory.

After this sequence, there is a kind of postlude. The second of its two poems is held together by an allusion to Goethe's 'Kennst du das Land, wo die Zitronen blühn?' ('Do you know the land where the lemon-trees blossom?' – Luke, 85; Smith, 113). More to the purpose, there follows a sequence of four sonnets, 'We Do What We Are', which constitutes a meditation on the art of writing: 'One wants words meat-hooked from the living steer' ('1. The Nihilist as Hero'); 'this open book . . . my open coffin' ('4. Reading Myself'). Dispersed in focus, by comparison, are the thirteen sonnets of the next sequence. It has been reported that there is a circular movement through all the *Notebooks* (Yenser, 10), and certainly this sequence is called 'Circles'. But it does not amount to more than self-questioning ('And I am still *in corpore sano*?'), parallels with Ulysses, a general sense of life ebbing. The first poem, 'Homing', anticipates a twentieth wedding anniversary; the penultimate one, 'The Lost Tune', declares 'I am too wise, or tired;/one's read the book, even the woman dies'.

The tiredness continues, unalleviated, into 'The Races', a set of ten sonnets to do with Eugene McCarthy's campaign, and the presidential election. The Republican Convention in Miami is touched upon; also the Democratic Convention in Chicago. But there is a sense that the rallying is over: 'I am so tired and had' ('6. After the Convention'). The alliance is altered: Eugene McCarthy withdrew from the campaign, Robert Kennedy, who came in late, was killed. Now the conflict is between the Democratic hack, Hubert Humphrey, and the Republican hawk, Richard Nixon. The poems of the sequence are political, but not informedly so: 'Nobody has won, nobody has lost . . . Will the election-winners ever pay us back?' ('10. November 7: From the Painter's Loft').

In most of the group of poems that follows, the 'Summer' sequence, Lowell takes refuge in the topography of Castine, where he spent most summers between 1957 and 1969 (Heymann, 438): 'Mostly it's a color; its change and yield/give easily, no stand except the headland' ('8. Castine Harbor'). But the seascape is a retreat, the retreat is illusory, and too much of the poetry is derived from chatter which it does not transcend: '11. Growth – ' "I'm talking the whole idea of life, and boys,/with Mother" '; '12. The Graduate' – ' "Transylvania's Greek Revival Chapel/is one of the best Greek Revival things in the South" '; '13. The Outlivers' – ' "If we could slow the world to what it changed/a hundred years ago" '. At the end of the sequence, the poet is left wishing he was a seal ('16').

As if to endorse that vain hope, the book concludes, like a Romantic symphony, several times over. There are two sonnets to Allen Tate, one of which, about a twin son that had died, was so tactless as to put severe strain even on that long-endured friendship (Heymann, 481). There are two sonnets called 'The End', the second of which consists of further conversational snippets pieced together. There is a sonnet to John Berryman, valorizing Lowell as well as his friend: 'John, we used the language as if we made it'. A poem called 'Close the Book' does not, in fact, close the book. It sounds a note of self-reproach: 'we too were students, and betrayed our hand'. A sequence of five poems ensues, remarking – as the opening of the book did – the poet's half-century. This is followed by an equivocal sonnet addressed to his wife, 'Obit': 'After loving you so much, can I forget/you for eternity, and have no other choice?'.

The book does not quite end, even with this. There is a prose 'Afterthought' to tell us that the separate poems and sections are opportunist and inspired by impulse, together with a list of significant dates. These are, then, poems looking for subjects. Though a sense of weariness prevails, it is worth mentioning that the period of writing, from September 1967 to the final revision of February 1969, was Lowell's longest time without a mental breakdown since *Lord Weary's Castle* in 1946.

By the end of 1969, Lowell had begun to revise *Notebook 1967–68* all over again. He enlisted a talented student from one of his writing classes, Frank Bidart, to help him. The revision was of a peculiar kind. There is nothing in *Notebook 1967–68* that does not recur in *Notebook*, which was to be published in 1970. However, forty of the original 277 poems are revised, some of them heavily. The initial 'Harriet' sequence is unchanged, but one poem – 'Here nature seldom feels the hand of man' – is added to the second sequence, 'Long Summer', and this is followed by a new poem on its own, 'Outlaws: A Goodbye'. After the tribute to Mary McCarthy, which remains unchanged, there is an additional poem, about a New York encounter, called 'Leaving'. The sequence 'Searchings' that follows has a third item substantially rewritten and is followed by a new poem, 'Les Mots', which tries to equate sport, love and art. 'Dream of the Fair Women' has two new poems added, 'The Last Resort' and 'The Walk', to make a sequence, 'The Backward'. But thereafter the sequences 'Five Dreams', 'Through the Night', 'October and November', 'Symbols' and 'Charles River' are virtually unchanged, this last retaining as the fourth item a version of the *Lord Weary's Castle* poem, 'Rebellion'. A new sequence, 'Thanksgiving', is created, based on the poem 'My Grandfather' (now called 'Two Farmers'), with three new poems added. 'Names', 'Harvard', 'Alcohol', 'In the Forties', 'Sleep', 'Mexico', and 'Those Older' are much the same. But two poems are added to the sequence 'Christmas and New Year'; two to 'Midwinter'; 'February and March' is expanded from thirteen to twenty-five poems; and 'April' from twelve to eighteen. Further expansions include 'Power' (from thirteen to twenty-two poems, with the title changed to 'The Powerful'); 'May' (from seventeen to twenty-four poems); 'To Summer' (from eleven to eighteen); 'Circles' (from thirteen to twenty); and the final 'Summer' sequence from sixteen to twenty-four poems.

These additional poems, among others, bring the total of the book up to 372, and swamp the basic plan. They supply little that is of poetic or structural advantage. 'Power' was not the most impressive sequence in the original and is not helped under its new title, 'The Powerful', by acquiring thumbnail sketches of Alexander, Anne Boleyn, Christopher Marlowe, Mary Stuart, Robespierre, Saint-Just, Coleridge, Presidents William Henry Harrison and Abraham Lincoln. The level of writing in these addenda is well below that of the originals. Of Lincoln, Lowell says 'You, our one genius in politics . . . you followed/the bull to the altar, death in unity./*J'accuse, j'accuse, j'accuse, j'accuse, j'accuse!*/Say it in American. Who'll shoot the deserters?'. This is incoherent, without even the virtue (found in one or two items of the original sequence) of random insight.

In *Notebook 1967–68* the verbal efficacy lay mainly with personal poems, and there is no doubt that items in sequences such as 'Symbols', 'Charles River' and 'Mexico' achieved a characteristic cadence, and sometimes more than that. In *Notebook*, on the other hand, the additional poems furnish endless explanations which blur the elegaic outlines of the original.

Notebook met with puzzlement: David Bromwich, for instance, found it privately allusive, a flow of turbid consciousness (*Commentary*, August 1971). *Notebook 1967–68*, on the other hand, deserves to be disseminated. Even though it is not likely to rank with *Life Studies* and *Imitations*, as a whole it is considerably more than the sum of its parts. It has the kind of attractiveness we associate with Pepys's *Diary* or Boswell's *Journals*. The authenticity is projected through the very rawness of expression. But, as Gerald Burns said, 'revising the book forces us to see it as a Work which needed revision' (*SouthWest Review*, Spring 1971).

By the time *Notebook* came out in October 1970, Lowell had lived to fulfil some of the premonitions that vibrated below the surface of *Notebook 1967–68*. He had accepted a Fellowship at All Souls College, Oxford, and a Visiting Professorship at the University of Essex. The latter had undergone student demonstrations not dissimilar to those which Lowell had chronicled as taking place at Columbia. Lowell came in to Essex two days a week, two terms a year, teaching a series of seminars on Shakespeare and a Minor course on modern English and American poetry. This lasted, in spite of personal complications, until the spring of 1973. Lowell's original plan had been for Elizabeth Hardwick and their daughter Harriet to join him for a year in London. In fact, however, some time after his arrival in April 1970, Lowell started a liaison with the novelist, Caroline Blackwood. This was quite different from the brief affairs with co-eds in and about Cambridge, Massachusetts. Then, Elizabeth Hardwick had been cast in the role of outraged parent and Lowell continued in his archetypal act as Naughty Bobby. Caroline Blackwood, however, was the mother of three daughters, and the veteran, like Lowell, of two previous marriages. There began a spirited series of communications from Elizabeth Hardwick, marooned in New York, on the subject of this new alliance. Under the pressure, Lowell collapsed, and in July was admitted to a London nursing home with what looked like a recurrence of his old malady (Hamilton, 400). Elizabeth Hardwick flew over to see him, but to no effect. Lowell, as ever, sought to handle the problem by writing it up, and began what amounted to a new *Notebook* (Hamilton, 408). Ninety poems were produced between

June and November, 1970. The situation seems to have been temporarily stabilized by Caroline Blackwood's discovery in February 1971 that she was pregnant. By May, Lowell thought he had finished the new book (Hamilton, 412). In September, his son, Sheridan, was born. More poems were added to *The Dolphin*, as the new book was called. Furthermore, throughout the time he had been composing *The Dolphin*, he had also been at work on the existent *Notebook*. Frank Bidart was brought over to England to help Lowell in what became the biggest publishing venture of the ageing author's career. By February 1972, Lowell and Bidart had turned the heavily revised *Notebook* into two further collections: *History* and *For Lizzie and Harriet*.

History was a reorganization of the more public and historical poems of *Notebook* into chronological order, augmented with a good many adaptations of pieces from the earlier books. The more personal poems of *Notebook* had been siphoned off and put into *For Lizzie and Harriet*. *The Dolphin* consisted of new poems, something after the notion behind Lawrence's cycle, *Look! We Have Come Through!*. It told the story of Lowell's liaison with Caroline Blackwood, the birth of their son, and their imminent marriage, which took place in October 1972. These poems included adaptations of several letters that Elizabeth Hardwick had sent. All three volumes were published in July 1973.

The achievement was hardly commensurate with the effort that had gone into it. *History* exhales an atmosphere of fidgeting and revamping. None of the adaptations of earlier poems represents an improvement. This can be demonstrated by indicating what happens in revision to an imitation which originally appeared in *Lord Weary's Castle*. 'War', as it is called, derives from Rimbaud's poem 'Le Mal'. Like the version of 'Spleen' in *Imitations*, discussed in Chapter Five, it replaces statements with images. The poem begins 'Where basilisk and mortar lob their lead/Whistling against the cloud sheep overhead'. This is quite a way from 'Tandis que les crachats rouges de la mitraille/Sifflent tout le jour par l'infini du ciel bleu' which has been translated as 'While the red gobs of spit of the grape-shot whistle all day through the infinitude of blue sky' (Bernard, 102). Lowell's poem in *Lord Weary's Castle* escapes the clichés which too close a rendering of the original would be likely to involve. However, the revised text that appears in *Imitations* is not so tactful: 'All

day the red spit of the chain-shot tore/whistling across the infinite
blue sky'. This is hardly an improvement. 'Infinite blue sky' is the
sort of phrase that has been done to death by a succession of
English poets. A further revision in *History* takes us away from
the felt life of the early rendering without getting us any nearer to
Rimbaud: 'All day the red spit of the grapeshot smears/whistling
across the infinite blue sky'. What has happened is that the poet
reverts to the French original in the second revision, that of
Imitations, and then in *History* attempts to turn it into something
which would look like an original poem in English. But the text
as revised for *History* has all the faults found in the *Imitations*
version, without any of its advantages.

Lowell made many other attempts to revise his imitations.
Sometimes, in contradistinction to the poem just discussed, the
author departed from his original the more he revised it. But this
does not, any more than the converse process, make for improvement. 'Napoleon after Sedan' appears in *Imitations* and is
adapted from Rimbaud's 'Rages des Césars'. In Lowell's first
version, as in the original text by Rimbaud, the poem is a
character-piece describing Napoleon III as a prisoner held by the
Prussians. Subsequent revisions take away the emphasis from
Napoleon and in its stead build up a description of Rimbaud. The
piece becomes, in version after version, a poem about the man
who wrote the poem about Napoleon. In each case, revision
results in a loss of lucidity and causes the poem to become
abstract, even cerebral. Consider these excerpts from each
version:

> The man waxy – he jogs along the fields
> in flower, black, a cigar between his teeth.
> The wax man thinks about the Tuilleries
> in flower. At times his mossy eye takes fire.
>
> Twenty years of orgy have made him drunk:
> he'd said: 'My hand will snuff out Liberty,
> politely, gently, as I snuff my stogie.'
> Liberty lives; the Emperor is out –
> (*Imitations*)

One said the normal flow of my aesthetic
energies was to use the other direction:
I, Rimbaud, servant of France I saved . . .
I was looking for writing I could trust;
but the man was waxy, he jogged along the fields
flowering, a black cigar between his teeth.
His twenty years orgy had made him drunk,
a hand prepared to stub out liberty.
(*Notebook*)

(Rimbaud, the servant of the France he saved,
feared the predestined flow of his aesthetic
energies was to use the wrong direction;
he was looking for writing he needn't hate –)
Napoleon is waxy, and walks the barrack's unflowering
garden, a black cigar between his teeth . . .
a hand once able to stub out liberty.
(*History*)

The verse movement grows less certain with each revision; in that done for *History*, it is near collapse.

Sometimes chunks from earlier poems are hacked out for later volumes, often with scant regard for context. We have already seen how the *Notebook* version of 'In the Forties' was torn from the narrative of 'The Mills of the Kavanaughs'; in *History*, there is a version that is even more obscure. The *procédé* in the later book seems arbitrary. 'Caligula', a poem which appears in *For the Union Dead*, is cut down to fourteen lines as 'Caligula 2'. It is passed off in *History* with an inferior version of the 'Spleen' which had appeared in *Imitations* and which is now called 'Caligula 1'. The renderings of Horace's Odes, II 7 and I 37, stylistically forced as they may seem in *Near the Ocean*, are certainly not improved by being squashed into fourteen lines apiece for inclusion in *History* as, respectively, 'Pardon for a Friend' and 'Nunc est bibendum, Cleopatra's Death'. It is difficult to feel that *History* is any more than a ransacking of Lowell's previous work in order to produce – in monotonous fourteen-line units – a chronological account of mankind. There are better ways of writing history than this, and the effect upon the poetry is ruinous.

It is really too bad to find such poems from *Lord Weary's Castle* as 'Rebellion' and 'The Shako' bulldozed into sonnets: 'There was rebellion . . .' in *Notebook* and 'Before Waterloo' in *History*. The relatively few good poems in *For the Union Dead* such as 'Water' and 'Night Sweat' are similarly manhandled. But there is no inbuilt magic in fourteen unrhymed lines. *Life Studies* has a poem called 'The Banker's Daughter'; in *History* it is arbitrarily split into two sonnets and called 'The Wife of Henri Quatre'. The revision of 'Heine Dying in Paris', also in *History*, may take us nearer to the German text, but, in so doing, it suffers a diminution: 'God, how hatefully bitter it is to die,/how snugly one lives in this snug earthly nest!'. The romantic evocation of the earlier 'frail and green-juice', is brought down to a safe and dull 'snug'. Similarly, fine poems in *Imitations*, such as 'Meditation' and 'The Abyss', both founded on Baudelaire, are battered into jerky and inconsequential rhythms: 'Pascal's abyss moved with him as he moved –/all void, alas – activity, desires, words!'.

Sometimes *History* draws upon the same detail as the earlier books, without actually rewriting the poem. 'Charles the Fifth and the Peasant' (*Lord Weary's Castle*) is paralleled by 'Charles V by Titian'. 'Ford Madox Ford' and 'To Delmore Schwartz', both in *Life Studies*, are paralleled by 'Ford Madox Ford and Others' and 'In Dreams Begin Responsibilities', the latter with a title taken from one of Schwartz's stories. 'The Flaw' in *For the Union Dead* has a companion piece of similar title in *History*. There are many other instances, but in each one the later parallel is inferior. A representative contrast is that between the startling glimpse of Ford lecturing at Boulder, Colorado, 'mouth pushed out/fish-fashion, as if you gagged for air' and the knowing summary of a man's career, abridged to conform with the procedure of *History*, 'Ford could pick up talent from the flyspeck'. Over and over again, atmosphere is suppressed in favour of generalization which seems only on the surface to be epigrammatic. There is, in fact, little wit in *History*. The volume basically consists of poems shaped earlier, but now compressed into monotonous ranks of unrhymed sonnets.

For Lizzie and Harriet is composed of sixty-seven personal poems excavated from *Notebook*: the sequences 'Summer', 'Through the Night', 'The Charles River', 'Mexico', etc. The collection as a whole tells of a breaking marriage, but it is hard to say how it improves on *Life Studies*:

It's the injustice . . . he is so unjust –
whiskey-blind, swaggering home at five.
(' "To Speak of the Woe That is In Marriage" ', *Life Studies*)

By miracle, I left the party half
an hour behind you, reached home five hours drunker.
('New Year's Eve', *For Lizzie and Harriet*)

In the earlier poem, Lowell actively creates a situation: 'Whiskey-blind, swaggering home at five'. In the later poem, the situation is passively noted down: 'reached home, five hours drunker'. Lowell's verbal energy – that quality that made his earlier books so remarkable – seems to have deserted him.

The Dolphin, which came out simultaneously with *For Lizzie and Harriet*, comprises 104 love poems, none previously collected. Unlike the other two books, it is not hived off from the mother lode of *Notebook*. But this need not be a redeeming factor. Lowell was never at his best as a positive love poet, and these pieces are, on the whole, sentimental, and even religiose. Like so much of Lowell's later output, they are sonnets in form, and repose a good deal of faith in their capacity to achieve a memorable closing line. The crypto-epigram of *History* is seen here as a portentous gesture or, worse, pious hope: 'They told us by harshness to win the stars'; 'like God, I almost doubt if you exist'; 'we are weak enough to enter heaven'; 'my eyes have seen what my hand did'. It may be argued that these are last lines unsupported by context. But there is precious little context to support them. Odd realistic details may back up this thin, characterless stream of reverie, but they seem brought in irrelevantly, arbitrary in themselves and factitious in context:

The bathroom is a daub of daylight,
the beefy, flustered pigeons swish their quills –
in time the pigeons will forget the window;
I cannot – I, in flight without a ledge.
('Morning Blue')

The analogy is far-fetched; the more vivacious words – 'daub', 'beefy' – are imprecise; the workaday words that keep the poem going are flat.

What is true locally is true of the whole. The concept of the 'Caroline' figure as a dolphin is culled from a *Notebook* poem called 'Dawn', reprinted in *For Lizzie and Harriet*. But the image is used at once inconsistently and without development. *The Dolphin* is perhaps best read as jottings towards a love sequence not complete within its own covers. What comes over with relative strength is the intervention of 'Lizzie', in the shape of the poet's recasting of her letters and telephone calls. Elizabeth Hardwick had a tangible effect on Lowell's verse (Oberg, 42–43), and this is not surprising. She is a strong writer; her literary criticism as remarkable for its manner as its matter. One can discern a degree of overlap between Hardwick's essays on William James and on Boston culture on the one hand and, on the other, the title poem of *For the Union Dead*. There would probably have been more frequent overlaps in style had Lowell been more drawn to the subjects with which Hardwick tended to engage. Nevertheless, an extent of congruence is visible in such shared interests as the question of literary partnership: 'Before the bright fire at tea-time, we can see these high-strung men and women clinging together, their inky fingers touching' (Hardwick 1962, 188); 'Our writers often/marry writers, are true, bright, clashing' ('George Eliot'). The latter quotation comes from Lowell, but it would fit quite well into one of Hardwick's essays.

So, given the peculiar nature of the occasion, it seems natural for Lowell to incorporate letters from his estranged partner into his sequence about himself and his new fiancée. The following has been (Willis; Corcoran; Perloff 1980) admired: ' "Your student wrote me, if he took a plane/past Harvard, at any angle, at any height,/he'd see a person missing, *Mr. Robert Lowell*" ' ('In the Mail'). The procedure brought, however, some sharp comment from the critics. Adrienne Rich wrote 'The inclusion of the letter-poems stands as one of the most vindictive and mean-spirited acts in the history of poetry, one for which I can think of no precedent' (*American Poetry Review*, September–October 1973). The reply to such a stricture would seem to be that the inclusion of anything in a work of art is justifiable *if it is a work of art*. A controversy ensued, in which the poetry was defended on biographical rather than literary grounds: 'Elizabeth comes off in the completed reading as an intelligent, sensitive woman who's been done dirt' (Watterlond); 'it is the portrait of a noble person of great gifts, piercingly intelligent in anger' (Williamson 1973).

Tributes such as these could be multiplied, and it is open to question whether they are not recognitions of the capabilities (Willis) or magnificences (Wakoski 1974) of Hardwick's prose rather than the efficacy or otherwise of Lowell's verse.

We need not doubt that a problem lies here; and it is an extraordinary fact that movement towards a solution can be found in *The Dolphin* itself, rather than in the comment it aroused. A new tone is emerging; tentatively, perhaps, but through its very incertitude reaching towards a way out of five volumes and six years of compulsive sonneteering:

> are we so conscience-dark and cataract-blind,
> we only blame in others what they blame in us?
> (The sentence writes *we*, when charity wants *I* . . .)
> It takes such painful mellowing to use error . . .
> I have stood too long on a chair or ladder,
> branch-lightning forking through my thought and veins –
> I cannot hang my heavy picture straight.
> ('1.Summer Between Terms')

The pattern is that of iambic breakdown, pulled together by a formal iambic line such as the final one of the quotation above. Usually such a line will contain a strong negative element. In some of the later sonnets one sees the form, now found constrictive, in a state of collapse. '6. Facing Oneself' consists of five lines, the last of which is prose:

> After a day indoors I sometimes see
> my face in the shaving mirror looks as old,
> frail and distinguished as my photographs –
> as established. But it doesn't make one feel
> the temptation to try to be a Christian.

Without the rhyme-scheme, abandoned for the most part since the 'Harriet' sequence of 1967, the atrophy of metrical framework indicates a process of giving way to the remarkable free verse of the final collection.

Day by Day, unlike the relatively subdued *Notebook*, is unmistakable in diction and movement; nonetheless so for being a sustained confession of failure. It is full of images of death and impotence:

> Summer is like Hope
> to engrave free verse on bronze –
> in this room,
> the air is blocked by its walls;
> I cannot walk to old friends,
> as if there were doors.
> ('Lives')

That locution, 'I cannot', is a mannerism in the book, varying in persona, constant in its sense of helplessness: 'I cannot bring back youth with a snap of my belt,/I cannot touch you' ('Logan Airport, Boston'); 'She cannot cure his hallucinations/he can bribe or stare/any woman he wants into orgasm' ('Ear of Corn'); most memorably, 'They cannot stay awake,/and keep their own hours,/like degenerates/drinking the day in' and 'Age is the bilge/ we cannot shake from the mop' ('Ulysses and Circe').

'Ulysses and Circe' is one of the most impressive poems of the book. It opens with the two in bed, a scene that sacrifices none of the author's graphic qualities in its late summer glow. But the 'uxorious . . . waking' is overseen by Penelope, for whom all this is a cycle out of which the Ulysses figure is powerless to break: 'Ulysses circles . . . ten years to and ten years fro'. The poem gains poignance because of the inescapable casting of the central characters: Lowell as the Adventurer, Caroline as the Temptress, Elizabeth as his Wife. In that sense, 'Ulysses and Circe' is more truly a 'confessional poem' than many of the *Life Studies*. Elizabeth Hardwick had asked in one of her most searching essays how the work of Sylvia Plath would read to us if the poet had lived to finish more poems (Hardwick 1974, 119). In much the same manner, we have to ask how *Day by Day* would read if we knew that Lowell were alive and well, and back with his second wife in New York. There is no doubt that rhizome, our knowledge of the tentacular relationships in the background, is liable to inform our interpretation. The very title of the book, which echoes the advice a doctor gives a depressive, reflects the life back upon the text.

Apart from 'Ulysses and Circe', perhaps the most distinguished poem in the volume is 'The Downlook':

> Last summer nothing dared impede
> the flow of the body's thousand rivulets of welcome,

winding effortlessly, yet with ambiguous invention –
safety in nearness.

Now the downlook, the downlook – small fuss,
nothing that could earn a line or picture
in the responsible daily paper we'll be reading,
an anthology of the unredeemable world . . .

Without any background knowledge, we should be able to see
that a relationship is coming to a term. But, given its placing near
the end of this volume and the biographical information impossible to keep from the reader, this, too, is a confessional poem. It
is limited by that description: clearly the liaison of 'Ulysses' and
'Circe' is coming apart. The confessional description also defines
the mode: it is poignant, as some of the earlier pieces are, but it
lacks the dramatic quality of *Life Studies* and *Imitations*. 'There's
no greater happiness in days of the downlook/than to turn back
to recapture former joy': these are retrospective poems, and they
enumerate old themes. Lowell revisits Phillips House, where his
grandfather died, and finds himself with a sharpened sense of
inferiority. He recalls his school, 'St. Mark's, 1933', and includes
insults left out of previous reminiscences: we now discover to
whom the adjective 'dimbulb', found in the earlier poem 'During
Fever', was first applied. The elder Mrs Lowell comes alive
again, at once ('To Mother') more human than her son had
thought her, and also ('Unwanted') more stupid. The poet
invokes his father ('Robert T. S. Lowell') and finds him, not the
failure described in 'Commander Lowell', but an *alter ego*: 'it's
your life, and dated like mine'. A former wife reappears ('Jean
Stafford, a Letter'); an image of his lost faith ('Home'). His most
formidable contemporary, now dead ('John Berryman'), turns
out to be an ikon: 'To my surprise, John,/I pray *to* not for you'.
This is a world of visitations, reminiscences, and failing health. In
hospital, we find Lowell drafting a poem on suicide: ' "When the
trees close branches and redden,/their winter skeletons are hard
to find" ' ('Notice'). These lines seem familiar, and we remember
that we saw them some 106 pages earlier, in a poem actually
called 'Suicide'. It is, however, a rejection of that way out, taken
though it was by so many of Lowell's acquaintances, including
Berryman himself.

In *Day by Day* we have an artistry devoted to decline. Yet
there is no decline in the artistry; rather, a rallying of resources.

However, not all the former force revived: there is, compared with the middle-period books, an etiolation, a narrowing of range. Lowell describes his poems as drab tapes that play back his own voice to him ('George III'); yet they are not drab to the reader. He complains that he can only tell his own story, 'talking to myself' ('Unwanted'); the reader overhears him, and is fascinated. The final poem gives the clue to the book: 'Pray for the grace of accuracy/Vermeer gave to the sun's illumination/ stealing like the tide across a map/to his girl solid with yearning' ('Epilogue'). If, as has been suggested (Deese, 186), *Woman in Blue Reading a Letter* is what Lowell had in mind, the parallel is just. We do not know the contents of the letter in Vermeer's painting, but the woman's solid presence in the light flowing through the window is unmistakable. So it is with Lowell's life. Why it was lived as it was remains a mystery, but the seventeen books he refined from his torment stand as the most distinguished *oeuvre* of the American half-century: 'We are poor passing facts,/ warned by that to give/each figure in the photographs/his living name'. Lowell's titles are more than ordinarily evocative: *Life Studies, Imitations*, 'Water', 'The Well', and, in this final collection, 'Shadow', 'Shifting Colors', 'The Downlook'. In 'Epilogue' he comments ruefully on his own 'blessèd structures, plot and rhyme'.

It would have been easy to write a study of Lowell as a confessional poet, using his verse to illuminate his life. After all, these final poems are confessional. But such an approach would have taken no account of what is positive: the character of the rhythm, the colour of the language, what he himself calls 'a humor for myself in images'. Lowell died on 12 September 1977, in the back of a New York taxi-cab taking him from Kennedy Airport to the flat on West 67th Street where he had lived with Elizabeth Hardwick. Perhaps the poem 'Ulysses and Circe' had proved prophetic: 'Ulysses circles . . ./She sees no feat/in his flight or his flight back'. The poet's heart gave out, enlarged by amateurishly self-administered lithium, exacerbated by alcohol, nicotine, and stress.

One could query whether the stress Lowell put himself through, and through which he put others, was justified by the poetry. But that is the wrong question to ask. Rather we should marvel that such an afflicted life could produce so much of value. Lowell seems to have inherited an unstable ego, partly as a result of the 'Spence negligence', which we would now call bipolar disorder. But being brought up in the framework of a loveless marriage, under the shadow of a Boston aristocracy, could not have helped. Lowell, however, long before the lithium treatment, found his own therapy. He developed his superb verbal gifts to create an area of his own. He evolved with a self-renewing power that enabled him to establish his fluctuating ego as a real presence in other people's lives. His life studies extended beyond his family, and yet were of it. One thinks of Jonathan Edwards, Anne Kavanaugh, Mother Marie Therese, the old man falling asleep over the *Aeneid*; the grandson, son, husband, father of *Life Studies* itself; Villon, Heine, Baudelaire, Rimbaud, in *Imitations*. The poet's face varies, apparently, from character to character. It is only when we peer further that we recognize the dissolving lineaments behind as a dispensable mask.

Acknowledgments

Acknowledgment is made to the following for permission to use copyright material:

Excerpts from 'The Dandelion Girls', 'The Cities' Summer Death', 'Death from Cancer', 'Death from Cancer on Easter', 'A Prayer for my Grandfather to Our Lady', copyright © 1988 by the Estate of Robert Lowell, reprinted by permission of the Estate of Robert Lowell and Farrar, Straus and Giroux, Inc., New York. Extracts from *Lord Weary's Castle*, copyright 1946, 1974 by Robert Lowell, reprinted by permission of Harcourt Brace Jovanovich, Inc., Orlando, Florida; these extracts included in *Poems 1938–1949* by Robert Lowell, reprinted with the permission of Faber and Faber Ltd, London. Extracts from *The Mills of the Kavanaughs*, copyright 1951 by Robert Lowell, renewed 1979 by Harriet W. Lowell, reprinted by permission of Harcourt Brace Jovanovich, Inc., Orlando, Florida; these extracts contained, except for the title-poem, in *Poems 1938–1949* by Robert Lowell, reprinted with the permission of Faber and Faber Ltd, London; title-poem included in *Robert Lowell: The First Twenty Years* by Hugh B. Staples, reprinted with the permission of Faber and Faber Ltd, London. Excerpts from *Life Studies* by Robert Lowell, copyright © 1956, 1959 by Robert Lowell, used by permission of Farrar, Straus and Giroux, Inc., New York, and Faber and Faber Ltd, London. Excerpts from *Imitations* by Robert Lowell, copyright © 1958, 1959, 1960, 1961 by Robert Lowell, used by permission of Farrar, Straus and Giroux Inc., New York, and Faber and Faber Ltd, London. Excerpts from *Phaedra* and *Figaro* by Robert Lowell and Jacques Barzun, copyright © 1960, 1961 by Robert Lowell, used by permission of Farrar, Straus and Giroux Inc., New York, and Faber and Faber Ltd, London. Excerpts from *For the Union Dead* by Robert Lowell, copyright © 1960, 1961, 1962, 1963, 1964 by Robert Lowell, used by permission of Farrar, Straus and Giroux Inc., New York, and Faber and Faber Ltd, London. Excerpts from 'My Kinsman, Major Molineux' from *The Old Glory* by Robert Lowell, copyright © 1945, 1965 by Robert Lowell, used by permission of Farrar, Straus and Giroux Inc., New York, and Faber and Faber Ltd, London. Excerpts from *Near the Ocean* by Robert Lowell, copyright © 1967 by Robert Lowell, used by permission of Farrar, Straus and Giroux Inc., New York, and Faber and Faber Ltd, London. Excerpts from *Prometheus Bound* by Robert Lowell, copyright © 1967, 1969 by Robert Lowell, used by permission of Farrar, Straus and Giroux Inc., New York, and Faber and Faber Ltd, London. Excerpts from *Notebook 1967–68* by Robert Lowell, copyright © 1967, 1968, 1969 by Robert Lowell, used by permission of Farrar,

Straus and Giroux Inc., New York. Excerpts from *Notebook* by Robert Lowell, copyright © 1967, 1968, 1969, 1970 by Robert Lowell, used by permission of Farrar, Straus and Giroux Inc., New York, and Faber and Faber Ltd, London. Excerpts from *History* by Robert Lowell, copyright © 1967, 1968, 1969, 1970, 1973 by Robert Lowell, used by permission of Farrar, Straus and Giroux Inc., New York, and Faber and Faber Ltd, London. Excerpts from *For Lizzie and Harriet* by Robert Lowell, copyright © 1973 by Robert Lowell, used by permission of Farrar, Straus and Giroux Inc., New York, and Faber and Faber Ltd, London. Excerpts from *The Dolphin* by Robert Lowell, copyright © 1973 by Robert Lowell, used by permission of Farrar, Straus and Giroux Inc., New York, and Faber and Faber Ltd, London. Excerpts from *Day by Day* by Robert Lowell, copyright © 1975, 1976, 1977 by Robert Lowell, used by permission of Farrar, Straus and Giroux, Inc., New York, and Faber and Faber Ltd, London. Excerpts from *The Oresteia* by Robert Lowell, copyright © 1978 by Robert Silvers and State Street Bank and Trust Company, used by permission of Farrar, Straus and Giroux Inc., New York, and Faber and Faber Ltd, London. Excerpt from *Collected Prose* by Robert Lowell, copyright © 1987 by Caroline Lowell, Harriet Lowell, Sheridan Lowell, reprinted by permission of Farrar, Straus and Giroux Inc., New York, and Faber and Faber Ltd, London. Excerpt from *His Toy, His Dream, His Rest* by John Berryman, copyright © 1964, 1965, 1966, 1967, 1968 by John Berryman, reprinted by permission of Farrar, Straus and Giroux Inc., New York, and Faber and Faber Ltd, London. Excerpt from *The Complete Poems 1927–1979* by Elizabeth Bishop, copyright © 1983 by Alice Helen Methfessel, copyright © 1957 by Elizabeth Bishop, reprinted by permission of Farrar, Straus and Giroux Inc., New York, and Chatto & Windus Ltd, London. Extract from *Catullus, Tibullus, Pervigilium Veneris*, edited and translated by F. W. Cornish and J. P. Postgate (1913, rep. and rev. 1968), used by permission of Harvard University Press, Cambridge, Mass. and Heinemann Ltd, London. Extract from *The Mystical Theology of Saint Bernard* by Étienne Gilson used by permission of Sheed and Ward Ltd, London. Extract from *Field Work*, copyright © 1979 by Seamus Heaney, used by permission of the author, Farrar, Straus and Giroux Inc., New York, and Faber and Faber Ltd, London. Extract from 'Violence in Poetry: a discussion edited by Philip Hobsbaum' used by permission of George MacBeth. Extract from *The Nightmare Factory* by Maxine Kumin (1970) used by permission of Harper & Row, Publishers, Inc., New York. Extract from *Ariel* by Sylvia Plath (1965) used by permission of Harper & Row, Publishers, Inc., and Faber and Faber Ltd, London. Extract from *All My Pretty Ones*, copyright © 1962 by Anne Sexton, reprinted by permission of Houghton Mifflin Company, Boston. Extract from *Nostalgia for the Present* by Andrei Voznesensky (1980) used by permission of Oxford University Press.

Bibliographical References

BOOKS BY ROBERT LOWELL

LAND OF UNLIKENESS (Cummington, Mass. 1944; partly contained in *Poems 1938–49*, London 1950)

LORD WEARY'S CASTLE (New York 1946; contained in *Poems 1938–49*, London 1950)

THE MILLS OF THE KAVANAUGHS (New York 1951; contained, except for the title-poem, in *Poems 1938–49*, London 1950; title-poem included in *Robert Lowell: The First Twenty Years* by Hugh B. Staples, London 1962)

LIFE STUDIES (New York 1959; London, except for '91 Revere Street', 1959)

IMITATIONS (New York 1961; London 1962)

PHAEDRA (New York 1961; London 1963)

FOR THE UNION DEAD (New York 1964; London 1965)

THE OLD GLORY (New York 1964, rev. 1968; London 1973)

NEAR THE OCEAN (New York and London 1967)

PROMETHEUS BOUND (New York 1969; London 1970)

NOTEBOOK 1967–68 (New York 1969)

NOTEBOOK (New York and London 1970)

HISTORY (New York and London 1973)

FOR LIZZIE AND HARRIET (New York and London 1973)

THE DOLPHIN (New York and London 1973)

DAY BY DAY (New York 1977; London 1978)

THE ORESTEIA OF AESCHYLUS (New York 1978; London 1979)

CRITICISM

Collections of articles by several hands:

ANZILOTTI — Rolando Anzilotti (ed.), *Robert Lowell: A Tribute* (Pisa 1979)

AXELROD AND DEESE 1986 — Steven Gould Axelrod and Helen Deese (eds.), *Robert Lowell: Essays on the Poetry* (Cambridge, England 1986)

LONDON AND BOYERS — Michael London and Robert Boyers (eds.), *Robert Lowell: A Portrait of the Artist in his Time* (New York 1970)

MAZZARO 1971 — Jerome Mazzaro (ed.), *Profile of Robert Lowell* (Columbus, Ohio 1971)

OSTROFF — Anthony Ostroff (ed.), *The Contemporary Poet as Artist and Critic* (Boston, Mass. and Toronto 1964)

PARKINSON — Thomas Parkinson (ed.), *Robert Lowell: A Collection of Critical Essays* (Englewood Cliffs, N. J. 1968)

PRICE — Jonathan Price (ed.), *Critics on Robert Lowell* (Miami, Florida 1972 and London 1974)

Books and Publications in periodicals:

AIKEN — Conrad Aiken, 'Varieties of Poetic Statement', *New Republic* III (23 October 1944; reviewing *Land of Unlikeness*), rep. *A Reviewer's ABC: Collected Criticism of Conrad Aiken from 1916 to the present*, Rufus A. Blanshard (ed.), (London 1961)

AKEY — John Akey, 'Lowell's "After the Surprising Conversions" ', *Explicator* IX (June 1951)

ALVAREZ — A. Alvarez, 'Something New in Verse', *The Observer* (London, 12 April 1959; reviewing *Life Studies*)

ANZILOTTI 1979 — Rolando Anzilotti, 'Translating Lowell' (in Anzilotti, above)

AXELROD 1971 — Steven Gould Axelrod, 'Baudelaire and the Poetry of Robert Lowell', *Twentieth Century Literature* 17 (October 1971)

AXELROD 1978 — Steven Gould Axelrod, *Robert Lowell: Life and Art* (Princeton, N. J. 1978)

AXELROD AND DEESE 1982 — Steven Gould Axelrod and Helen Deese, *Robert Lowell: a Reference Guide* (Boston, Mass. 1982)

BAKER — Mary Jane Baker, 'Classes with a Poet', *Mademoiselle* (November 1954)

BARO — Gene Baro, 'New Richness from an American Poet', *New York Herald Tribune Book Review* (22 April 1951; reviewing *The Mills of the Kavanaughs*)

BAUMEL — Judith Baumel, 'Robert Lowell: The Teacher', *Harvard Advocate* CXIII (November 1979)

BELITT — Ben Belitt, *Adam's Dream: A Preface to Translation* (New York 1978)

BELL — Vereen M. Bell, *Robert Lowell: Nihilist as Hero* (Cambridge, Mass. 1983)

BENNETT — Joseph Bennett, 'Two Americans, A Brahmin, and the Bourgeoisie', *Hudson Review* XII (Autumn 1959; reviewing *Life Studies*; in London and Boyers, above)

BENTLEY — Eric Bentley, 'Comment' (on *Phaedra*), *Kenyon Review* 24 (Winter 1962)

BERRYMAN 1947 — John Berryman, 'Lowell, Thomas etc.', *Partisan Review* 14 (January–February 1947), rep. as 'Robert Lowell and Others', *The Freedom of the Poet* (New York 1976; reviewing *Lord Weary's Castle*)

BERRYMAN 1964 — John Berryman, 'Despondency and Madness: On Lowell's "Skunk Hour" ' (in Ostroff, and Parkinson, above), rep. *The Freedom of the Poet* (New York 1976)

BEWLEY — Marius Bewley, 'Aspects of Modern American Poetry', *Scrutiny* 17 (March 1951), rep. in rev. version *The Complex Fate* (London 1952; in London and Boyers, above)

BIDART — Frank Bidart, 'A Note on the Text' in *The Oresteia of Aeschylus* by Robert Lowell (New York 1978; London 1979)

BLACKMUR — R. P. Blackmur, 'Notes on Eleven Poets', *Kenyon Review* 7 (Spring 1945; reviewing *Land of Unlikeness*), rep. as 'Notes on Seven Poets', *Language as Gesture: Essays on Poetry* (London 1954; in Parkinson, above)

BRANSCOMB — Jack Branscomb, 'Robert Lowell's Painters: Two Sources', *English Language Notes* 15 (December 1977)

BROMWICH — David Bromwich, 'Reading Robert Lowell', *Commentary* 52 (August 1971; reviewing *Notebook*)

BRUSTEIN — Robert Brustein, 'Introduction' to *The Old Glory* by Robert Lowell (New York 1964; in London and Boyers, and Price, above)

BURNS — Gerald Burns, 'What to Make of an Unfinished Thing', *Southwest Review* 56 (Spring 1971; reviewing *Notebook*)

CARNE-ROSS — Donald Carne-Ross, 'The Two Voices of Translation' (in Parkinson, above)

CARRUTH 1962 — Hayden Carruth, ' "Towards, Not Away From": *Imitations* by Robert Lowell', *Poetry* 100 (April 1962)

CARRUTH 1967 — Hayden Carruth, 'A Meaning of Robert Lowell', *Hudson Review* XX (Autumn 1967; reviewing *Near the Ocean*; in London and Boyers, above)

CHADWICK — C. Chadwick, 'Meaning and Tone', *Essays in Criticism* 13 (October 1963; note on *Imitations*; in Price, above)

CHAMBERS — Barry Chambers, *Robert Lowell* (Milton Keynes 1976)

CLARK — Blair Clark, 'On Robert Lowell', *Harvard Advocate* CXIII (November 1979)

COOPER — Philip Cooper, *The Autobiographical Myth of Robert Lowell* (Chapel Hill, N. C. 1970)

CORCORAN — Neil Corcoran, 'Lowell Retiarius: Towards *The Dolphin*', *Agenda* 18 (Autumn 1980)

COSGRAVE — Patrick Cosgrave, *The Public Poetry of Robert Lowell* (New York 1970)

CRICK — J. F. Crick, *Robert Lowell* (Edinburgh 1974)

CRUTTWELL — Patrick Cruttwell, 'Six *Phaedras* in Search of One *Phèdre*', *Delos* 2 (1968)

DAVIE — Donald Davie, '*Life Studies* by Robert Lowell', *Granta* LXIV (17 October 1959)

DEESE — Helen Deese, 'Lowell and the Visual Arts' (in Axelrod and Deese 1986, above)

DUBROW — Heather Dubrow, 'The Marine in the Garden: Pastoral Elements in Lowell's "Quaker Graveyard"', *Philological Quarterly* (Spring 1983)

EBERHART 1947 — Richard Eberhart, 'Four Poets', *Sewanee Review* LV (Spring 1947; reviewing *Lord Weary's Castle*; in Parkinson, above)

EBERHART 1952 — Richard Eberhart, 'Five Poets' *Kenyon Review* 14 (Winter 1952; reviewing *The Mills of the Kavanaughs*; in London and Boyers, above)

EBERHART 1959 — Richard Eberhart, 'A Poet's People', *New York Times Book Review* (3 May 1959; reviewing *Life Studies*)

EHRENPREIS — Irvin Ehrenpreis, 'The Age of Lowell', *American Poetry*: *Stratford upon Avon Studies* 7, John Russell Brown and Bernard Harris (eds.), (London 1965; in Parkinson, and Price, above)

EULERT — Donald Eulert, 'Robert Lowell and W. C. Williams: Sterility in "Central Park"', *English Language Notes* 5 (December 1967)

FEIN — Richard J. Fein, *Robert Lowell* (2nd edition; Boston, Mass. 1979)

FENDER — Stephen Fender, 'What Really Happened to Warren Winslow?', *Journal of American Studies* 7 (August 1973)

FITTS — Dudley Fitts, '*The Mills of the Kavanaughs*', *Furioso* VI (Fall 1951; in Mazzaro 1971, above)

FRASER — G. S. Fraser, 'Amid the Horror, a Song of Praise', *New York Times Book Review* (4 October 1964; reviewing *For the Union Dead*; in Mazzaro 1971, above)

GIFFORD — Henry Gifford, '*Imitations* by Robert Lowell', *Critical Quarterly* 5 (Spring 1963)

HAMILTON — Ian Hamilton, *Robert Lowell: A Biography* (London 1983)

HECHT — Roger Hecht, 'Rilke in Translation', *Sewanee Review* 71 (Summer 1963)

HERRNSTEIN SMITH — Barbara Herrnstein Smith, *Poetic Closure: A Study of How Poems End* (Chicago 1968)

HEYMANN — C. David Heymann, *American Aristocracy: The Life and Times of James Russell, Amy and Robert Lowell* (New York 1980)

HILL — Geoffrey Hill, 'Robert Lowell: "Contrasts and Repetitions"', *Essays in Criticism* 13 (April 1963; in Price, above)

HOBSBAUM 1976 — Philip Hobsbaum, 'Robert Lowell: The Mask Behind The Face', *Lines Review* 58 (June 1976)

HOBSBAUM 1985 — Philip Hobsbaum, '"Lycidas": The Sonic Boomerang', *Words* 1 (June 1985)

HOBSBAUM 1986 — Philip Hobsbaum, 'Eliot, Lowell and the New Critics', *Studies in Modern English and American Poetry: a Festschrift on the Sixtieth Birthday of Professor Chi-gyu Kim*, The Festschrift Committee (eds.), (Seoul 1986)

HOFFMAN — Daniel Hoffman, 'Robert Lowell's *Near the Ocean*: The Greatness and Horror of Empire', *The Hollins Critic* IV (February 1967)

HOLDER — Alan Holder, *The Imagined Past: Portrayals of Our History in Modern American Literature* (London and Toronto 1980)

HOWARD 1964 — Richard Howard, 'Voice of a Survivor', *Nation* 199 (26 October 1964; reviewing *For the Union Dead*)

HOWARD 1967 — Richard Howard,

'Fuel on the Fire', *Poetry* 110 (September 1967 ; reviewing *Near the Ocean*)

HUDSON — Derek Hudson, 'Blunden versus Lowell', *Spectator* 206 (4 February 1966)

JARRELL 1985 — Mary Jarrell (ed.), *Randall Jarrell's Letters: An Autobiographical and Literary Selection* (London 1986)

JARRELL 1945 — Randall Jarrell, 'Poetry in War and Peace', *Partisan Review* 12 (Winter 1945), rep. *Kipling, Auden & Co.: Essays and Reviews 1935–64* (New York 1980; Manchester 1986; reviewing *Land of Unlikeness*)

JARRELL 1947 — Randall Jarrell, 'From the Kingdom of Necessity', *Nation* 164 (18 January 1947), rep. *Poetry and the Age* (London 1955; reviewing *Lord Weary's Castle*; in London and Boyers, Parkinson, and Price, above)

JARRELL 1951 — Randall Jarrell, 'A View of Three Poets', *Partisan Review* 18 (November–December 1951), rep. as 'Three Books', *Poetry and the Age* (London 1955; reviewing *The Mills of the Kavanaughs*; in Parkinson, above)

KAVANAGH — Paul Kavanagh, 'The Nation Past and Present: a Study of Robert Lowell's "For the Union Dead" ', *Journal of American Studies* 5 (1971)

KERMODE — Frank Kermode, 'Talent and More', *Spectator* 202 (1 May 1959; reviewing *Life Studies*)

LANE — Lauriat Lane, Jr., 'Robert Lowell: the Problems and Power of Allusion', *Dalhousie Review* 60 (Winter 1980–81)

LARKIN — Philip Larkin, 'Collected Poems', *Manchester Guardian Weekly* (21 May 1959; reviewing *Life Studies*)

LEIBOWITZ — Herbert Leibowitz, 'The Muse and the News', *Hudson Review* 22 (August 1969; reviewing *Notebook 1967–68*)

LOWELL 1943 — Robert Lowell, 'A Review of *Four Quartets*', *Sewanee Review* 51 (Summer 1943; in Lowell 1987, below)

LOWELL 1944 — Robert Lowell, 'A Note' (on Gerard Manley Hopkins), *Kenyon Review* 6 (Autumn 1944), rep. as 'Hopkins's Sanctity' in *Gerard Manley Hopkins* by The Kenyon Critics (New York 1945; in Lowell 1987, below)

LOWELL 1946 — Robert Lowell, 'Current Poetry', *Sewanee Review* 54 (Winter 1946; reviewing Edmund Blunden)

LOWELL 1959 — Robert Lowell, 'Visiting the Tates', *Sewanee Review* 67 (Autumn 1959; in Lowell 1987, below)

LOWELL 1961A — Robert Lowell, 'An Interview with Frederick Seidel', *Paris Review* (Winter–Spring 1961), rep. *Writers at Work*, Second Series, Malcolm Cowley (ed.), (New York 1963); also *Modern Poets on Modern Poetry*, James Scully (ed.), (London 1966; in London and Boyers, and Parkinson, above, and Lowell 1987, below)

LOWELL 1961B — Robert Lowell, 'William Carlos Williams', *Hudson Review* 14 (Winter 1961–62), rep. *William Carlos Williams: A Collection of Critical Essays*, J. Hillis Miller (ed.), (Englewood Cliffs, N. J. 1966; in Lowell 1987, below)

LOWELL 1963 — Robert Lowell, 'In Conversation with A. Alvarez', *Observer* (21 July 1963; in Mazzaro 1971, above, and Lowell 1987, below)

LOWELL 1964A — Robert Lowell, 'On Robert Lowell's "Skunk Hour" ' (in Ostroff, above, and Lowell 1987, below)

LOWELL 1964B — Robert Lowell, 'Talk with Robert Lowell' (by Stanley Kunitz), *New York Times Book Review* (October 4 1964; in Mazzaro 1971, above)

LOWELL 1966 — Robert Lowell, 'On Two Poets' (Ford Madox Ford and Sylvia Plath), *New York Review of Books* (12 May 1966; in Lowell 1987, below)

LOWELL 1967 — Robert Lowell, 'Randall Jarrell, 1914–1965: An Appreciation' in *The Lost World* by Randall Jarrell (New York 1966) and *Randall Jarrell 1914–1965*, Robert Lowell, Peter Taylor and Robert Penn Warren (eds.),

(New York 1967; in Lowell 1987, below)

LOWELL 1968A — Robert Lowell, *The Voyage and other versions of poems by Charles Baudelaire*, illustrated by Sidney Nolan (New York 1968)

LOWELL 1968B — Robert Lowell, 'Conversation with Robert Lowell' (by D. S. Carne-Ross), *Delos* I (1968; in Mazzaro 1971, above)

LOWELL 1987 — Robert Lowell, *Collected Prose*, Robert Giroux (ed.), (New York and London 1987)

LUCIE-SMITH 1959 — Edward Lucie-Smith, 'A Boston Brahmin', *Gemini* 2 (Autumn 1959; reviewing *Life Studies*)

LUCIE-SMITH 1966 — Edward Lucie-Smith, 'An Address to the Electors of Oxford', *Spectator* 206 (28 January 1966)

LUCIE-SMITH AND PORTER — Edward Lucie-Smith and Peter Porter, 'Talent and More' (letter about *Life Studies*), *Spectator* 202 (15 May 1959)

MACCAIG — Norman MacCaig, 'Poetry', *Saltire Review* 6 (Autumn 1959; reviewing *Life Studies*)

McCALL — Dan McCall, 'Robert Lowell's "Hawthorne" ', *New England Quarterly* XXXIX (June 1966)

McFADDEN — George McFadden, ' "Life Studies" – Robert Lowell's Comic Breakthrough', *PMLA* 90 (January 1975)

McLACHLAN — W. I. McLachlan, 'The Problem of Understanding: Structure and Image in Robert Lowell's Imitations of Rimbaud', *Australian Universities' Language and Literature Association: Proceedings and Papers of the Twelfth Congress* (1969)

MARTIN — Jay Martin, *Robert Lowell* (Minneapolis 1970)

MAZZARO 1965 — Jerome Mazzaro, *The Poetic Themes of Robert Lowell* (Ann Arbor, Michigan 1965)

MAZZARO 1969 — Jerome Mazzaro, 'Robert Lowell and the Kavanaugh Collapse', *University of Windsor Review* V (Fall 1969)

MAZZARO 1973 — Jerome Mazzaro, '*Imitations*', *American Poetry Review* II (September 1973)

MILLER — Jonathan Miller, 'Director's Note', *The Old Glory* by Robert Lowell (London 1966)

MIZENER — Arthur Mizener, 'Recent Poetry', *Accent* I (Winter 1945; reviewing *Land of Unlikeness*)

MOORE 1977 — Andy J. Moore, 'Frost – and Lowell – at Midnight', *The Southern Quarterly* (USA) 15 (April 1977)

MOORE 1973 — Stephen Moore, 'Politics and the Poetry of Robert Lowell', *Georgia Review* 27 (Summer 1973)

MOSS — Howard Moss, 'Ten Poets', *Kenyon Review* 9 (Spring 1947; reviewing *Lord Weary's Castle*)

NIMS — John Frederick Nims, 'On Robert Lowell's "Skunk Hour" ' (in Ostroff, above)

OBERG — Arthur Oberg, *Modern American Lyric: Lowell, Berryman, Creeley, and Plath* (New Brunswick, N. J. 1978)

O'CONNOR — Flannery O'Connor, *The Habit of Being: Letters*, Sally Fitzgerald (ed.), (New York 1979)

PEARCE — Roy Harvey Pearce, 'Lowell's "After the Surprising Conversions" ', *Explicator* IX (June 1951)

PEARSON — Gabriel Pearson, 'Robert Lowell', *The Review* 20 (March 1969), rep. as 'Lowell's Marble Meanings', *The Survival of Poetry*, Martin Dodsworth (ed.), (London 1970); last half, *Contemporary Poetry in America*, Robert Boyers (ed.), (New York 1974)

PERLOFF 1973 — Marjorie G. Perloff, *The Poetic Art of Robert Lowell* (Ithaca and London 1973)

PERLOFF 1980 — Marjorie G. Perloff, 'Robert Lowell's Last Poems', *Agenda* 18 (Autumn 1980)

PHILLIPS — Robert Phillips, *The Confessional Poets* (Carbondale and Edwardsville, Southern Illinois 1973)

PRAMPOLINI — Gaetano Prampolini, 'Robert Lowell's Dante' (in Anzilotti, above)

PROCOPIOW 1976 — Norma Procopiow, 'William Carlos Williams and the Origin of the Confessional Poem', *Ariel* 7 (April 1976)

PROCOPIOW 1984 — Norma Procopiow,

Robert Lowell: The Poet and his Critics (Chicago 1984)

RAFFEL 1980 — Burton Raffel, 'Robert Lowell's *Imitations*', *Translation Review* 5 (Summer 1980)

RAFFEL 1981 — Burton Raffel, *Robert Lowell* (New York 1981)

RANSOM — John Crowe Ransom, 'A Look Backward and a Note of Hope', *Harvard Advocate* XCIV (November 1961)

REEVES — James Reeves, 'Blunden versus Lowell', *Spectator* 206 (4 February 1966)

RICH — Adrienne Rich, 'Caryatid: A Column', *American Poetry Review* II (September–October 1973; remarks on *The Dolphin*)

RICKS — Christopher Ricks, 'The Three Lives of Robert Lowell', *New Statesman* (26 March 1965; in Price, above)

RIZZARDI — Alfredo Rizzardi, 'Robert Lowell's Imitations of Italian Poetry' (in Anzilotti, above)

ROLLINS 1979A — J. Barton Rollins, 'An Early Version of Lowell's "The Drunken Fisherman" ', *Notes on Modern American Literature* 3 (1979)

ROLLINS 1979B — J. Barton Rollins, 'Young Robert Lowell's Poetics of Revision', *Journal of Modern Literature* 7 (September 1979)

ROSENTHAL — M. L. Rosenthal, 'Poetry as Confession', *Nation* 190 (19 September 1959), rev. and rep. *The Modern Poets* (New York 1960; reviewing *Life Studies*; in Price, and, rev. version, London and Boyers, and Parkinson, above)

RUDMAN — Mark Rudman, *Robert Lowell: An Introduction to the Poetry* (New York 1985)

SIMON — John Simon, 'Abuse of Privilege: Lowell as Translator', *Hudson Review* 20 (Winter 1967–68; in London and Boyers, above)

SIMPSON — Eileen Simpson, *Poets in their Youth: A Memoir* (London 1982, rep. 1984)

SMITH — Vivian Smith, *The Poetry of Robert Lowell* (Sydney 1974)

STANDERWICK — DeSales Standerwick, 'Pieces too Personal', *Renascence* XIII (Autumn 1960; reviewing *Life Studies*; in Mazzaro 1971, and

Price, above)

STAPLES — Hugh B. Staples, *Robert Lowell: The First Twenty Years* (London 1962)

SWALLOW — Alan Swallow, 'A Review of Some Recent Poetry', *New Mexico Quarterly Review* 15 (Spring 1945; reviewing *Land of Unlikeness*)

TATE 1944 — Allen Tate, Preface to *Land of Unlikeness* by Robert Lowell (Cummington, Mass. 1944), rep. *The Poetry Reviews of Allen Tate*, Ashley Brown and Frances Neel Cheney (eds.), (Baton Rouge, Louisiana and London 1983; in London and Boyers, Parkinson, and Price, above)

TILLINGHAST — Richard Tillinghast, 'Robert Lowell in the Sixties', *Harvard Advocate* CXIII (November 1979)

TOMLINSON — Charles Tomlinson, 'Recent American Verse', *Listen* 3 (Spring 1960; reviewing *Life Studies*)

VENDLER — Helen Vendler, 'Lowell in the Classroom', *Harvard Advocate* CXIII (November 1979)

WAKOSKI 1974 — Diane Wakoski, 'The Craft of Carpenters, Plumbers, & Mechanics: A Column', *American Poetry Review* III (January–February 1974; remarks on *The Dolphin*)

WATTERLOND — Michael Watterlond, 'All that Grandeur of Imperfection', *Works* 4 (Summer 1974; reviewing *The Dolphin*)

WEALES — Gerald Weales, 'Robert Lowell as a Dramatist', *Shenandoah* 20 (Autumn 1968)

WHITTEMORE — Reed Whittemore, 'Packing Up for Devil's Island', *Kenyon Review* 24 (Spring 1962; reviewing *Imitations*)

WILLIAMS — William Carlos Williams, 'In a Mood of Tragedy', *New York Times Book Review* (22 April 1951), rep. *Selected Essays of William Carlos Williams* (New York 1954; reviewing *The Mills of the Kavanaughs*; in London and Boyers, Parkinson, and Price, above)

WILLIAMSON 1973 — Alan Williamson, Letter (on 'The Dolphin'),

American Poetry Review 2
(November–December 1973)
WILLIAMSON 1974 — Alan Williamson,
*Pity the Monsters: The Political
Vision of Robert Lowell* (New
Haven, Conn. and London
1974)
WILLIAMSON 1979 — Alan Williamson,

'A Reminiscence', *Harvard
Advocate* CXIII (November 1979)
WILLIS — G. D. Willis, 'Afloat on
Lowell's *Dolphin'*, *Critical
Quarterly* 17 (Winter 1975)
YENSER — Stephen Yenser, *Circle to
Circle: The Poetry of Robert Lowell*
(Berkeley, California 1975)

BACKGROUND

ATLAS — James Atlas, *Delmore
Schwartz: The Life of an American
Poet* (New York 1977)
BARNSTONE — Willis Barnstone (ed.),
Modern European Poetry, (New
York 1966, rep. 1970)
BERNARD — Oliver Bernard (tr.),
Rimbaud: Selected Verse
(Harmondsworth, Middlesex 1962)
BERRYMAN 1969 — John Berryman,
His Toy, His Dream, His Rest
(New York 1968; London 1969)
BERRYMAN 1973 — John Berryman,
Recovery (London 1973)
BISHOP 1953 — Elizabeth Bishop, 'In
the Village', *New Yorker* (19
December 1953), rep. *Questions of
Travel* (New York 1965)
BISHOP 1984 — Elizabeth Bishop, *The
Complete Poems 1927–1979*
(New York 1983; London 1984)
BRANSCOMBE — Peter Branscombe
(tr.), *Heine: Selected Verse*
(Harmondsworth, Middlesex 1967)
BRATFOS AND HAUG — Ole Bratfos and
John Otto Haug, 'The Course of
Manic-Depressive Psychosis', *Acta
Psychiatrica Scandinavica* 44(1)
(1968)
BRIDGEWATER — Patrick Bridgewater
(ed. & tr.), *Twentieth-Century
German Verse* (Harmondsworth,
Middlesex 1963)
BURCHARD — Peter Burchard,
*One Gallant Rush: Robert Gould
Shaw and his Brave Black
Regiment* (New York 1965)
CAMBON — Glauco Cambon (ed.),
*Selected Poems by Eugenio
Montale* (Edinburgh 1965)
CAMERON 1942 — Norman Cameron
(tr.), *Selected Verse Poems by
Arthur Rimbaud* (London 1942)
CAMERON 1966 — Norman Cameron
(tr.), *Poems of François Villon*

(New York 1966)
CARLSON AND GOODWIN — Gabrielle
A. Carlson and Frederick K.
Goodwin, 'The Stages of Mania',
Archives of General Psychiatry 28
(February 1973)
CLARK 1956 — Kenneth Clark, *The
Nude: A Study in Ideal Form*
(Princeton, N. J. 1956)
CORNISH — F. W. Cornish, J. P.
Postgate, and J. W. Mackail (eds.
& trs.), *Catullus, Tibullus,
Pervigilium Veneris* (London and
Cambridge, Mass. 1913, rep. and
rev. 1968)
CUTRER — Thomas W. Cutrer,
*Parnassus on the Mississippi: The
Southern Review and the Baton
Rouge Literary Community 1935–
1942* (Baton Rouge, Louisiana and
London 1984)
EMPSON 1930 — William Empson,
Seven Types of Ambiguity (London
1930)
EMPSON 1961 — William Empson, MS
Note on Wyatt and Peter Porter
written on the draft of a Ph.D
thesis later published as *A Theory
of Communication*, Philip
Hobsbaum (London and
Bloomington, Indiana 1970)
FORSTER — Leonard Forster (ed. &
tr.), *The Penguin Book of German
Verse* (Harmondsworth, Middlesex
1957, rev. 1959)
FRAZER — James G. Frazer, *The
Golden Bough: A Study in Magic
and Religion* (abridged edn.),
(London 1922, rep. 1949)
GILSON 1924 — Étienne Gilson, *The
Philosophy of St. Thomas Aquinas,*
Edward Bullough (tr.),
(Cambridge 1924)
GILSON 1936 — Étienne Gilson, *The
Spirit of Mediaeval Philosophy:*

Gifford Lectures 1931–1932, A. H.
C. Downes (tr.), (London 1936)
GILSON 1938 — Étienne Gilson, *The
Unity of Philosophical Experience*
(London 1938)
GILSON 1940 — Étienne Gilson, *The
Mystical Theology of Saint
Bernard,* A. H. C. Downes (tr.),
(London and New York 1940)
GREENSLET — Ferris Greenslet, *The
Lowells and Their Seven Worlds*
(London 1947)
HARDWICK 1962 — Elizabeth
Hardwick, *A View of My Own:
Essays in Literature and Society*
(New York 1962 and London
1964)
HARDWICK 1974 — Elizabeth
Hardwick, *Seduction and Betrayal:
Women and Literature* (New York
and London 1974)
HARDWICK 1980 — Elizabeth
Hardwick, *Sleepless Nights* (New
York 1979; London 1980)
HARTLEY — Anthony Hartley (ed. &
tr.), *The Penguin Book of French
Verse* 3. 'The Nineteenth Century'
(Harmondsworth, Middlesex 1957,
rev. 1958)
HENDERSON — Robert Henderson
(tr.), *Phèdre* by Jean Racine in *Six
Plays by Corneille and Racine,* Paul
Landis (ed.), (New York 1931)
INNES — Mary M. Innes (tr.), *The
Metamorphoses of Ovid*
(Harmondsworth, Middlesex 1955)
JAMES — William James, *Memories
and Studies* (London 1911)
KINNELL — Galway Kinnell (tr.), *The
Poems of François Villon* (New
York 1965)
KUMIN — Maxine Kumin, *The
Nightmare Factory* (New York and
London 1970)
LARNER — Jeremy Larner, *Nobody
Knows: Reflections on the
McCarthy Campaign of 1968* (New
York 1970)
LATTIMORE — Richmond Lattimore
(tr.), *Aeschylus I: Oresteia*
(Chicago and London 1953, rep.
1969)
LEAVIS — F. R. Leavis, *F. R. Leavis
discusses 'Xenia' by Eugenio
Montale, The Listener* 86 (16
December 1971)
LOWE-PORTER — H. T. Lowe-Porter
(tr.), *'Death in Venice' and Seven

Other Stories* (New York 1930, rep.
1936, rep. 1954)
LUKE — David Luke (tr.), *Goethe:
Selected Verse* (Harmondsworth,
Middlesex 1964)
MACINTYRE — C. F. MacIntyre (tr.),
*Selected Poems of Rainer Maria
Rilke* (Berkeley, California 1947,
rep. 1957)
MAILER — Norman Mailer, *The
Armies of the Night* (New York and
London 1968, rep.
Harmondsworth, Middlesex 1970)
MARITAIN — Jacques Maritain, *Art and
Scholasticism and the Frontiers of
Poetry,* Joseph W. Evans (tr.),
(New York 1962; Notre Dame,
Indiana and London 1974;
originally Paris, 3rd edn. 1935)
MICHIE — James Michie (tr.), *The
Poems of Catullus* (London 1969,
rep. 1972)
PADDOCK — Harold J. Paddock (ed.),
*Languages in Newfoundland and
Labrador: Preliminary Version* (for
discussion of R. T. S. Lowell's *The
New Priest in Conception Bay* by
Philip Hiscock; St John's,
Newfoundland 1977)
PASTERNAK 1958 — Boris Pasternak,
*Safe Conduct: an autobiography
and other writings,* Beatrice Scott,
Robert Payne, C. M. Bowra,
Babette Deutsch (trs.), (New York
1949, rep. 1958)
PASTERNAK 1961 — Boris Pasternak,
Doctor Zhivago, Max Hayward
and Manya Harari (trs.), (London
1958, rep. 1961)
PAYKEL — E. S. Paykel (ed.),
Handbook of Affective Disorders
(Edinburgh and New York 1982)
PLATH 1965 — Sylvia Plath, *Ariel*
(New York and London 1965)
PLATH 1966 — Sylvia Plath, *The Bell
Jar* (London 1963, rep. 1966)
PORTER — Peter Porter, *Collected
Poems* (Oxford 1983)
POUND 1928 — Ezra Pound, *Selected
Poems,* Preface by T. S. Eliot
(London 1928)
POUND 1930 — Ezra Pound, *A Draft of
XXX Cantos* (1930), rep. *The
Cantos of Ezra Pound* (London
1954)
POUND 1949 — Ezra Pound, *The Pisan
Cantos* (1949), rep. *The Cantos of
Ezra Pound* (London 1954)

PRIEN, KLETT, CAFFEY — Robert F. Prien, James Klett and Eugene M. Caffey, 'Lithium Carbonate and Imipramine in Prevention of Affective Episodes', *Archives of General Psychiatry* 29 (September 1973)

RICHARDSON — Joanna Richardson (tr.), *Baudelaire: Selected Poems* (Harmondsworth, Middlesex 1975)

ROCHE — Paul Roche (tr.), *Aeschylus: Prometheus Bound* (New York 1964)

SANTAYANA — George Santayana, *The Letters of George Santayana*, Daniel Cory (ed.), (London 1955)

SCARFE — Francis Scarfe (tr.), *Baudelaire: The Complete Verse* (London 1986)

SEXTON — Anne Sexton, *All My Pretty Ones* (Boston, Mass. 1962)

SNODGRASS — W. D. Snodgrass, *Heart's Needle* (Hessle, Yorkshire 1960)

SNOW — Edith Abercrombie Snow (tr.), *Poems by Franz Werfel* (Princeton, N. J. 1945)

SQUIRES — Radcliffe Squires, *Allen Tate: A Literary Biography* (New York 1971)

STAFFORD 1944 — Jean Stafford, *Boston Adventure* (New York 1944; London 1946)

STAFFORD 1945 — Jean Stafford, *Children are Bored on Sunday* (New York 1945)

STAFFORD 1954 — Jean Stafford, 'New England Winter', *Holiday* XV (February 1954)

STAFFORD 1978 — Jean Stafford, 'An Influx of Poets', *New Yorker* (6 November 1978)

STEVENS — Wallace Stevens, *Collected Poems* (New York and London 1955)

SULLIVAN AND O'TOOLE — Robert E. Sullivan and James M. O'Toole, *Catholic Boston: Studies in Religion and Community 1870–1970* (Boston 1985)

TATE 1969 — Allen Tate, *Essays of Four Decades* (Chicago 1969; London 1970)

TATE 1970 — Allen Tate, *The Swimmers and Other Selected Poems* (London 1970)

TATE 1976 — Allen Tate, *Memories and Essays Old and New 1926–1974* (Manchester 1976)

TAYLOR AND ABRAMS — Michael Taylor and Richard Abrams, 'Manic States: A Genetic Study of Early and Late Onset Affective Disorders', *Archives of General Psychiatry* 28 (May 1973)

TAYLOR — Peter Taylor, *The Collected Stories of Peter Taylor* (New York, 3rd printing 1979)

THOMSON AND SALGÃDO — Peter Thomson and Gãmini Salgãdo, *The Everyman Companion to the Theatre* (London 1985)

WAKOSKI 1968 — Diane Wakoski, *Inside the Blood Factory* (New York 1968)

WATKIN — E. I. Watkin, *Catholic Art and Culture* (London 1942)

WHITFIELD — John Humphreys Whitfield (tr.), *Leopardi's 'Canti'* (Naples 1962)

WILLIAMS 1963 — William Carlos Williams, *Paterson* Books I–V (New York 1963; London 1964)

WINTERS 1932 — Yvor Winters, 'Traditional Mastery', *Hound and Horn* V (January–March 1932), rep. *Uncollected Essays and Reviews*, Francis Murphy (ed.), (Chicago 1973; reviewing *The Shorter Poems* of Robert Bridges)

WINTERS 1947 — Yvor Winters, *In Defense of Reason* (Denver, Colorado 1947; London 1960)

WINTERS 1960 — Yvor Winters, *Collected Poems* (Denver, Colorado 1960; London 1962)

YEATS — W. B. Yeats, *Collected Poems* (London 1950)

YOUNG — Thomas Daniel Young, *Gentleman in a Dustcoat: A Biography of John Crowe Ransom* (Baton Rouge, Louisiana 1976)

Index

WORKS OF ROBERT LOWELL: